Charles Kingsley

At last: a Christmas in the West Indies

Charles Kingsley

At last: a Christmas in the West Indies

ISBN/EAN: 9783741181641

Manufactured in Europe, USA, Canada, Australia, Japa

Cover: Foto ©Andreas Hilbeck / pixelio.de

Manufactured and distributed by brebook publishing software (www.brebook.com)

Charles Kingsley

At last: a Christmas in the West Indies

A CHRISTMAS IN THE WEST INDIES.

BY
CHARLES KINGSLEY.

WITH ILLUSTRATIONS.

IN TWO VOLUMES.
VOL. II.

London and New York
MACMILLAN AND CO.
1871.

CONTENTS.

CHAPTER IX.

SAN JOSEF . . . . PAGE 1

CHAPTER X.

NAPARIMA AND MONTSERRAT 27

CHAPTER XI.

THE NORTHERN MOUNTAIN 91

CHAPTER XII.

THE SAVANNA OF ARIPO 164

CHAPTER XIII.

THE COCAL 185

CHAPTER XIV.

THE "EDUCATION QUESTION" IN TRINIDAD . 224

CHAPTER XV.

THE RACES—A LETTER . . 259

CHAPTER XVI.

A PROVISION GROUND. . 268

CHAPTER XVII. (AND LAST).

HOMEWARD BOUND . 292

LIST OF ILLUSTRATIONS.

		PAGE
A MANGROVE SWAMP.	*Front.*	
COOLIE AND NEGRO		1
A COOLIE FAMILY . . .		47
BANANA . . .		61
TORTUGA	*To face*	81
COOLIE GROUP . . .		85
FILLETTE	*To face*	107
AVOCADO PEAR		109
CANNON-BALL TREE . . .		114
A TROPIC BEACH	*To face*	160
YOUNG COCO-PALM .		198
THE COCAL	*To face*	200
COOLIE SACRIFICING .		257

LIST OF ILLUSTRATIONS.

		PAGE
WAITING FOR THE RACES .	*To face*	260
THE LAST OF THE GIANTS .	,,	268
BREAD-FRUIT		269
YAM . .		274
SWEET POTATO . .		275
GUAVA . .		290

Coolie and Negro.

AT LAST.

A CHRISTMAS IN THE WEST INDIES.

CHAPTER IX.

SAN JOSEF.

THE road to the ancient capital of the island is pleasant enough, and characteristic of the West Indies. Not, indeed, as to its breadth, make, and material, for they, contrary to the wont of West India roads, are as good as they would be in England, but on account of the quaint travellers along it, and the quaint sights which are to be seen over every hedge. You pass all the races of the island going to and from town or fieldwork, or washing clothes in some clear brook, beside which a solemn Chinaman sits catching for his dinner strange fishes, known to my learned friend, Dr. Günther, and perhaps to one or two other men in Europe: but certainly not to me. Always somebody or something new and strange is to be seen, for eight most pleasant miles.

The road runs at first along a low cliff foot, with an ugly Mangrove swamp, looking just like an alder-bed at home, between you and the sea; a swamp which it would be worth while to drain by a steam-pump, and then plant with coco-nuts or bamboos; for its miasma makes the southern corner of Port of Spain utterly pestilential. You cross a railroad, the only one in the island, which goes to a limestone quarry, and so out along a wide straight road, with Negro cottages right and left, embowered in fruit and flowers. They grow fewer and finer as you ride on; and soon you are in open country, principally of large paddocks. These paddocks, like all West Indian ones, are apt to be ragged with weeds and scrub. But the coarse broad-leaved grasses seem to keep the mules in good condition enough, at least in the rainy season. Most of these paddocks have, I believe, been under cane cultivation at some time or other; and have been thrown into grass during the period of depression dating from 1845. It has not been worth while, as yet, to break them up again, though the profits of sugar-farming are now, or at least ought to be, very large. But the soil along this line is originally poor and sandy; and it is far more profitable to break up the rich vegas, or low alluvial lands, even at the trouble of clearing them of forest. So these paddocks are left, often with noble trees standing about in them, putting one in mind—if it were not for the Palmistes and Bamboos and the crowd of black vultures over an occasional dead animal—of English parks.

But few English parks have such backgrounds. To the right, the vast southern flat, with its smoking engine-house chimneys and bright green cane-pieces, and, beyond all, the black wall of the primæval forest; and to the left, some half mile off, the steep slopes of the green northern mountains blazing in the sun, and sending down, every two or three miles, out of some charming glen, a clear pebbly brook, each winding through its narrow strip of vega. The vega is usually a highly cultivated cane-piece, where great lizards sit in the mouths of their burrows, and watch the passer-by with intense interest. Coolies and Negros are at work in it: but only a few; for the strength of the hands is away at the engine-house, making sugar day and night. There is a piece of cane in act of being cut. The men are hewing down the giant grass with cutlasses; the women stripping off the leaves, and then piling the cane in carts drawn by mules, the leaders of which draw by rope traces two or three times as long as themselves. You wonder why such a seeming waste of power is allowed, till you see one of the carts stick fast in a mud-hole, and discover that even in the West Indies there is a good reason for everything, and that the Creoles know their own business best. For the wheelers, being in the slough with the cart, are powerless: but the leaders, who have scrambled through, are safe on dry land at the end of their long traces, and haul out their brethren, cart and all, amid the yells, and, I am sorry to say blows, of the black gentlemen in attendance. But cane-cutting is altogether a busy, happy scene. The heat is awful, and all limbs rain perspiration: yet no one seems to mind the heat; all look fat and jolly; and they have cause to do so, for all, at every spare moment, are sucking sugar-cane.

You pull up, and take off your hat to the party. The Negros shout, " Marnin', sa !" The Coolies salaam gracefully, hand to forehead. You return the salaam, hand to heart, which is considered the correct thing on the part of a superior in rank; whereat the Coolies look exceedingly pleased; and then the whole party, without visible reason, burst into shouts of laughter.

The manager rides up, probably under an umbrella, as you are, and a pleasant and instructive chat follows, wound up, usually, if the house be not far off, by an invitation to come in and have a light drink; an invitation which, considering the state of the thermometer, you will be tempted to accept, especially as you know that the claret and water will be excellent. And so you dawdle on, looking at this and that new and odd sight, but most of all feasting your eyes on the beauty of the northern mountains, till you reach the gentle rise on which stands, eight miles from Port of Spain, the little city of San Josef. We should call it, here in England, a village: still, it is not every village in England which has fought the Dutch, and earned its right to be called a city, by beating some of the bravest sailors of the seventeenth century. True, there is not a single shop in it with plate-glass windows: but what matters that, if its citizens have all that civilized people need, and more, and will heap what they have on the stranger so hospitably that they almost pain him by the trouble which they take? True, no carriages and pairs, with powdered footmen, roll about the streets; and the most splendid vehicles you are likely to meet are American buggies—four-wheeled gigs with heads, and aprons through which the reins can be passed in wet weather. But what matters that, as long as the buggies keep out sun and rain effectually, and as long as those who sit in them be real gentlemen, and those who wait for them at home, whether in the city or the estates around, be real ladies? As for the rest—peace, plenty, perpetual summer, time to think and read —(for there are no daily papers in San Josef)—and what can man want more on earth? So I thought more than once, as I looked at San Josef nestling at the mouth of its noble glen, and said to myself,—If the telegraph cable were but laid down the islands, as it will be in another year or two, and one could hear a little more swiftly and loudly the beating of the Great Mother's heart at home, then would San Josef be about the most delectable spot which I have ever seen for a cultivated and civilized man to live, and work, and think, and die in.

San Josef has had, nevertheless, its troubles and excitements more than once since it defeated the Dutch. Even as late as 1837, it was, for a few hours, in utter terror and danger from a mutiny of free black recruits. No one in the island, civil or military, seems to have been to blame for the mishap. It was altogether owing to the unwisdom of military authorities at home, who seem to have fancied that they could transform, by a magical spurt of the pen, heathen savages into British soldiers.

The whole tragedy—for tragedy it was—is so curious, and so illustrative of the Negro character, and of the effects of the slave trade, that I shall give it at length, as it stands in that clever little History of Trinidad, by M. Thomas, which I have quoted more than once :—

"Donald Stewart, or rather Dâaga,[1] was the adopted son of Madershee, the old and childless king of the tribe called Paupaus, a race that inhabit a tract of country bordering on that of the Yarrabas. These races are constantly at war with each other.

"Dâaga was just the man whom a savage, warlike, and depredatory tribe would select for their chieftain, as the African Negros choose their leaders with reference to their personal prowess. Dâaga stood six feet six inches without shoes. Although scarcely muscular in proportion, yet his frame indicated in a singular degree the union of irresistible strength and activity. His head was large; his features had all the peculiar traits which distinguish the Negro in a remarkable degree; his jaw was long, eyes large and protruded, high cheek-bones, and flat nose: his teeth were large and regular. He had a singular cast in his eyes, not quite amounting to that obliquity of the visual organs denominated a squint, but sufficient to give his features a peculiarly forbidding appearance;—his forehead, however, although small in proportion to his enormous head, was remarkably compact and well formed. The whole head was disproportioned, having the greater part of the brain behind the

[1] Pronounced like the Spanish noun Daga.

ears; but the greatest peculiarity of this singular being was his voice. In the course of my life I never heard such sounds uttered by human organs as those formed by Dâaga. In ordinary conversation he appeared to me to endeavour to soften his voice—it was a deep tenor; but when a little excited by any passion (and this savage was the child of passion) his voice sounded like the low growl of a lion, but when much excited it could be compared to nothing so aptly as the notes of a gigantic brazen trumpet.

"I repeatedly questioned this man respecting the religion of his tribe. The result of his answers led me to infer that the Paupaus believed in the existence of a future state; that they have a confused notion of several powers, good and evil, but these are ruled by one supreme being called Holloloo. This account of the religion of Dâaga was confirmed by the military chaplain who attended him in his last moments. He also informed me that he believed in predestination;—at 'east he said that Holloloo, he knew, had ordained that he should come to white man's country and be shot.

"Dâaga having made a successful predatory expedition into the country of the Yarrabas, returned with a number of prisoners of that nation. These he, as usual, took, bound and guarded, towards the coast to sell to the Portuguese. The interpreter, his countryman, called these Portuguese WHITE GENTLEMEN. The white gentlemen proved themselves more than a match for the black gentlemen; and the whole transaction between the Portuguese and Paupaus does credit to all concerned in this gentlemanly traffic in human flesh.

"Dâaga sold his prisoners; and under pretence of paying him, he and his Paupau guards were enticed on board a Portuguese vessel;—they were treacherously overpowered by the Christians, who bound them beside their late prisoners, and the vessel sailed over 'the great salt water.'

"This transaction caused in the breast of the savage a deep hatred against all white men—a hatred so intense that he frequently, during and subsequent to the mutiny, declared he would eat the first white man he killed; yet this cannibal was made to swear allegiance to our Sovereign on the Holy Evangelists, and was then called a British soldier.

"On the voyage the vessel on board which Dâaga had been entrapped was captured by the British. He could not comprehend that his new captors liberated him: he had been over-reached and trepanned by one set of white men, and he naturally looked on his second captors as more successful rivals in the human, or rather inhuman, Guinea trade; therefore this event lessened not his hatred for white men in the abstract.

"I was informed by several of the Africans who came with him that when, during the voyage, they upbraided Dâaga with being the cause of their capture, he pacified them by promising that when they should arrive in white man's country, he would repay their perfidy by attacking them in the night. He further promised that if the Paupaus and Yarrabas would follow him, he would fight his way back to Guinea. This account was fully corroborated by many of the mutineers, especially those who were shot with Dâaga: they all said the revolt never would have happened but for Donald Stewart, as he was called by the officers; but Africans who were not of his tribe called him Longa-longa, on account of his height.

"Such was this extraordinary man, who led the mutiny I am about to relate.

"A quantity of captured Africans having been brought hither from the islands of Grenada and Dominica, they were most imprudently induced to enlist as recruits in the 1st West India Regiment. True it is, we have been told they did this voluntarily: but, it may be asked, if they had any will in the matter, how could they understand the duties to be imposed on them by becoming soldiers, or how comprehend the nature of an oath of allegiance? without which they could not, legally speaking, be considered as soldiers. I attended the whole of the trials of these men, and well know how difficult it was to make them comprehend any idea which was at all new to them by means of the best interpreters procurable,

"It has been said that by making those captured Negros soldiers, a service was rendered them: this I doubt. Formerly it was most true that a soldier in a black regiment was better off than a slave; but certainly a free African in the West Indies now is infinitely in a better situation than a soldier, not only in a pecuniary point of view, but in almost every other respect.

"To the African savage, while being drilled into the duties of a soldier, many things seem absolute tyranny which would appear to a civilized man a mere necessary restraint. To keep the restless body of an African Negro in a position to which he has not been accustomed—to cramp his splay-feet, with his great toes standing out, into European shoes made for feet of a different form—to place a collar round his neck, which is called a stock, and which to him is cruel torture—above all, to confine him every night to his barracks—are almost insupportable. One unacquainted with the habits of the Negro cannot conceive with what abhorrence he looks on having his disposition to nocturnal rambles checked by barrack regulations.[1]

"Formerly the 'King's man,' as the black soldier loved to call himself, looked (not without reason) contemptuously on the planter's slave, although he himself was after all but

---

[1] See Bryan Edwards on the character of the African Negros; also Chanvelon's Histoire de la Martinique.

a slave to the State: but these recruits were enlisted shortly after a number of their recently imported countrymen were wandering freely over the country, working either as free labourers, or settling, to use an apt American phrase, as squatters; and to assert that the recruit, while under military probation, is better off than the free Trinidad labourer, who goes where he lists and earns as much in one day as will keep him for three days, is an absurdity. Accordingly we find that Lieutenant-Colonel Bush, who commanded the 1st West India Regiment, thought that the mutiny was mainly owing to the ill-advice of their civil, or, we should rather say, un-military countrymen. This, to a certain degree, was the fact: but, by the declaration of Dâaga and many of his countrymen, it is evident the seeds of mutiny were sown on the passage from Africa.

"It has been asserted that the recruits were driven to mutiny by hard treatment of their commanding officers. There seems not the slightest truth in this assertion; they were treated with fully as much kindness as their situation would admit of, and their chief was peculiarly a favourite of Colonel Bush and the officers, notwithstanding Dâaga's violent and ferocious temper often caused complaints to be brought against him.

"A correspondent of the *Naval and Military Gazette* was under an apprehension that the mutineers would be joined by the prædial apprentices of the circumjacent estates: not the slightest foundation existed for this apprehension. Some months previous to this Dâaga had planned a mutiny, but this was interrupted by sending a part of the Paupau and Yarraba recruits to St. Lucia. The object of all those conspiracies was to get back to Guinea, which they thought they could accomplish by marching to eastward.

"On the night of the 17th of June, 1837, the people of San Josef were kept awake by the recruits, about 280 in number, singing the war-song of the Paupaus. This wild song consisted of a short air and chorus. The tone was, although wild, not inharmonious, and the words rather euphonious. As near as our alphabet can convey them, they ran thus:—

> 'Dangkarrée
> Au fey,
> Oluu werrei,
> Au lay.'

which may be rendered almost literally by the following couplet:—

> Air by the chief: 'Come to plunder, come to slay;'
> Chorus of followers: 'We are ready to obey.'

"About three o'clock in the morning their war-song (highly characteristic of a predatory tribe) became very loud, and they commenced uttering their war-cry. This is different from what we conceive the Indian war-whoop to be: it seems to be a kind of imitation of the growl of wild beasts, and has a most thrilling effect.

"Fire now was set to a quantity of huts built for the accommodation of African soldiers to the northward of the barracks, as well as to the house of a poor black woman called Dalrymple. These burnt briskly, throwing a dismal glare over the barracks and picturesque town of San Josef, and overpowering the light of the full moon, which illumined a cloudless sky. The mutineers made a rush at the barrack-room, and seized on the muskets and fusees in the racks. Their leader, Dâaga, and a daring Yarraba named Ogston, instantly charged their pieces; the former of these had a quantity of ball-cartridges, loose powder, and ounce and pistol-balls, in a kind of grey worsted cap. He must have provided himself with these before the mutiny. How he became possessed of them, especially the pistol-balls, I never could learn.; probably he was supplied by his unmilitary countrymen: pistol-balls are never given to infantry. Previous to this Dâaga and three others made a rush at the regimental store-room, in which was deposited a quantity of powder. An old African soldier, named Charles Dixon, interfered to stop them, on which Maurice Ogston, the Yarraba chief, who had armed himself with a sergeant's sword, cut down the faithful African. When down Dâaga said, in English, 'Ah, you old soldier, you knock down.' Dixon

ITS CHILDISHNESS. 15

was not Dâaga's countryman, hence he could not speak to him in his own language. The Paupau then levelled his musket and shot the fallen soldier, who groaned and died. The war-yells, or rather growls, of the Paupaus and Yarabbas now became awfully thrilling, as they helped themselves to cartridges: most of them were fortunately blank, or without ball. Never was a premeditated mutiny so wild and ill planned. Their chief, Dâaga, and Ogston. seemed to have had little command of the subordinates, and the whole acted more like a set of wild beasts who had broken their cages than men resolved on war.

"At this period, had a rush been made at the officers' quarters by one half (they were more than 200 in number), and the other half surrounded the building, not one could have escaped. Instead of this they continued to shout their war-song, and howl their war-notes; they loaded their pieces with ball-cartridge, or blank-cartridge and small stones, and commenced firing at the long range of white buildings in which Colonel Bush and his officers slept. They wasted so much ammunition on this useless display of fury that the buildings were completely riddled. A few of the old soldiers opposed them, and were wounded; but it fortunately happened that they were, to an inconceivable degree, ignorant of the right use of fire-arms—holding their muskets in their hands when they discharged them, without allowing the butt-end to rest against their shoulders, or any part of their bodies. This fact accounts for the comparatively little mischief they did in proportion to the quantity of ammunition thrown away.

"The officers and sergeant-major escaped at the back of the building, while Colonel Bush and Adjutant Bentley came down a little hill. The colonel commanded the mutineers to lay down their arms, and was answered by an irregular discharge of balls, which rattled amongst the leaves of a tree under which he and the adjutant were standing. On this Colonel Bush desired Mr. Bentley to make the best of his way to St. James's Barracks for all the disposable force of the 89th Regiment. The officers made good their retreat, and the adjutant got into the stable where his horse was. He saddled and bridled the animal while the shots were coming into the stable, without either man or beast getting injured. The officer mounted, but had to make his way through the mutineers before he could get into San Josef, the barracks standing on an eminence above the little town. On seeing the adjutant mounted, the mutineers set up a thrilling howl, and commenced firing at him. He discerned the gigantic figure of Dâaga (alias Donald Stewart), with his musket at the trail: he spurred his horse through the midst of them; they were grouped, but not in line. On looking back he saw Dâaga aiming at him; he stooped his head beside his horse's neck, and effectually sheltered himself from about fifty shots aimed at him. In this position he rode furiously down a steep hill leading from the barracks to the church, and was out of danger. His escape appears extraordinary: but he got safe to town, and thence to St. James's, and in a short time, considering it is eleven miles distant, brought out a strong detachment of European troops; these, however, did not arrive until the affair was over.

"In the meantime a part of the officers' quarters was bravely defended by two old African soldiers, Sergeant Merry and Corporal Plague. The latter stood in the gallery near the room in which were the colours; he was ineffectually fired at by some hundreds, yet he kept his post, shot two of the mutineers, and, it is said, wounded a third. Such is the difference between a man acquainted with the use of fire-arms and those who handle them as mops are held.

"In the meantime Colonel Bush got to a police-station above the barracks, and got muskets and a few cartridges from a discharged African soldier who was in the police establishment. Being joined by the policemen, Corporal Craven[1] and Ensign Pogson, they concealed themselves on an eminence above, and as the mutineers (about 100 in number) approached, the fire of muskets opened on them from the little

[1] This man, who was a friend of Dâaga's, owed his life to a solitary act of humanity on the part of the chief of this wild tragedy. A musket was levelled at him, when Dâaga pushed it aside, and said, "Not this man."

VOL. II.   C

ambush. The little party fired separately, loading as fast as they discharged their pieces; they succeeded in making the mutineers change their route.

"It is wonderful what little courage the savages in general showed against the Colonel and his little party; who absolutely beat them, although but a twenty-fifth of their number, and at their own tactics, *i.e.* bush fighting.

"A body of the mutineers now made towards the road to Maraccas, when the colonel and his three assistants contrived to get behind a silk-cotton tree, and recommenced firing on them. The Africans hesitated and set forward, when the little party continued to fire on them; they set up a yell, and retreated down the hill.

"A part of the mutineers now concealed themselves in the bushes about San Josef barracks. These men, after the affair was over, joined Colonel Bush, and with a mixture of cunning and effrontery smiled as though nothing had happened, and as though they were glad to see him; although, in general, they each had several shirts and pairs of trousers on preparatory for a start to Guinea, by way of Band de l'Est.[1]

"In the meantime the San Josef militia were assembled, to the number of forty. Major Giuseppi, and Captain and

---

[1] People will smile at the simplicity of those savages; but it should be recollected that civilized convicts were lately in the constant habit of attempting to escape from New South Wales in order to walk to China.

Adjutant Rousseau, of the second division of militia forces took command of them. They were in want of flints, powder, and balls—to obtain these they were obliged to break open a merchant's store; however, the adjutant so judiciously distributed his little force as to hinder the mutineers from entering the town, or obtaining access to the militia arsenal, wherein there was a quantity of arms. Major Chadds and several old African soldiers joined the militia, and were by them supplied with arms.

"A good deal of skirmishing occurred between the militia and detached parties of the mutineers, which uniformly ended in the defeat of the latter. At length Dâaga appeared to the right of a party of six, at the entrance of the town; they were challenged by the militia, and the mutineers fired on them, but without effect. Only two of the militia returned the fire, when all but Dâaga fled. He was deliberately reloading his piece, when a militia-man, named Edmond Luce, leaped on the gigantic chief, who would have easily beat him off, although the former was a strong young man of colour: but Dâaga would not let go his gun; and, in common with all the mutineers, he seemed to have no idea of the use of the bayonet. Dâaga was dragging the militia-man away, when Adjutant Rousseau came to his assistance, and placed a sword to Dâaga's breast. Doctor Tardy and several others rushed on the tall Negro, who was soon, by the united efforts of several, thrown down and secured. It was at this period that he repeatedly exclaimed, while he bit his own shoulder, 'The first white man I catch after this I will eat him.'[1]

"Meanwhile about sixteen of the mutineers, led by the daring Ogston, took the road to Arima; in order, as they said, to commence their march to Guinea: but fortunately the militia of that village, composed principally of Spaniards, Indians, and Sambos, assembled. A few of these met them and stopped their march. A kind of parley (if intercourse carried on by signs could be so called) was carried on between the parties. The mutineers made signs that they wished to go forward, while the few militia-men endeavoured to detain them, expecting a reinforcement momently. After a time the militia agreed to allow them to approach the town; as they were advancing they were met by the commandant, Martin Sorzano, Esq., with sixteen more militia-men. The commandant judged it imprudent to allow the Africans to enter the town with their muskets full cocked and poised ready to fire. An interpreter was now procured, and the mutineers were told that if they would retire to their barracks the gentlemen present would intercede for their pardon. The Negros refused to accede to these terms, and while the interpreter was addressing some, the rest tried to push forward. Some of the

---

[1] I had this anecdote from one of his countrymen, an old Paupan soldier, who said he did not join the mutiny.

militia opposed them by holding their muskets in a horizontal position, on which one of the mutineers fired, and the militia returned the fire. A mêlée commenced, in which fourteen mutineers were killed and wounded. The fire of the Africans produced little effect: they soon took to flight amid the woods which flanked the road. Twenty-eight of them were taken, amongst whom was the Yarraba chief, Ogston. Six had been killed, and six committed suicide by strangling and hanging themselves in the woods. Only one man was wounded amongst the militia, and he but slightly, from a small stone fired from a musket of one of the Yarrabas.

"The quantity of ammunition expended by the mutineers, and the comparatively little mischief done by them, was truly astonishing. It shows how little they understood the use of fire-arms. Dixon was killed, and several of the old African soldiers were wounded, but not one of the officers was in the slightest degree hurt.

"I have never been able to get a correct account of the number of lives this wild mutiny cost, but believe it was not less than forty, including those slain by the militia at Arima; those shot at San Josef; those who died of their wounds (and most of the wounded men died); the six who committed suicide; the three that were shot by sentence of the court-martial, and one who was shot while endeavouring to escape (Satchell).

"A good-looking young man, named Torrens, was brought as prisoner to the presence of Colonel Bush. The Colonel wished to speak to him, and desired his guards to liberate him; on which the young savage shook his sleeve, in which was concealed a razor, made a rush at the Colonel, and nearly succeeded in cutting his throat. He slashed the razor in all directions until he made an opening; he rushed through this: and, notwithstanding he was fired at, and I believe wounded, he effected his escape, was subsequently re-taken; and again made his escape with Satchell, who after this was shot by a policeman.

"Torrens was re-taken, tried, and recommended to mercy. Of this man's fate I am unable to speak, not knowing how far the recommendation to mercy was attended to. In appearance he seemed the mildest and best-looking of the mutineers, but his conduct was the most ferocious of any. The whole of the mutineers were captured within one week of the mutiny, save this man, who was taken a month after.

"On the 19th of July, Donald Stewart, otherwise Dâaga, was brought to a court-martial. On the 21st William Satchell was tried. On the 22d a court-martial was held on Edward Coffin; and on the 24th one was held on the Yarraba chief, Maurice Ogston, whose country name was, I believe, Mawee. Torrens was tried on the 29th.

"The sentences of these courts-martial were unknown until the 14th of August, having been sent to Barbados in order to be submitted to the Commander-in-Chief, Lieutenant-General Whittingham, who approved of the decision of the courts, which was that Donald Stewart (Dâaga), Maurice Ogston, and Edward Coffin, should suffer death by being shot; and that William Satchell should be transported beyond seas during the term of his natural life. I am unacquainted with the sentence of Torrens.

"Donald Stewart, Maurice Ogston, and Edward Coffin were executed on the 16th of August, 1837, at San Josef Barracks. Nothing seemed to have been neglected which could render the execution solemn and impressive; the scenery and the weather gave additional awe to the melancholy proceedings. Fronting the little eminence where the prisoners were shot was the scene where their ill-concerted mutiny commenced. To the right stood the long range of building on which they had expended much of their ammunition for the purpose of destroying their officers. The rest of the panorama was made up of an immense view of forest below them, and upright masses of mountains above them. Over those, heavy bodies of mist were slowly sailing, giving a sombre appearance to the primæval woods which, in general, covered both mountains and plains. The atmosphere indicated an inter-tropical morning during the rainy season, and the sun shone resplendently between dense columns of clouds.

"At half-past seven o'clock the condemned men asked to be allowed to eat a hearty meal, as they said persons about to be executed in Guinea were always indulged with a good repast. It is remarkable that these unhappy creatures ate most voraciously, even while they were being brought out of their cell for execution.

"A little before the mournful procession commenced the condemned men were dressed from head to foot in white habiliments trimmed with black; their arms were bound with cords. This is not usual in military executions, but was deemed necessary on the present occasion. An attempt to escape, on the part of the condemned, would have been productive of much confusion, and was properly guarded against.

"The condemned men displayed no unmanly fear. On the contrary, they steadily kept step to the Dead March which the band played; yet the certainty of death threw a cadaverous and ghastly hue over their black features, while their singular and appropriate costume, and the three coffins being borne before them, altogether rendered it a frightful picture: hence it was not to be wondered at that two of the European soldiers fainted.

"The mutineers marched abreast. The tall form and horrid looks of Dâaga were almost appalling. The looks of Ogston were sullen, calm, and determined; those of Coffin seemed to indicate resignation.

"At eight o'clock they arrived at the spot where three graves were dug; here their coffins were deposited. The condemned men were made to face to westward; three sides of a hollow square were formed, flanked on one side by a detachment of the 89th Regiment and a party of artillery, while the recruits, many of whom shared the guilt of the culprits, were appropriately placed in the line opposite them. The firing party were a little in advance of the recruits.

"The sentence of the courts-martial, and other necessary documents, having been read by the fort adjutant, Mr. Meehan, the chaplain of the forces read some prayers appropriated for these melancholy occasions. The clergyman then shook hands with the three men about to be sent into another state of existence. Dâaga and Ogston coolly gave their hands: Coffin wrang the chaplain's hand affectionately, saying, in tolerable English, 'I am now done with the world.'

"The arms of the condemned men, as has been before stated, were bound, but in such a manner as to allow them to bring their hands to their heads. Their night-caps were drawn over their eyes. Coffin allowed his to remain, but Ogston and Dâaga pushed theirs up again. The former did this calmly; the latter showed great wrath, seeming to think himself insulted; and his deep metallic voice sounded in anger above that of the provost-marshal,[1] as the latter gave the words 'Ready! present!' But at this instant his vociferous daring forsook him. As the men levelled their muskets at him, with inconceivable rapidity he sprang bodily round, still preserving his squatting posture, and received the fire from behind; while the less noisy, but more brave, Ogston, looked the firing-party full in the face as they discharged their fatal volley.

"In one instant all three fell dead, almost all the balls of the firing-party having taken effect. The savage appearance and manner of Dâaga excited awe. Admiration was felt for the calm bravery of Ogston, while Edward Coffin's fate excited commiseration.

"There were many spectators of this dreadful scene, and amongst others a great concourse of Negros. Most of these expressed their hopes that after this terrible example the recruits would make good soldiers."

Ah, stupid savages. Yes: but also—ah, stupid civilized people.

[1] One of his countrymen explained to me what Dâaga said on this occasion, viz.—"The curse of Holloloo on white men. Do they think that Dâaga fears to fix his eyeballs on death?"

CHAPTER X.

NAPARIMA AND MONTSERRAT.

I HAD a few days of pleasant wandering in the centre of the island, about the districts which bear the names of Naparima and Montserrat; a country of such extraordinary fertility, as well as beauty, that it must surely hereafter become the seat of a high civilization. The soil seems inexhaustibly rich. I say inexhaustibly; for as fast as the upper layer is impoverished, it will be swept over by the tropic rains, to mingle with the vegas, or alluvial flats below, and thus enriched again, while a fresh layer of virgin soil is exposed above. I have seen, cresting the highest ridges of Montserrat, ten feet at least of fat earth, falling clod by clod right and left upon the gardens below. There are, doubtless, comparatively barren tracts of gravel toward the northern mountains; there are poor sandy lands, likewise, at the southern part of the island, which are said, nevertheless, to be specially fitted for the growth of cotton: but from San

Fernando on the west coast to Manzanilla on the east, stretches a band of soil which seems to be capable of yielding any conceivable return to labour and capital, not omitting common sense.

How long it has taken to prepare this natural garden for man is one of those questions of geological time which have been well called of late " appalling." How long was it since the " older Parian " rocks (said to belong to the Neocomian, or green-sand, era) of Point a Pierre were laid down at the bottom of the sea? How long since a still unknown thickness of tertiary strata in the Nariva district laid down on them? How long since not less than six thousand feet of still later tertiary strata laid down on them again? What vast, though probably slow, processes changed that seabottom from one salt enough to carry corals and limestones, to one brackish enough to carry abundant remains of plants, deposited probably by the Orinoco, or by some river which then did duty for it? Three such periods of disturbance have been distinguished, the net result of which is, that the strata (comparatively recent in geological time) have been fractured, tilted, even set upright on end, over the whole lowland. Trinidad seems to have had its full share of those later disturbances of the earth-crust, which carried tertiary strata up along the shoulders of the Alps; which upheaved the chalk of the Isle of Wight, setting the tertiary beds of Alum Bay upright against it; which even, after the Age of Ice, thrust up the Isle of Moen in Denmark, and the Isle of Ely in Cambridgeshire, entangling the boulder clay among the chalk—how long ago? Long enough ago, in Trinidad at least, to allow water —probably the estuary waters of the Orinoco—to saw all the upheaved layers off at the top into one flat sea-bottom once more, leaving as projections certain harder knots of rock, such as the limestones of Mount Tamana; and, it may be, the curious knoll of hard clay rock under which nestles the town of San Fernando. Long enough ago, also, to allow that whole sea-bottom to be lifted up once more, to the height, in one spot, of a thousand feet, as the lowland which occupies six-sevenths of the Isle of Trinidad. Long enough ago, again, to allow that lowland to be sawn out into hills and valleys, ridges and gulleys, which are due to the action of Colonel George Greenwood's geologic panacea, "Rain and Rivers," and to nothing else. Long enough ago, once more, for a period of subsidence, as I suspect, to follow the period of upheaval; a period at the commencement of which Trinidad was perhaps several times as large as it is now, and has gradually been eaten away by the surf, as fresh pieces of the soft cliffs have been brought, by the sinking of the land, face to face with its slow, but sure destroyer.

And how long ago began the epoch—the very latest which

this globe has seen, which has been long enough for all this? The human imagination can no more grasp that time than it can grasp the space between us and the nearest star.

Such thoughts were forced upon me as the steamer stopped off San Fernando; and I saw, some quarter of a mile out at sea, a single stack of rock, which is said to have been joined to the mainland in the memory of the fathers of this generation; and on shore, composed, I am told, of the same rock, that hill of San Fernando which forms a beacon by sea and land for many a mile around. An isolated boss of the older Parian, composed of hardened clay which has escaped destruction, it rises, though not a mile long and a third of a mile broad, steeply to a height of nearly six hundred feet, carrying on its cliffs the remains of a once magnificent vegetation. Now its sides are quarried for the only road-stone met with for miles around; cultivated for pasture, in which the round-headed mango-trees grow about like oaks at home; or terraced for villas and gardens, the charm of which cannot be told in words. All round it, rich sugar estates spread out, with the noble Palmistes left standing here and there along the roads and terraces; and everywhere is activity and high cultivation, under the superintendence of gentlemen who are prospering, because they deserve to prosper.

Between the cliff and the shore nestles the gay and growing little town, which was, when we took the island in 1795, only a group of huts. In it I noted only one thing which looked unpleasant. The Negro houses, however roomy and comfortable, and however rich the gardens which surrounded them, were mostly patched together out of the most heterogeneous and wretched scraps of wood; and on inquiry I found that the materials were, in most cases, stolen; that when a Negro wanted to build a house, instead of buying the materials, he pilfered a board here, a stick there, a nail somewhere else, a lock or a clamp in a fourth place, about the sugar estates, regardless of the serious injury which he caused to working buildings; and when he had gathered a sufficient pile, hidden safely away behind his neighbour's house, the new hut rose as if by magic. This continual pilfering, I was assured, was a serious tax on the cultivation of the estates around. But I was told, too, frankly enough, by the very gentleman who complained, that this habit was simply an heirloom from the bad days of slavery, when the pilfering of the slaves from other estates was connived at by their own masters, on the ground that if A's Negros robbed B, B's Negros robbed C, and so all round the alphabet; one more evil instance of the demoralizing effect of a state of things which, wrong in itself, was sure to be the parent of a hundred other wrongs.

Being, happily for me, in the Governor's suite, I had opportunities of seeing the interior of the island which an average traveller could not have; and I looked forward with interest to visiting new settlements in the forests of the interior, which very few inhabitants of the island, and certainly no strangers, had as yet seen. Our journey began by landing on a good new jetty, and being transferred at once to the tramway which adjoined it. A truck, with chairs on it, as usual here, carried us off at a good mule-trot; and we ran in the fast-fading light through a rolling hummocky country, very like the lowlands of Aberdeenshire, or the neighbourhood of Waterloo, save that, as night came on, the fireflies flickered everywhere among the canes, and here and there the palms and ceibas stood up, black and gaunt, against the sky. At last we escaped from our truck, and found horses waiting, on which we floundered, through mud and moonlight, to a certain hospitable house, and found a hungry party, who had been long waiting for a dinner worth the waiting.

It was not till next morning that I found into what a charming place I had entered overnight. Around were books, pictures, china, vases of flowers, works of art, and all appliances of European taste, even luxury: but in a house utterly un-European. The living rooms, all on the first floor, opened into each other by doorless doorways, and the walls were of cedar and other valuable woods, which good taste had left still unpapered. Windowless bay windows, like great port-holes, opened from each of them into a gallery which ran round the house, sheltered by broad sloping eaves. The deep shade of the eaves contrasted brilliantly with the bright light outside: and contrasted too with the wooden pillars which held up the roof, and which seemed on their southern sides white-hot in the blazing sunshine.

What a field was there for native art; for richest ornamentation of these pillars and those beams. Surely Trinidad, and the whole of northern South America, ought to become some day the paradise of wood-carvers, who, copying even a few of the numberless vegetable and animal forms around, may far surpass the old wood-carving schools of Burmah and Hindostan. And I sat dreaming of the lianes which might be made to wreathe the pillars; the flowers, fruits, birds, butterflies, monkeys, kinkajous, and what not, which might cluster about the capitals, or swing along the beams. Let men who have such materials, and such models, proscribe all tawdry and poor European art—most of it a bad imitation of bad Greek, or worse Renaissance—and trust to Nature and the facts which lie nearest them. But when will a time come for the West Indies when there will be wealth and civilization enough to make such an art possible? Soon, if all the employers of labour were like the gentleman at whose house we were that day, and like some others in the same island.

And through the windows and between the pillars of the gallery, what a blaze of colour and light. The ground-floor was hedged in, a few feet from the walls, with high shrubs, which would have caused unwholesome damp in England, but were needed here for shade. Foreign Crotons, Dracænas, Cereuses, and a dozen more curious shapes—among them a "cup-tree," with concave leaves, each of which would hold water. It was said to come from the East, and was unknown to me. Among them, and over the door, flowering creepers tangled and tossed, rich with flowers; and beyond them a circular lawn (rare in the West Indies), just like an English one, save that the shrubs and trees which bounded it were hot-house plants. A few Carat-palms[1] spread their huge fan-leaves among the curious flowering trees; other foreign palms, some of them very rare, beside them; and on the lawn opposite my bedroom window stood a young Palmiste, which had been planted barely eight years, and was now thirty-eight feet in height, and more than six feet in girth at the butt. Over the roofs of the outhouses rose scarlet Bois immortelles, and tall clumps of Bamboo reflecting blue light from their leaves even under a cloud; and beyond them and below them to the right, a park just like an English one

[1] Sabal.

carried stately trees scattered on the turf, and a sheet of artificial water. Coolies, in red or yellow waistcloths, and Coolie children, too, with nothing save a string round their stomachs (the smaller ones at least), were fishing in the shade. To the left, again, began at once the rich cultivation of the rolling cane-fields, among which the Squire had left standing, somewhat against the public opinion of his less tasteful neighbours, tall Carats, carrying their heads of fan-leaves on smooth stalks from fifty to eighty feet high, and Ceibas—some of them the hugest I had ever seen. Below in the valley were the sugar-works; and beyond this half-natural, half-artificial scene, rose, some mile off, the lowering wall of the yet untouched forest.

It had taken only fifteen years, but fifteen years of hard work, to create this paradise. And only the summer before all had been well-nigh swept away again. During the great drought the fire had raged about the woods. Estate after estate around had been reduced to ashes. And one day our host's turn came. The fire burst out of the woods at three different points. All worked with a will to stop it by cutting traces. But the wind was wild; burning masses from the tree-tops were hurled far among the canes, and all was lost. The canes burnt like shavings, exploding with a perpetual crackle at each joint. In a few hours the whole estate, works, Coolie barracks, Negro huts, was black ash; and the house only, by extreme exertion, saved. But the ground had scarcely cooled when replanting and rebuilding commenced; and now the canes were from ten to twelve feet high, the works nearly ready for the coming crop-time, and no sign of the fire was left, save a few leafless trees, which we found, on riding up to them, to be charred at the base.

And yet men say that the Englishman loses his energy in a tropic climate.

We had a charming Sunday there, amid charming society, down even to the dogs and cats; and not the least charming object among many was little Franky, the Coolie butler's child, who ran in and out with the dogs, gay in his little cotton shirt, and melon-shaped cap, and silver bracelets, and climbed on the Squire's knee, and nestled in his bosom, and played with his seals; and looked up trustingly into our faces with great soft eyes, like a little brown guazu-pita fawn out of the forest. A happy child, and in a happy place.

Then to church at Savannah Grande, riding, of course; for the mud was abysmal, and it was often safer to ride in the ditch than on the road. The village, with a tramway through it, stood high and healthy. The best houses were those of Chinese. The poorer Chinese find peddling employments and trade about the villages, rather than hard work on the estates; while they cultivate on ridges, with minute care, their favourite sweet potato. Round San Fernando, a Chinese will rent from a sugar-planter a bit of land which seems hopelessly infested with weeds, even of the worst of all sorts,—the creeping Para grass[1]—which was introduced a generation since, with some trouble, as food for cattle, and was supposed at first to be so great a boon that the gentleman who brought it in received public thanks and a valuable testimonial. The Chinaman will take the land for a single year, at a rent, I believe, as high as a pound an acre, grow on it his sweet potato crop, and return it to the owner, cleared, for the time being, of every weed. The richer shopkeepers have each a store : but they disdain to live at it. Near by each you see a comfortable low house, with verandahs, green jalousies, and often pretty flowers in pots ; and catch glimpses inside of papered walls, prints, and smart moderator-lamps, which seem to be fashionable among the Celestials. But for one fashion of theirs, I confess, I was not prepared.

We went to church—a large, airy, clean, wooden one—which ought to have had a verandah round to keep off the intolerable sunlight, and which might, too, have had another pulpit. For in getting up to preach in a sort of pill-box on a long stalk, I found the said stalk surging and nodding so

[1] Panicum sp.

under my weight, that I had to assume an attitude of most dignified repose, and to beware of "beating the drum ecclesiastic," or "danging the Bible to shreds," for fear of toppling into the pews of the very smart, and really very attentive, brown ladies below. A crowded congregation it was, clean, gay, respectable and respectful, and spoke well both for the people and for their clergyman. But—happily not till the end of the sermon—I became aware, just in front of me, of a row of smartest Paris bonnets, net-lace shawls, brocades and satins, fit for duchesses; and as the centre of each blaze of finery— " offam non faciem," as old Ammianus Marcellinus has it— the unmistakable visage of a Chinese woman. Whether they understood one word; what they thought of it all; whether they were there for any purpose save to see and be seen, were questions to which I tried in vain, after service, to get an answer. All that could be told was, that the richer Chinese take delight in thus bedizening their wives on high days and holidays; not with tawdry cheap finery, but with things really expensive, and worth what they cost, especially the silks and brocades; and then in sending them, whether for fashion or for loyalty's sake, to an English church. Be that as it may, there they were, ladies from the ancient and incomprehensible Flowery Land, like fossil bones of an old world sticking out amid the vegetation of the new; and we will charitably hope that they were the better for being there.

After church we wandered about the estate to see huge trees. One Ceiba, left standing in a cane-piece, was very grand, from the multitude and mass of its parasites and its huge tresses of lianes; and grand also from its form. The prickly board-wall spurs were at least fifteen feet high, some of them, where they entered the trunk; and at the summit of the trunk, which could not have been less than seventy or eighty feet, one enormous limb (itself a tree) stuck out quite horizontally, and gave a marvellous notion of strength. It seemed as if its length must have snapped it off, years since, where it joined the trunk; or as if the leverage of its weight must have toppled the whole tree over. But the great vegetable had known its own business best, and had built itself up right cannily; and stood, and will stand for many a year, perhaps for many a century, if the Matapalos do not squeeze out its life. I found, by the bye, in groping my way to that tree through canes twelve feet high, that one must be careful, at least with some varieties of cane, not to get cut. The leaf-edges are finely serrated; and more, the sheaths of the leaves are covered with prickly hairs, which give the Coolies sore shins if they work barelegged. The soil here, as everywhere, was exceedingly rich, and sawn out into rolling mounds and steep gullies—sometimes almost too steep for cane-cultivation—by the tropic rains. If, as cannot be doubted, denudation by rain has gone on here, for thousands of years, at the same pace at which it goes on now, the amount of soil removed must be very great; so great, that the Naparimas may have been, when they were first uplifted out of the Gulf, hundreds of feet higher than they are now.

Another tree we went to see in the home park, of which I would have gladly obtained a photograph. A Poix doux,[1] some said it was; others that it was a Figuier.[2] I incline to the former belief, as the leaves seemed to me pinnated: but the doubt was pardonable enough. There was not a leaf on the tree which was not nigh one hundred feet over our heads. For size of spurs and wealth of parasites the tree was almost as remarkable as the Ceiba I mentioned just now. But the curiosity of the tree was a Carat-palm which had started between its very roots; had run its straight and slender stem up parallel with the bole of its companion, and had then pierced through the head of the tree, and all its wilderness of lianes, till it spread its huge flat crown of fans among the highest branches, more than a hundred feet aloft. The contrast between the two forms of vegetation, each so grand, but as utterly different in every line as they are in botanical affinities, and yet both living together in such close embrace, was very noteworthy; a good example of the rule, that while competition is most severe between forms most

[1] Inga. [2] Ficus.

closely allied, forms extremely wide apart may not compete at all, because each needs something which the other does not.

On our return I was introduced to the "Uncle Tom" of the neighbourhood, who had come down to spend Sunday at the Squire's house. He was a middle-sized Negro, in cast of features not above the average, and Isaac by name. He told me how he had been born in Baltimore, a slave to a Quaker master; how he and his wife Mary, during the second American war, ran away, and after hiding three days in the bush, got on board a British ship of war, and so became free. He then enlisted into one of the East Indian regiments, and served some years; as a reward for which he had given him his five acres of land in Trinidad, like others of his corps. These Negro yeomen-veterans, let it be said in passing, are among the ablest and steadiest of the coloured population. Military service has given them just enough of those habits of obedience of which slavery gives too much—if the obedience of a mere slave, depending not on the independent will, but on brute fear, is to be called obedience at all.

Would that in this respect, as in some others, the white subject of the British crown were as well off as the black one. Would that during the last fifty years we had followed the wise policy of the Romans, and by settling our soldiers on our colonial frontiers, established there communities of loyal, able, and valiant citizens. Is it too late to begin now ? Is there no colony left as yet not delivered over to a self-government which actually means, more and more—according to the statements of those who visit the colonies—government by an Irish faction; and which will offer a field for settling our soldiers when they have served their appointed time; so strengthening ourselves, while we reward a class of men who are far more respectable, and far more deserving, than most of those on whom we lavish our philanthropy ?

Surely such men would prove as good subjects as old Isaac and his comrades. For fifty-three years, I was told, he had lived and worked in Trinidad, always independent; so independent indeed, that the very last year, when all but starving, like many of the coloured people, from the long drought which lasted nearly eighteen months, he refused all charity, and came down to this very estate to work for three months in the stifling cane-fields, earning—or fancying that he earned—his own livelihood. A simple, kindly, brave Christian man he seemed, and all who knew him spoke of him as such. The most curious fact, however, which I gleaned from him was his recollection of his own "conversion." His Mary, of whom all spoke as a woman of a higher intellect than he, had "been in the Gospel" several years before him, and used to read and talk to him; but, he said, without effect. At last he had a severe fever; and when he fancied himself dying, had a vision. He saw a grating in the floor, close by his bed, and through it the torments of the lost. Two souls he remembered specially; one "like a singed hog," the other "all over black like a charcoal spade." He looked in fear, and heard a voice cry, "Behold your sins." He prayed; promised, if he recovered, to try and do better; and felt himself forgiven at once.

This was his story, which I have set down word for word; and of which I can only say, that its imagery is no more gross, its confusion between the objective and subjective no more unphilosophical, than the speech on similar matters of many whom we are taught to call divines, theologians, and saints.

At all events, this crisis in his life produced, according to his own statement, not merely a religious, but a moral change. He became a better man henceforth. He had the reputation, among those who knew him well, of being altogether a good man. If so, it matters little what cause he assigned for the improvement. Wisdom is justified of all her children; and, I doubt not, of old black Isaac among the rest.

In 1864 he had a great sorrow. Old Mary, trying to smoke the mosquitos out of her house with a charcoal-pan, set fire, in her short-sightedness, to the place; and everything was burned—the savings of years, the precious Bible among the rest. The Squire took her down to his house, and nursed her: but she died in two days of cold and fright; and Isaac had to begin life again alone. Kind folks built up his ajoupa, and started him afresh; and, to their astonishment, Isaac grew young again, and set to work for himself. He had depended too much for many years on his wife's superior intellect: now he had to act for himself; and he acted. But he spoke of her, like any knight of old, as of a guardian goddess—his guardian still in the other world, as she had been in this.

He was happy enough, he said: but I was told that he had to endure much vexation from the neighbouring Negros, who were Baptists, narrow and conceited; and who—just as the Baptists of the lower class in England would be but too apt to do—tormented him by telling him that he was not sure of heaven, because he went to church instead of joining their body. But he, though he went to chapel in wet weather, clung to his own creed like an old soldier; and came down to Massa's house to spend the Sunday whenever there was a Communion, walking some five miles thither, and as much back again.

So much I learnt concerning old Isaac. And when in the afternoon he toddled away, and back into the forest, what wonder if I felt like Wordsworth after his talk with the old leech-gatherer?—

> "And when he ended,
> I could have laughed myself to scorn to find
> In that decrepit man so firm a mind;
> God, said I, be my help and stay secure,
> I'll think of thee, leech-gatherer, on the lonely moor."

On the Monday morning there was a great parade. All the Coolies were to come up to see the Governor; and after breakfast a long line of dark people arrived up the lawn, the women in their gaudiest muslins, and some of them in cotton velvet jackets of the richest colours. The Oriental instinct for harmonious hues, and those at once rich and sober, such as may be seen in Indian shawls, is very observable even in these Coolies, low-caste as most of them are. There were bangles and jewels among them in plenty; and as it was a high day and a holiday, the women had taken out the little gold or silver stoppers in their pierced nostrils, and put in their place the great gold ring which hangs down over the mouth, and is considered by them, as learned men tell us it was by Rebekah at the well, a special ornament. The men stood by themselves; the women by themselves; the children grouped in front; and a merrier, healthier, shrewder-looking party I have seldom seen. Complaints there were none. All seemed to look on the Squire as a father, and each face brightened when he spoke to them by name. But the great ceremony was the distributing by the Governor of red and yellow sweetmeats to the children out of a huge dish held up by the Hindoo butler, while Franky, in a long night-shirt of crimson cotton velvet, acted as aide-de-camp, and took his perquisites freely. Each of the little brown darlings got its share, the boys putting them into the flap of their waist-cloths, the girls into the front of their veils; and some of the married women seemed ready enough to follow the children's example; some of them, indeed, were little more than children themselves. The pleasure of the men at the whole ceremony was very noticeable, and very pleasant. Well fed, well cared for, well taught (when they will allow themselves to be so), and with a local medical man appointed for their special benefit, Coolies under such a master ought to be, and are, prosperous and happy. Exceptions there are, and must be. Are there none among the workmen of English manu-facturers and farmers? Abuses may spring up, and do. Do none spring up in London and elsewhere? But the Govern-ment has the power to interfere, and uses that power. These poor people are sufficiently protected by law from their white employers; what they need most is protection for the new-comers against the usury, or swindling, by people of their own race, especially Hindoos of the middle class, who are covetous and ill-disposed, and who use their experience of the island for their own selfish advantage. But that evil also

Government is doing its best to put down. Already the Coolies have a far larger amount of money in the savings'-banks of the island than the Negros; and their prosperity can be safely trusted to wise and benevolent laws, enforced by men who can afford to stand above public opinion, as

A Coolie Family.

well as above private interest. I speak, of course, only of Trinidad, because only Trinidad I have seen. But what I say I know intimately to be true.

The parade over—and a pleasant sight it was, and one not easily to be forgotten—we were away to see the Salse, or "mud-volcano," near Monkey Town, in the forest to the south-east. The cross-roads were deep in mud, all the worse because it was beginning to dry on the surface, forming a tough crust above the hasty-pudding which, if broken through, held the horse's leg suspended as in a vice, and would have thrown him down, if it were possible to throw down a West-Indian horse. We passed in one place a quaint little relic of the older world; a small sugar-press, rather than mill, under a roof of palm-leaf, which was worked by hand, or a donkey, just as a Spanish settler would have worked it three hundred years ago. Then on through plenty of garden cultivation, with all the people at their doors as we passed, fat and grinning: then up to a good high-road, and a school for Coolies, kept by a Presbyterian clergyman, Mr. Morton—I must be allowed to mention his name—who, like a sensible man, wore a white coat instead of the absurd regulation black one, too much affected by all well-to-do folk, lay as well as clerical, in the West Indies. The school seemed good enough in all ways. A senior class of young men— including one who had had his head nearly cut off last year by misapplication of that formidable weapon the cutlass, which every coloured man and woman carries in the West Indies— could read pretty well; and the smaller children—with as much clothing on as they could be persuaded to wear—were a sight pleasant to see. Among them, by the bye, was a little lady who excited my astonishment. She was, I was told, twelve years old. She sat summing away on her slate, bedizened out in gauze petticoat, velvet jacket—between which and the petticoat, of course, the waist showed just as nature had made it—gauze veil, bangles, necklace, nose-jewel; for she was a married woman, and her Papa (Anglicè, husband) wished her to look her best on so important an occasion.

This over-early marriage among the Coolies is a very serious evil, but one which they have brought with them from their own land. The girls are practically sold by their fathers while yet children, often to wealthy men much older than they. Love is out of the question. But what if the poor child, as she grows up, sees some one, among that overplus of men, to whom she for the first time in her life takes a fancy? Then comes a scandal; and one which is often ended swiftly enough by the cutlass. Wife-murder is but too common among these Hindoos, and they cannot be made to see that it is wrong. "I kill my own wife. Why not? I kill no other man's wife," was said by as pretty, gentle, graceful a lad of two-and-twenty as one need see; a convict performing, and perfectly, the office of housemaid in a friend's house. There is murder of wives, or quasi-wives now and then, among the baser sort of Coolies—murder because a poor girl will not give her ill-earned gains to the ruffian who considers her as his property. But there is also law in Trinidad, and such offences do not go unpunished.

Then on through Savannah Grande and village again, and past more sugar estates, and past beautiful bits of forest, left, like English woods, standing in the cultivated fields. One patch of a few acres on the side of a dell was very lovely. Huge Figuiers and Huras were mingled with palms and rich undergrowth, and lighted up here and there with purple creepers.

So we went on, and on, and into the thick forest, and what was, till Sir Ralph Woodford taught the islanders what an European road was like, one of the pattern royal roads of the island. Originally an Indian trace, it had been widened by the Spaniards, and transformed from a line of mud six feet broad to one of thirty. The only pleasant reminiscence which I have about it was the finding in flower a beautiful parasite, undescribed by Griesbach;[1] a "wild pine" with a branching spike of crimson flowers, purple tipped; which shone in the darkness of the bush like a great bunch of rose-buds growing among lily-leaves.

The present Governor, like Sir Ralph Woodford before him, has been fully aware of the old saying—which the Romans knew well, and which the English did not know,

[1] Æchmæa Augusta.

and only re-discovered some century since—that the "first step in civilization is to make roads; the second, to make more roads; and the third, to make more roads still."

Through this very district (aided by men whose talents he had the talent to discover and employ) he has run wide, level, and sound roads, either already completed or in progress through all parts of the island which I visited, save the precipitous glens of the northern shore.

Of such roads we saw more than one in the next few days. That day we had to commit ourselves, when we turned off the royal road, to one of the old Spanish-Indian jungle tracks. And here is a recipe for making one :—Take a railway embankment of average steepness, strew it freely with wreck, rigging and all, to imitate the fallen timber, roots, and lianes—a few flagstones and boulders here and there will be quite in place; plant the whole with the thickest pheasant-cover; set a field of huntsmen to find their way through it at the points of least resistance three times a week during a wet winter; and if you dare follow their footsteps, you will find a very accurate imitation of a forest-track in the wet season.

At one place we seemed to be fairly stopped. We plunged and slid down into a muddy brook, luckily with a gravel bar on which the horses could stand, at least one by one; and found opposite us a bank of smooth clay, bound with slippery roots, some ten feet high. We stood and looked at it, and the longer we looked—in hunting phrase—the less we liked it. But there was no alternative. Some one jumped off, and scrambled up on his hands and knees; his horse was driven up the bank to him—on its knees, likewise, more than once—and caught staggering among boughs and mud; and by the time the whole cavalcade was over, horses and men looked as if they had been brick-making for a week.

But here again the cunning of these horses surprised me. On one very steep pitch, for instance, I saw before me two logs across the path, two feet and more in diameter, and what was worse, not two feet apart. How the brown cob meant to get over I could not guess: but as he seemed not to falter or turn tail, as an English horse would have done, I laid the reins on his neck and watched his legs. To my astonishment, he lifted a fore-leg out of the abyss of mud, put it between the logs, where I expected to hear it snap; clawed in front, and shuffled behind; put the other over the second log, the mud and water splashing into my face, and then brought the first freely out from between the logs, and—horrible to see—put a hind one in. Thus did he fairly walk through the whole; stopped a moment to get his breath; and then staggered and scrambled upward again, as if he had done nothing remarkable. Coming back, by the bye, those two logs lay heavy on my heart for a mile ere I neared them. He might get up over them: but how would he get down again? And I was not surprised to hear more than one behind me say, "I think I shall lead over." But being in front, if I fell, I could only fall into the mud, and not on the top of a friend. So I let the brown cob do what he would, determined to see how far a tropic horse's legs could keep him up; and, to my great amusement, he quietly leapt the whole, descending five or six feet into a pool of mud, which shot out over him and me, half blinding us for the moment; then slid away on his haunches downward; picked himself up; and went on as usual, solemn, patient, and seemingly stupid as any donkey.

We had some difficulty in finding our quest, the Salse, or mud volcano. But at last, out of a hut half buried in verdure on the edge of a little clearing, there tumbled the quaintest little old black man, cutlass in hand, and, without being asked, went on ahead as our guide. Crook-backed, round-shouldered, his only dress a ragged shirt and ragged pair of drawers, he had evidently thriven upon the forest life for many a year. He did not walk nor run, but tumbled along in front of us, his bare feet plashing from log to log and mud-heap to mud-heap, his grey woolly head wagging right and left, and his cutlass brushing almost instinctively at every bough he passed, while he turned round every moment to jabber something, usually in Creole French, which of course I could not understand.

He led us well, up and down, and at last over a flat of rich muddy ground, full of huge trees, and of their roots likewise, where there was no path at all. The solitude was awful; so was the darkness of the shade; so was the stifling heat; and right glad we were when we saw an opening in the trees, and the little man quickened his pace, and stopped with an air of triumph not unmixed with awe on the edge of a circular pool of mud and water some two or three acres in extent.

"Dere de debbil's woodyard," said he, with somewhat bated breath. And no wonder; for a more doleful, uncanny, half-made spot I never saw. The sad forest ringed it round with a green wall, feathered down to the ugly mud, on which, partly perhaps from its saltness, partly from the changeableness of the surface, no plant would grow, save a few herbs and creepers which love the brackish water. Only here and there an Echites had crawled out of the wood and lay along the ground, its long shoots gay with large cream-coloured flowers and pairs of glossy leaves; and on it, and on some dead brushwood, grew a lovely little parasitic Orchis, an Oncidium, with tiny fans of leaves, and flowers like swarms of yellow butterflies.

There was no track of man, not even a hunter's footprint;

but instead, tracks of beasts in plenty. Deer, quenco[1] and lapo,[2] with smaller animals, had been treading up and down, probably attracted by the salt-water. They were safe enough, the old man said. No hunter dare approach the spot. There were "too much jumbies" here; and when one of the party expressed a wish to lie out there some night, in the hope of good shooting, the Negro shook his head. He would "not do that for all the world. De debbil come out here at night, and walk about;" and he was much scandalized when the young gentleman rejoined, that the chance of such a sight would be an additional reason for bivouacking there.

So we walked out upon the mud, which was mostly hard enough, past shallow pools of brackish water, smelling of asphalt, toward a group of little mud-volcanos on the further side. These curious openings into the nether-world are not permanent. They choke up after awhile, and fresh ones appear in another part of the area, thus keeping the whole clear of plants.

They are each some two or three feet high, of the very finest mud, which leaves no feeling of grit on the fingers or tongue, and dries, of course, rapidly in the sun. On the top, or near the top, of each, is a round hole, a finger's-breadth, polished to exceeding smoothness, and running down through

[1] Dicoteles (Peccary hog).   [2] Cœlogenys paca.

the cone as far as we could dig. From each oozes perpetually, with a clicking noise of gas-bubbles, water and mud; and now and then, losing their temper, they spirt out their dirt to a considerable height; a feat which we did not see performed, but which is so common that we were in something like fear and trembling, while we opened a cone with our cutlasses. For though we could hardly have been made dirtier than we were, an explosion in our faces of mud with " a faint bituminous smell," and impregnated with "common salt, a notable proportion of iodine, and a trace of carbonate of soda and carbonate of lime,"[1] would have been both unpleasant and humiliating. But the most puzzling thing about the place is, that out of the mud comes up — not jumbies, but—a multitude of small stones, like no stones in the neighbourhood; we found concretions of iron sand, and scales which seemed to have peeled off them; and pebbles, quartzose, or jasper, or like in appearance to flint; but all evidently long rolled on a sea-beach. Messrs. Wall and Sawkins mention pyrites and gypsum as being found: but we saw none, as far as I recollect. All these must have been carried up from a considerable depth by the force of the same gases which make the little mud volcanos.

Now and then this "Salse," so quiet when we saw it, is

[1] Dr. Davy (West Indies, art. *Trinidad*).

said to be seized with a violent paroxysm. Explosions are heard, and large discharges of mud, and even flame, are said to appear. Some seventeen years ago (according to Messrs. Wall and Sawkins) such an explosion was heard six miles off; and next morning the surface was found quite altered, and trees had disappeared, or been thrown down. But—as they wisely say—the reports of the inhabitants must be received with extreme caution. In the autumn of last year, some such explosion is said to have taken place at the Cedros Salse, a place so remote, unfortunately, that I could not visit it. The Negros and Coolies, the story goes, came running to the overseer at the noise, assuring him that something terrible had happened; and when he, in defiance of their fears, went off to the Salse, he found that many tons of mud—I was told thousands—had been thrown out. How true this may be, I cannot say. But Messrs. Wall and Sawkins saw with their own eyes, in 1856, about two miles from this Cedros Salse, the results of an explosion which had happened only two months before, and of which they give a drawing. A surface two hundred feet round had been upheaved fifteen feet, throwing the trees in every direction; and the sham earthquake had shaken the ground for two hundred or three hundred yards round, till the natives fancied that their huts were going to fall.

There is a third Salse near Poole river, on the Upper

Ortoire, which is extinct, or at least quiescent; but this, also, I could not visit. It is about seventeen miles from the sea, and about two hundred feet above it. As for the causes of these Salses, I fear the reader must be content, for the present, with a somewhat muddy explanation of the muddy mystery. Messrs. Wall and Sawkins are inclined to connect it with asphalt springs and pitch lakes. "There is," they say, "easy gradation from the smaller Salses to the ordinary naphtha or petroleum springs." It is certain that in the production of asphalt, carbonic acid, carburetted hydrogen, and water are given off. "May not," they ask, "these orifices be the vents by which such gases escape? And in forcing their way to the surface, is it not natural that the liquid asphalt and slimy water should be drawn up and expelled?" They point out the fact, that wherever such volcanos exist, asphalt or petroleum is found hard by. The mud volcanos of Turbaco, in New Granada, famous from Humboldt's description of them, lie in an asphaltic country. They are much larger than those of Trinidad, the cones being, some of them, twenty feet high. When Humboldt visited them in 1801, they gave off hardly anything save nitrogen gas. But in the year 1850, a "bituminous odour" had begun to be diffused; asphaltic oil swam on the surface of the small openings; and the gas issuing from any of the cones could be ignited. Dr. Daubeny found the mud volcanos of

Macaluba giving out bitumen, and bubbles of carbonic acid and carburetted hydrogen. The mud-volcano of Saman, in the Western Caucasus, gives off, with a continual stream of thick mud, ignited gases, accompanied with mimic earthquakes like those of the Trinidad Salses; and this out of a soil said to be full of bituminous springs, and where (as in Trinidad) the tertiary strata carry veins of asphalt, or are saturated with naphtha. At the famous sacred Fire wells of Baku, in the Eastern Caucasus, the ejections of mud and inflammable gas are so mixed with asphaltic products, that Eichwald says "they should be rather called naphtha volcanos than mud volcanos, as the eruptions always terminate in a large emission of naphtha."

It is reasonable enough, then, to suppose a similar connection in Trinidad. But whence come, either in Trinidad or at Turbaco, the sea-salts and the iodine? Certainly not from the sea itself, which is distant, in the case of the Trinidad Salses, from two to seventeen miles. It must exist already in the strata below. And the ejected pebbles, which are evidently sea-worn, must form part of a tertiary sea-beach, covered by sands, and covering, perhaps, in its turn, vegetable débris which, as it is converted into asphalt, thrusts the pebbles up to the surface.

We had to hurry away from the strange place; for night was falling fast, or rather ready to fall, as always here, in a moment, without twilight, and we were scarce out of the forest before it was dark. The wild game was already moving, and a deer crossed our line of march, close before one of the horses. However, we were not benighted; for the sun was hardly down ere the moon rose, bright and full; and we floundered home through the mud, to start again next morning into mud again.

Through rich rolling land covered with cane; past large sugar-works, where crop-time and all its bustle was just beginning; along a tramway, which made an excellent horse-road, and then along one of the new roads, which are opening up the yet untouched riches of this island. In this district alone, thirty-six miles of good road and thirty bridges have been made, where formerly there were only two abominable bridle-paths. It was a solid pleasure to see good engineering round the hill-sides; gullies which but a year or two before were break-neck scrambles into fords often impassable after all, bridged with baulks of incorruptible timber, on piers sunk, to give a hold in that sea of hasty-pudding, sixteen feet below the river-bed; and side supports sunk as far into the banks; a solid pleasure to congratulate the warden (who had joined us) on his triumphs, and to hear how he had sought for miles around in the hasty-pudding sea, ere he could find either gravel or stone for road metal, and had found it after all; or how in places, finding no stone at all, he had been forced to metal the way with burnt clay, which, as I can testify, is an excellent substitute; or how again he had coaxed and patted the too-comfortable natives into being well paid for doing the very road-making which, if they had any notion of their own interests, they would combine to do for themselves. And so we rode on chatting,

"While all the land,
Beneath a broad and equal-blowing breeze,
Smelt of the coming summer;"

for it was winter then, and only 80° in the shade, till the road entered the virgin forest, through which it has been driven, on the American principle of making land valuable by beginning with a road, and expecting settlers to follow it. Some such settlers we found, clearing right and left; among them a most satisfactory sight; namely, more than one Coolie family, who had served their apprenticeship, saved money, bought Government land, and set up as yeomen; the foundation, it is to be hoped, of a class of intelligent and civilized peasant proprietors.

Banana.

These men, as soon as they have cleared as much land as their wives and children, with their help, can keep in order, go off, usually, in gangs of ten to fifteen, to work, in many instances, on the estates from which they originally came. This fact practically refutes the opinion which was at first held by some attorneys and managers of sugar-estates, that the settling of free Indian immigrants would materially affect the labour supply of the colony. I must express an earnest hope that neither will any planters be short-sighted enough to urge such a theory on the present Governor, nor will the present Governor give ear to it. The colony at large must gain by the settlement of Crown lands by civilized people like the Hindoos, if it be only through the increased exports and imports; while the sugar estates will become more and more sure of a constant supply of labour, without the heavy expense of importing fresh immigrants. I am assured, that the only expense to the colony is the fee for survey, amounting to eighteen dollars for a ten-acre allotment, as the Coolie prefers the thinly-wooded and comparatively poor lands, from the greater facility of clearing them; and these lands are quite unsaleable to other customers. Therefore, for less than 4*l.*, an acclimatized Indian labourer with his family (and it must be remembered, that, while the Negro families increase very slowly, the Coolies increase very rapidly, being more kind and careful parents) are permanently settled in the colony, the man to work five days a week on sugar estates, the family to grow provisions for the market, instead of being shipped back to India at a cost, including gratuities and etceteras, of not less than 50*l*.

One clearing we reached—were I five-and-twenty, I should like to make just such another next to it—of a higher class still. A cultivated Scotchman, now no longer young, but hale and mighty, had taken up three hundred acres, and already cleared a hundred and fifty; and there he intended to pass the rest of a busy life, not under his own vine and fig-tree, but under his own castor-oil and cacao-tree. We were welcomed by as noble a Scot's face as I ever saw, and as keen a Scot's eye; and taken in and fed, horses and men, even too sumptuously, in a palm and timber house. Then we wandered out to see the site of his intended mansion, with the rich wooded hills of the Latagual to the north, and all around the unbroken forest, where, he told us, the howling monkeys shouted defiance morning and evening at him who did

"Invade their ancient solitary reign."

Then we went down to see the Coolie barracks, where the folk seemed as happy and well cared for as they were certain to be under such a master; then down a rocky pool in the river, jammed with bare white logs (as in some North American forest), which had been stopped in flood by one enormous trunk across the stream; then back past the site of the ajoupa, which had been our host's first shelter, and which had disappeared by a cause strange enough to English ears. An enormous silk-cotton near by was felled, in spite of the Negros' fears. Its boughs, when it fell, did not reach the ajoupa by twenty feet or more; but the wind of its fall did, and blew the hut clean away. This may sound like a story out of Munchausen: but there was no doubt of the fact; and to us who saw the size of the tree which did the deed it seemed probable enough.

We rode away again, and into the "Morichal," the hills where Moriche palms are found; to see certain springs and a certain tree; and well worth seeing they were. Out of the base of a limestone hill, amid delicate ferns, under the shade of enormous trees, a clear pool bubbled up and ran away, a stream from its very birth, as is the wont of limestone springs. It was a spot fit for a Greek nymph; at least for an Indian damsel: but the nymph who came to draw water in a tin bucket, and stared stupidly and saucily at us, was anything but Greek, or even Indian, either in costume or manners. Be it so. White men are responsible for her being there; so white men must not complain. Then we went in search of the tree. We had passed as we rode up some Huras (sandbox trees), which would have been considered giants in England; and I had been laughed at more than once for asking, "Is that the tree? or that?" I soon knew why. We scrambled up a steep bank of broken limestone, through ferns and Balisiers, for perhaps a hundred feet; and then were suddenly aware of a bole which justified the saying of one of our party—that, when surveying for a road he had come suddenly on it, he "felt as if he had run against a church tower." It was a Hura, seemingly healthy, undecayed, and growing vigorously. Its girth—we measured it carefully—was forty-four feet, six feet from the ground, and as I laid my face against it and looked up, I seemed to be looking up a ship's side. It was perfectly cylindrical, branchless, and smooth, save, of course, the tiny prickles which beset the bark, for a height at which we could not guess, but which we luckily had an opportunity of measuring. A wild pine grew in the lowest fork, and had kindly let down an air-root into the soil. We tightened the root, set it perpendicular, cut it off exactly where it touched the ground, and then pulled carefully till we brought the plant, and half-a-dozen more strange vegetables, down on our heads. The length of the air-root was just seventy-five feet. Some twenty feet or more above that first fork was a second fork; and then the tree began. Where its head was we could not see. We could only, by laying our faces against the bole, and looking up, discern a wilderness of boughs carrying a green cloud of leaves, most of them too high for us to discern their shape without the glasses. We walked up the slope, and round about, in hopes of seeing the head of the tree clear enough to guess at its total height: but in vain. It was only when we had ridden some half mile up the hill that we could discern its masses rising, a bright green mound, above the darker foliage of the forest. It looked of any height, from one hundred and fifty to two hundred feet; less it could hardly be. " It made," says a note by one of our party, " other huge trees look like shrubs." I am not surprised that my friend Mr. St. Luce D'Abadie, who measured the tree since my departure, found it to be one hundred and ninety-two feet in height.

I was assured that there were still larger trees in the island. A certain Locust-tree and a Ceiba were mentioned. The Moras, too, of the southern hills, were said to be far taller. And I can well believe it; for if huge trees were as shrubs beside that Sandbox, it would be a shrub by the side of those Locusts figured by Spix and Martius, which fifteen Indians with outstretched arms could just embrace. At the bottom they were eighty-four feet round, and sixty where the boles became cylindrical. By counting the rings of such parts as could be reached, they arrived at the conclusion that they were of the age of Homer, and 332 years old in the days of Pythagoras. One estimate, indeed, reduced their antiquity to 2,052 years old; while another (counting,

I presume, two rings of fresh wood for every year) carried it up to 4,104.

So we rode on and up the hills, by green and flowery paths, with here and there a cottage and a garden, and groups of enormous Palmistes towering over the tree-tops in every glen, talking over that wondrous weed, whose head we saw still far below. For weed it is, and nothing more. The wood is soft and almost useless, save for firing; and the tree itself, botanists tell us, is neither more nor less than a gigantic Spurge, the cousin-german of the milky garden weeds with which boys burn away their warts. But if the modern theory be true, that when we speak (as we are forced to speak) of the relationships of plants, we use no metaphor, but state an actual fact; that the groups into which we are forced to arrange them indicate not merely similarity of type, but community of descent—then how wonderful is the kindred between the Spurge and the Hura—indeed, between all the members of the Euphorbiaceous group, so fantastically various in outward form; so abundant, often huge, in the Tropics, while in our remote northern island their only representatives are a few weedy Spurges, two Dog's Mercuries—weeds likewise—and the Box. Wonderful it is if only these last have had the same parentage—still more if they have had the same parentage, too, with forms so utterly different from them as the prickly-stemmed scarlet-flowered Euphorbia common in our hothouses; as the huge succulent cactus-like Euphorbia of the Canary Islands; as the gale-like Phyllanthus; the many-formed Crotons, which in the West Indies alone comprise, according to Griesbach, at least twelve genera and thirty species; the hemp-like Maniocs, Physic-nuts, Castor oils; the scarlet Poinsettia which adorns dinner-tables in winter; the pretty little pink and yellow Dalechampia, now common in hothouses; the Manchineel, with its glossy poplar-like leaves; and this very Hura, with leaves still more like a poplar, and a fruit which differs from most of its family in having not three but many divisions, usually a multiple of three, up to fifteen; a fruit which it is difficult to obtain, even where the tree is plentiful: for hanging at the end of long branches, it bursts when ripe with a crack like a pistol, scattering its seeds far and wide; from whence its name of Hura crepitans.

But what if all these forms are the descendants of one original form? Would that be one whit more wonderful, more inexplicable, than the theory that they were each and all, with their minute and often imaginary shades of difference, created separately and at once? But if it be—which I cannot allow—what can the theologian say, save that God's works are even more wonderful than we always believed them to be? As for the theory being impossible: who are we, that we should limit the power of God? "Is anything too hard for the Lord?" asked the prophet of old; and we have a right to ask it as long as time shall last. If it be said that natural selection is too simple a cause to produce such fantastic variety: we always knew that God works by very simple, or seemingly simple, means; that the universe, as far as we could discern it, was one organization of the most simple means; it was wonderful (or ought to have been) in our eyes, that a shower of rain should make the grass grow, and that the grass should become flesh, and the flesh food for the thinking brain of man; it was (or ought to have been) yet more wonderful in our eyes, that a child should resemble its parents, or even a butterfly resemble—if not always, still usually—its parents likewise. Ought God to appear less or more august in our eyes if we discover that His means are even simpler than we supposed? We held Him to be almighty and allwise. Are we to reverence Him less or more if we find that His might is greater, His wisdom deeper, than we had ever dreamed? We believed that His care was over all His works; that His providence watched perpetually over the universe. We were taught, some of us at least, by Holy Scripture, to believe that the whole history of the universe was made up of special providences: if, then, that should be true which Mr. Darwin says—"It may be metaphorically said that natural selection is daily and hourly scrutinizing, throughout the world, every variation, even the slightest; rejecting that which is bad, preserving and adding up all that is good; silently and insensibly working, whenever and wherever opportunity offers, at the improvement of each organic being in relation to its organic and inorganic conditions of life,"— if this, I say, were proved to be true, ought God's care, God's providence, to seem less or more magnificent in our eyes? Of old it was said by Him without whom nothing is made— " My Father worketh hitherto, and I work." Shall we quarrel with physical science, if she gives us evidence that these words are true? And if it should be proven that the gigantic Hura and the lowly Spurge sprang from one common ancestor, what would the orthodox theologian have to say to it, saving—" I always knew that God was great: and I am not surprised to find Him greater than I thought Him?"

So much for the giant weed of the Morichal, from which we rode on and up through rolling country growing lovelier at every step, and turned out of our way to see wild pine-apples in a sandy spot, or "Arenal" in a valley beneath. The meeting of the stiff marl and the fine sand was abrupt, and well marked by the vegetation. On one side of the ravine the tall fan-leaved Carats marked the rich soil; on the other, the sand and gravel loving Cocorites appeared at once, crowding their ostrich plumes together.

Most of them were the common species of the island[1] in which the pinnæ of the leaves grow in fours and fives, and at different angles from the leaf-stalk, giving the whole a brushy appearance, which takes off somewhat from the perfectness of its beauty. But among them we saw—for the first and last time in the forest—a few of a far more beautiful species,[2] common on the mainland. In it, the pinnæ are set on all at the same distance apart, and all in the same plane, in opposite sides of the stalk, giving to the whole foliage a grand simplicity; and producing, when the curving leaf-points toss in the breeze, that curious appearance which I mentioned in an earlier chapter, of green glass wheels with rapidly revolving spokes. At their feet grew the pine-apples, only in flower or unripe fruit, so that we could not quench our thirst with them, and only looked with curiosity at the small wild type of so famous a plant. But close by, and happily nearly ripe, we found a fair substitute for pine-apples in the fruit of the Karatas. This form of Bromelia, closely allied to the Pinguin of which hedges are made, bears a straggling plume of prickly leaves, six or eight feet long each, close to the ground. The forester looks for a plant in which the leaves droop outwards—a sign that the fruit is ripe. After beating it cautiously (for snakes are very fond of coiling under its shade) he opens the centre, and finds, close to

[1] Maximiliana Caribæa.   [2] M. regia.

the ground, a group of whitish fruits, nearly two inches long; peels carefully off the skin, which is beset with innumerable sharp hairs, and eats the sour-sweet refreshing pulp: but not too often, for there are always hairs enough left to make the tongue bleed if more than one or two are eaten.

With lips somewhat less parched, we rode away again to see the sight of the day; and a right pleasant sight it was. These Montserrat hills had been, within the last three years, almost the most lawless and neglected part of the island. Principally by the energy and tact of one man, the wild inhabitants had been conciliated, brought under law, and made to pay their light taxes, in return for a safety and comfort enjoyed perhaps by no other peasants on earth.

A few words on the excellent system, which bids fair to establish in this colony a thriving and loyal peasant proprietary. Up to 1847 crown-lands were seldom alienated. In that year a price was set upon them, and persons in illegal occupation ordered to petition for their holdings. Unfortunately, though a time was fixed for petitioning, no time was fixed for paying; and consequently the vast majority of petitioners never took any further steps in the matter. Unfortunately, too, the price fixed—£2 per acre—was too high; and squatting went on much as before.

It appeared to the late Governor that this evil would best be dealt with experimentally and locally; and he accordingly erected the chief squatting district, Montserrat, into a ward, giving the warden large discretionary powers as Commissioner of crown-lands. The price of crown-lands was reduced, in 1869, to £1 per acre; and the Montserrat system extended, as far as possible, to other wards; a movement which the results fully justified.

In 1867 there were in Montserrat 400 squatters, holding lands of from three to 120 acres, planted with cacao, coffee, or provisions. Some of the cacao plantations were valued at £1,000. These people lived without paying taxes, and almost without law or religion. The Crown woods had been, of course, sadly plundered by squatters, and by others who should have known better. At every turn magnificent cedars might have been seen levelled by the axe, only a few feet of the trunk being used to make boards and shingles, while the greater part was left to rot or burn. These irregularities have been now almost stopped; and 266 persons, in Montserrat alone, have taken out grants of land, some of 400 acres. But this by no means represents the number of purchasers, as nearly an equal number have paid for their estates though they have not yet received their grants, and nearly 500 more have made application. Two villages have been formed; one of which is that where we rested, containing the church. The other contains the warden's residence and office, the police-station, and a numerously attended school.

The squatters are of many races, and of many hues of black and brown. The half-breeds from the neighbouring coast of Venezuela, a mixture, probably of Spanish, Negro, and Indian, are among the most industrious; and their cacao plantations, in some cases, hold 8,000 to 10,000 trees. The south-west corner of Montserrat[1] is almost entirely settled by Africans of various tribes—Mandingos, Foulahs, Homas, Yarribas, Ashantees, and Congos. The last occupy the lowest position in the social scale. They lead, for the most part, a semi-barbarous life, dwelling in miserable huts, and subsisting on the produce of an acre or two of badly cultivated land, eked out with the pay of an occasional day's labour on some neighbouring estate. The social portion of some of the Yarribas forms a marked contrast to that of the Congos. They inhabit houses of cedar, or other substantial materials. Their gardens are, for the most part, well stocked and kept. They raise crops of yam, cassava, Indian corn, &c.; and some of them subscribe to a fund on which they may draw in case of illness or misfortune. They are, however (as is to be ex-

---

[1] I quote mostly from a report of my friend Mr. Robert Mitchell, who, almost alone, did this good work, and who has, since my departure, been sent to Demerara to assist at the investigation into the alleged ill-usage of the Coolie immigrants there. No more just or experienced public servant could have been employed on such an errand.

pected from superior intellect while still uncivilized), more difficult to manage than the Congos, and highly impatient of control.

These Africans, Mr. Mitchell says, all belong nominally to some denomination of Christianity: but their lives are more influenced by their belief in Obeah. While the precepts of religion are little regarded, they stand in mortal dread of those who practise this mischievous imposture. Well might the Commissioner say, in 1867, that several years must elapse before the chaos which reigned could be reduced to order. The wonder is, that in three years so much has been done. It was very difficult, at first, even to find the whereabouts of many of the squatters. The Commissioner had to work by compass through the pathless forest. Getting little or no food but cassava cakes and "guango" of maize, and now and then a little coffee and salt fish, without time to hunt the game which passed him, and continually wet through, he stumbled in suddenly on one squatting after another, to the astonishment of its owner, who could not conceive how he had been found out, and had never before seen a white man alone in the forest. Sometimes he was in considerable danger of a rough reception from people who could not at first understand what they had to gain by getting legal titles, and buying the lands the fruit of which they had enjoyed either for nothing, or for payment of a small annual assessment for the cultivated portion. In another quarter—Toco—a notoriously lawless squatter had expressed his intention of shooting the Government official. The white gentleman walked straight up to the little forest fortress hidden in bush, and confronted the Negro, who had gun in hand.

"I could have shot you if I had liked, buccra."

"No, you could not. I should have cut you down first: so don't play the fool," answered the official quietly, hand on cutlass.

The wild man gave in; paid his rates; received the crown title for his land; and became (as have all these sons of the forest) fast friends with one whom they have learnt at once to love and fear.

But among the Montserrat hills, the Governor had struck on a spot so fit for a new settlement, that he determined to found one forthwith. The quick-eyed Jesuits had founded a Mission on the same spot many years before. But all had lapsed again into forest. A group of enormous Palmistes stand on a plateau, flat, and yet lofty and healthy. The soil is exceeding fertile. There are wells and brooks of pure water all around. The land slopes down for hundreds of feet in wooded gorges, full of cedar and other admirable timber, with Palmistes towering over them everywhere. Far away lies the lowland; and every breeze of heaven sweeps over the crests of the hills. So one peculiarly tall palm was chosen for a central land-mark, an ornament to the town square such as no capital in Europe can boast. Traces were cut, streets laid out, lots of crown-lands put up for sale, and settlers invited in the name of the Government.

Scarcely eighteen months had passed since then, and already there Mitchell Street, Violin Street, Duboulay Street, Farfan Street, had each its new houses built of cedar and thatched with palm. Two Chinese shops had celestials with pig-tails and thick-soled shoes grinning behind cedar counters, among stores of Bryant's safety matches, Huntley and Palmer's biscuits, and Allsop's pale ale. A church had been built, the shell at least, and partly floored, with a very simple, but not tasteless, altar; the Abbé had a good house, with a gallery, jalousies, and white china handles to the doors. The mighty palm in the centre of Gordon Square had a neat railing round it, as befitted the Palladium of the village. Behind the houses, among the stumps of huge trees, maize and cassava, pigeon-peas and sweet potatoes, fattened in the sun, on ground which till then had been shrouded by vegetation a hundred feet thick; and as we sat at the head man's house, with French and English prints upon the walls, and drank beer from a Chinese shop, and looked out upon the loyal, thriving little settlement, I envied the two young men who could say, "At least, we have not lived in vain; for we have made this out of the primæval forest." Then on again. "We mounted" (I quote now from the notes of one to whom the existence of the settlement was due) "to the crest of the hills, and had a noble view southwards, looking over the rich mass of dark wood, flecked here and there with a scarlet stain of Bois immortelle, to the great sea of bright green sugar cultivation in the Naparimas, studded by white works and villages, and backed far off by a hazy line of forest, out of which rose the peaks of the Moruga Mountains. More to the west lay San Fernando hill, the calm gulf, and the coast toward La Brea and Cedros melting into mist. M—— thought we should get a better view of the northern mountains by riding up to old Nicano's house; so we went thither, under the cacao rich with yellow and purple pods. The view was fine: but the northern range, though visible, was rather too indistinct, and the mainland was not to be seen at all."

Nevertheless, the panorama from the top of Montserrat is at once the most vast, and the most lovely, which I have ever seen. And whosoever chooses to go and live there may buy any reasonable quantity of the richest soil at one pound per acre.

Then down off the ridge toward the northern lowland, lay a headlong old Indian path, by which we travelled, at last, across a rocky brook, and into a fresh paradise.

I must be excused for using this word so often: but I use it in the original Persian sense, as a place in which natural beauty has been helped by art. An English park or garden would have been called of old a paradise; and the enceinte of a West Indian house, even in its present half-wild condition, well deserves the same title. That Art can help Nature there can be no doubt. "The perfection of Nature" exists only in the minds of sentimentalists, and of certain well-meaning persons, who assert the perfection of Nature when they wish to controvert science, and deny it when they wish to prove this earth fallen and accursed. Mr. Nesfield can make landscapes, by obedience to certain laws which Nature is apt to disregard in the struggle for existence, more beautiful than they are already by Nature; and that without introducing foreign forms of vegetation. But if foreign forms, wisely chosen for their shapes and colours, be added, the beauty may be indefinitely increased. For the plants most capable of beautifying any given spot do not always grow therein, simply because they have not yet arrived there; as may be seen by comparing any wood planted with Rhododendrons and Azaleas with the neighbouring wood in its native state. Thus may be obtained somewhat of that variety and richness which is wanting everywhere, more or less, in the vegetation of our northern zone, only just recovering slowly from the destructive catastrophe of the glacial epoch;

a richness which, small as it is, vanishes as we travel northward, till the drear landscape is sheeted more and more with monotonous multitudes of heather, grass, fir, or other social plants. But even in the Tropics the virgin forest, beautiful as it is, is without doubt much less beautiful, both in form and colours, than it might be made. Without doubt, also, a mere clearing, after a few years, is a more beautiful place than the forest; because by it distance is given, and you are enabled to see the sky, and the forest itself beside; because new plants, and some of them very handsome ones, are introduced by cultivation, or spring up in the rastrajo; and lastly, but not least, because the forest on the edge of the clearing is able to feather down to the ground, and change what is at first a bare tangle of stems and boughs into a softly rounded bank of verdure and flowers. When, in some future civilization, the art which has produced, not merely a Chatsworth or a Dropmore, but an average English shrubbery or park, is brought to bear on tropic vegetation, then Nature, always willing to obey when conquered by fair means, will produce such effects of form and colour around tropic estates and cities as we cannot fancy for ourselves.

Mr. Wallace laments (and rightly) the absence in the tropic forests of such grand masses of colour as are supplied by a heather moor, a furze or broom-croft, a field of yellow charlock, blue bugloss, or scarlet poppy. Tropic landscape gar-

Tortuga.

dening will supply that defect; and a hundred plants of yellow Allamanda, or purple Dolichos, or blue Clitoria, or crimson Norantea, set side by side, as we might use a hundred Calceolarias or Geraniums, will carry up the forest walls, and over the tree-tops, not square yards, but I had almost said square acres of richest positive colour. I can conceive no limit to the effects—always heightened by the intense sunlight and the peculiar tenderness of the distances—which landscape gardening will produce when once it is brought to bear on such material as it has never yet attempted to touch, at least in the West Indies, save in the Botanic Garden at Port of Spain.

And thus the little paradise at Tortuga to which we descended to sleep, though cleared out without any regard to art, was far more beautiful than the forest out of which it had been hewn three years before. The two first settlers regretted the days when the house was a mere palm-thatched hut, where they sat on stumps which would not balance, and ate potted meat with their pocket-knives. But it had grown now into a grand place, fit to receive ladies: such a house, or rather shed, as those South Sea Island ones which may be seen in Hodges' Illustrations to Cook's Voyages, save that a couple of bedrooms have been boarded off at the back, a little office on one side, and a bulwark, like that of a ship, put round the gallery. And as we looked down through the purple gorges, and up at the mountain woods, over which the stars were flashing out bright and fast, and listened to the soft strange notes of the forest birds going to roost, again the thought came over me—Why should not gentlemen and ladies come to such spots as these to live "the Gentle Life?"

We slept that night, some in beds, some in hammocks, some on the floor, with the rich warm night wind rushing down through all the house; and then were up once more in the darkness of the dawn, to go down and bathe at a little cascade, where a feeble stream dribbled under ferns and balisiers over soft square limestone rocks like the artificial rocks of the Serpentine, and those—copied probably from the rocks of Fontainebleau—which one sees in old French landscapes. But a bathe was hardly necessary. So drenched was the vegetation with night dew, that if one had taken off one's clothes at the house, and simply walked under the bananas, and through the tanias and maize which grew among them, one would have been well washed ere one reached the stream. As it was, the bathers came back with their clothes wet through. No matter. The sun was up, and half an hour would dry all again.

One object, on the edge of the forest, was worth noticing, and was watched long, through the glasses; namely, two or three large trees, from which dangled a multitude of the pendant nests of the Merles:[1] birds of the size of a jackdaw, brown and yellow, and mocking-birds, too, of no small ability. The pouches, two feet long and more, swayed in the breeze, fastened to the end of the boughs with a few threads. Each had, about half-way down, an opening into the round sac below, in and out of which the Merles crept and fluttered, talking all the while in twenty different notes. Most tropic birds hide their nests carefully in the bush: the Merles hang theirs fearlessly in the most exposed situations. They find, I presume, that they are protected enough from monkeys, wild cats, and gato-melaos (a sort of ferret), by being hung at the extremity of the bough. So thinks M. Léotaud, the accomplished describer of the birds of Trinidad. But he adds with good reason: "I do not, however, understand how birds can protect their nestlings against ants; for so large is the number of these insects in our climes, that it would seem as if everything would become their prey."

And so everything will, unless the bird-murder be stopped. Already the parasol-ants have formed a warren close to Port of Spain, in what was forty years ago highly cultivated ground, from which they devastate at night the northern gardens. The forests seem as empty of birds as the neighbourhood of the city; and a sad answer will soon have to be given to M. Léotaud's question:—

[1] Cassicus.

"The insectivorous tribes are the true representatives of our ornithology. There are so many which feed on insects and their larvæ, that it may be asked with much reason, What would become of our vegetation, of ourselves, should these insect destroyers disappear? Everywhere may be seen" (M. L. speaks, I presume, of five-and-twenty years ago; my experience would make me substitute for his words, "Hardly anywhere can be seen,") "one of these insectivora in pursuit or seizure of its prey, either on the wing or on the trunks of trees; in the coverts of thickets, or in the calices of flowers. Whenever called to witness one of those frequent migrations from one point to another, so often practised by ants, not only can the Dendrocolaptes (connected with our Creepers) be seen following the moving trail, and preying on the ants and the eggs themselves, but even the black Tanager abandons his usual fruits for this more tempting delicacy. Our frugivorous and baccivorous genera are also pretty numerous, and most of them are so fond of insect food that they unite, as occasion offers, with the insectivorous tribes."

So it was once. Now a traveller, accustomed to the swarms of birds which, not counting the game, inhabit an average English cover, would be surprised and pained by the scarcity of birds in the forests of this island.

We rode down toward the northern lowland, along a broad new road of last year's making, terraced, with great labour, along the hill, and stopped to visit one of those excellent Government schools which do honour, first to that wise legislator, Lord Harris, and next to the late Governor. Here in the depths of the forest, where never policeman or schoolmaster had been before, was a house of satin-wood and cedar

Coolie group.

not two years old, used at once as police-station and school, with a shrewd Spanish-speaking schoolmaster, and fifty-two decent little brown children on the school-books, and getting, when their lazy parents will send them, as good an education as they would get in England. I shall have more to say on the education system of Trinidad. All it seems to me to want, with its late modifications, is compulsory attendance.

Soon, turning down an old Indian path, we saw the Gulf once more, and between us and it the sheet of cane cultivation, of which one estate ran up to our feet, " like a bright green bay entered by a narrow strait among the dark forest." Just before we came to it we passed another pleasant sight: more Coolie settlers, who had had lands granted them in lieu of the return passage to which they were entitled, were all busily felling wood, putting up bamboo and palm-leaf cabins, and settling themselves down each one his own master, yet near enough to the sugar estates below to get remunerative work whenever needful.

Then on, over slow miles (you must not trot beneath the burning midday sun) of sandy stifling flat, between high canes, till we saw with joy, through long vistas of straight traces, the Mangrove shrubbery which marked the sea. We turned into large sugar-works, to be cooled with sherry and ice by a hospitable manager, whose rooms were hung with good prints, and stored with good books and knick-knacks from Europe, showing the signs of a lady's hand. And here our party broke up. The rest carried their mud back to Port of Spain; I in the opposite direction back to San Fernando, down a little creek which served as a port to the estate.

Plastered up to the middle like the rest of the party, besides splashes over face and hat, I could get no dirtier than I was already. I got without compunction into a canoe some three feet wide; and was shoved by three Negros down a long winding ditch of mingled mud, water, and mangrove-roots. To keep one's self and one's luggage from falling out during the journey was no easy matter; at one moment, indeed, it threatened to become impossible. For where the mangroves opened on the sea, the creek itself turned sharply northward along shore, leaving (as usual) a bed of mud between it and the sea some quarter of a mile broad; across which we had to pass as a short-cut to the boat, which lay far out. The difficulty was, of course, to get the canoe out of the creek up the steep mud-bank. To that end she was turned on her side, with me on board. I could just manage, by jamming my luggage under my knees, and myself against the two gunwales, to keep in, holding on chiefly by my heels and the back of my neck. But it befel, that in the very agony of the steepest slope, when the Negros (who worked like really good fellows) were nigh waist-deep in mud, my eye fell, for the first time in my life, on a party of Calling Crabs, who had been down to the water to fish, and were now scuttling up to their burrows among the mangrove-roots; and at the sight of the pairs of long-stalked eyes, standing upright like a pair of opera-glasses, and the long single arms which each brandished, with frightful menaces, as of infuriated Nelsons, I burst into such a fit of laughter that I nearly fell out into the mud. The Negros thought for the instant that the "buccra parson" had gone mad: but when I pointed with my head (I dare not move a finger) to the crabs, off they went in a true Negro guffaw, which, when once begun, goes on and on, like thunder echoing round the mountains, and can no more stop itself than a Blackcap's song. So all the way across the mud the jolly fellows, working meanwhile like horses, laughed for the mere pleasure of laughing; and when we got to the boat, the Negro in charge of her saw us laughing, and laughed too for company, without waiting to hear the joke; and as two of them took the canoe home, we could hear them laughing still in the distance, till the lonely loathsome place rang again. I plead guilty to having given the men, as payment, not only for their work but for their jollity, just twice what they asked, which, after all, was very little.

But what are Calling-Crabs? I must ask the reader to conceive a moderate-sized crab, the front of whose carapace is very broad and almost straight, with a channel along it, in which lie, right and left, his two eyes, each on a footstalk half as long as the breadth of his body; so that the crab, when at rest, carries his eyes as epaulettes, and peeps out at the joint of each shoulder. But when business is to be done, the eyestalks jump bolt upright side by side, like a pair of little lighthouses, and survey the field of battle in a fashion utterly ludicrous. Moreover, as if he were not ridiculous enough even thus, he is (as Mr. Wood well puts it) like a small man gifted with one arm of Hercules, and another of Tom Thumb. One of his claw arms, generally the left, has dwindled to a mere nothing, and is not seen; while along the whole front of his shell lies folded one mighty right arm, on which he trusts; and with that arm, when danger appears, he beckons the enemy to come on, with such wild defiance, that he has gained therefrom the name of Gelasimus Vocans—"The Calling Laughable:" and it were well if all scientific names were as well fitted. He is, as might be guessed, a shrewd fighter, and uses the true old "Bristol guard" in boxing, holding his long arm across his body, and fencing and biting therewith swiftly and sharply enough. Moreover, he is a respectable animal, and has a wife, and takes care of her; and to see him in his glory, it is said, he should be watched sitting in the mouth of his burrow, his spouse packed safe behind him inside, while he beckons and brandishes, proclaiming to all passers-by the treasure which he protects, while he defies them to touch it.

Such is the "Calling-Crab," of whom I must say, that if he was not made on purpose to be laughed at, then I should be induced to suspect that nothing was made for any purpose whatsoever.

After which sight, and weary of waiting, not without some fear that—as the Negros would have put it—" If I tap da wan momant ma, I catch da confection," while of course a bucket or two of hot water was emptied on us out of a passing cloud, I got on board the steamer, and away to San Fernando, to wash away dirt and forget fatigue, amid the hospitality of educated and high-minded men, and of even more charming women.

CHAPTER XI.

THE NORTHERN MOUNTAINS.

I HAD heard and read much of the beauty of mountain scenery in the Tropics. What I had heard and read is not exaggerated. I saw, it is true, in this little island no Andes, with such a scenery among them and below them as Humboldt alone can describe—a type of the great and varied tropical world as utterly different from that of Trinidad as it is from that of Kent—or Siberia. I had not even the chance of such a view as that from the Silla of Caraccas described by Humboldt, from which you look down at a height of nearly six thousand feet, through layer after layer of floating cloud, which increases the seeming distance to an awful depth, upon the blazing shores of the Northern Sea.

That view our host and his suite had seen themselves the year before; and they assured me that Humboldt had not overstated its grandeur. The mountains of Trinidad do not much exceed 3,000 feet in height, and I could hope at most to see among them what my fancy had pictured among the serrated chines and green gorges of St. Vincent, Guadaloupe, and St. Lucia, hanging gardens compared with which those of Babylon of old must have been Cockney mounds. The rock among these mountains, as I have said already, is very seldom laid bare. Decomposed rapidly by the tropic rain and heat, it forms, even on the steepest slopes, a mass of soil many feet in depth, ever increasing, and ever sliding into the valleys, mingled with blocks and slabs of rock still undecomposed. The waste must be enormous now. Were the forests cleared, and the soil no longer protected by the leaves and bound together by the roots, it would increase at a pace of which we in this temperate zone can form no notion, and the whole mountain-range slide down in deluges of mud, as, even in the temperate zone, the Mont Ventoux and other hills in Provence are sliding now, since they have been rashly cleared of their primæval coat of woodland.

To this degrading influence of mere rain and air must be attributed, I think, those vast deposits of boulder which encumber the mouths of all the southern glens, sometimes to a height of several hundred feet. Did one meet them in Scotland, one would pronounce them at once to be old glacier-moraines. But Messrs. Wall and Sawkins, in their geological survey of this island, have abstained from expressing any such opinion; and I think wisely. They are more simply explained as the mere leavings of the old sea-worn mountain wall, at a time when the Orinoco, or the sea, lay along their southern, as it now does along their northern, side. The terraces in which they rise mark successive periods of upheaval; and how long these periods were, no reasonable man dare guess. But as for traces of ice-action, none, as far as I can ascertain, have yet been met with. He would be a bold man who should deny that, during the abyss of ages, a cold epoch may have spread ice over part of that wide land which certainly once existed to the north of Trinidad and the Spanish Main: but if so, its traces are utterly obliterated. The commencement of the glacial epoch, as far as Trinidad is concerned, may be safely referred to the discovery of Wenham Lake ice, and the effects thereof sought solely in the human stomach and the increase of Messrs. Haley's well-earned profits. Is it owing to this absence of any ice-action that there are no lakes, not even a tarn, in the northern mountains? Far be it from me to thrust my somewhat empty head into the battle which has raged for some time past between those who attribute all lakes to the scooping action of glaciers and those who attribute them to original depressions in the earth's surface: but it was impossible not to contrast the lakeless mountains of Trinidad with the mountains of Kerry, resembling them so nearly in shape and size, but swarming with lakes and tarns. There are no lakes throughout the West Indies, save such as are extinct craters, or otherwise plainly attributable to volcanic action, as I presume are the lakes of Tropical Mexico and Peru. Be that as it may, the want of water, or rather of visible water, takes away much from the beauty of these mountains, in which the eye grows tired toward the end of a day's journey with the monotonous surges of green woodland; and hails with relief, in going northward, the first glimpse of the sea horizon; in going south, the first glimpse of the hazy lowland, in which the very roofs and chimney-stalks of the sugar estates are pleasant to the eye from the repose of their perpendicular and horizontal lines after the perpetual unrest of rolling hills and tangled vegetation.

We started, then (to begin my story), a little after five one morning, from a solid old mansion in the cane-fields, which bears the name of Paradise, and which has all the right to the name which beauty of situation and goodness of inhabitants can bestow.

As we got into our saddles the humming-birds were whirring round the tree-tops; the Qu'est-ce qu'il dits inquiring the subject of our talk. The black vultures sat about looking on in silence, hoping that something to their advantage might be dropped or left behind—possibly that one of our horses might die.

Ere the last farewell was given, one of our party pointed to a sight which I never saw before, and perhaps shall never see again. It was the Southern Cross. Just visible in that winter season on the extreme southern horizon in early morning, it hung upright amid the dim haze of the lowland and the smoke of the sugar-works. Impressive as was, and always must be, the first sight of that famous constellation, I could not but agree with those who say that they are disappointed by its inequality, both in shape and in the size of its stars. However, I had but little time to make up my mind about it; for in five minutes more it had melted away into a blaze of sunlight, which reminded us that we ought to have been on foot half an hour before.

So away we went over the dewy paddocks, through broad-leaved grasses, and the pink balls of the sensitive-plants and blue Commelyna, and the upright Negro Ipecacuanha,[1] with its scarlet and yellow flowers, gayest and commonest of weeds; then down into a bamboo copse, and across a pebbly brook, and away toward the mountains.

Our party consisted of a bât-mule, with food and clothes, two or three Negros, a horse for me, another for general use in case of break-down; and four gentlemen who preferred walking to riding. It seemed at first a serious undertaking on their part; but one had only to see them begin to move, long, lithe, and light as deer-hounds, in their flannel shirts and trousers, with cutlass and pouch at their waists, to be sure

[1] Asclepias curassavica.

that they could both go and stay, and were as well able to get to Blanchisseuse as the horses beside which they walked.

The ward of Blanchisseuse, on the north coast, whither we were bound, was of old, I understand, called Blanchi Sali, or something to that effect, signifying the white cliffs. The French settlers degraded the name to its present form, and that so hopelessly, that the other day an old Negress in Port of Spain puzzled the officer of Crown property by informing him that she wanted to buy "a carré in what you call de washerwoman's." It had been described to me as possibly the remotest, loneliest, and unhealthiest spot in her Majesty's tropical dominions. No white man can live there for more than two or three years without ruin to his health. In spite of the perpetual trade-wind, and the steepness of the hill-sides, malaria hangs for ever at the mouth of each little mountain torrent, and crawls up inland to leeward to a considerable height above the sea.

But we did not intend to stay there long enough to catch fever and ague. We had plenty of quinine with us; and cheerily we went up the valley of Caura, first over the great boulder and pebble ridges, not bare like those of the Moor of Dinnet, or other Dee-side stone heap, but clothed with cane-pieces and richest rastrajo copses; and then entered the narrow gorge, which we had to follow into the heart of the hills, as our leader, taking one parting look at the broad green lowland behind us, reminded us of Shelley's lines about the plains of Lombardy seen from the Euganean hills :—

> "Beneath me lies like a green sea
> The waveless plain of Lombardy,
> *   *   *   *
> Where a soft and purple mist,
> Like a vaporous amethyst,
> Or an air-dissolvèd stone,
> Mingling light and fragrance, far
> From the curved horizon's bound
> To the point of heaven's profound,
> Fills the overflowing sky ;
> And the plains that silent lie
> Underneath, the leaves unsodden
> Where the infant frost has trodden
> With his morning-wingèd feet,
> Whose bright fruit is gleaming yet ;
> And the red and golden vines
> Piercing with their trellised lines
> The rough dark-skirted wilderness."

But there the analogy stopped. It hardly applied even so far. Between us and the rough dark-skirted wilderness of the high forests on Montserrat the infant frost had never trodden; all basked in the equal heat of the perpetual summer; awaiting, it may be, in ages to come, a civilization higher even than that whose decay Shelley deplored as he looked down on fallen Italy.

No clumsy words of mine can give an adequate picture of the beauty of the streams and glens which run down from either slope of the Northern Mountain. The reader must fancy for himself the loveliest brook which he ever saw in Devonshire or Yorkshire, Ireland or Scotland ; crystal-clear, bedded with grey pebbles, broken into rapids by rock-ledges or great white quartz boulders, swirling under steep cliffs, winding through flats of natural meadow and copse. Then let him transport his stream into the great Palm-house at Kew, stretch out the house up hill and down dale, five miles in length and two thousand feet in height; pour down on it from above a blaze which lights up every leaf into a gem, and deepens every shadow into blackness, and yet that very blackness full of inner light—and if his fancy can do as much as that, he can imagine to himself the stream up which we rode or walked, now winding along the narrow track a hundred feet or two above, looking down on the upper surface of the forest, on the crests of palms, and the broad sheets of the Balisier copse, and often on the statelier fronds of true bananas, which had run wild along the stream-side, flowering and fruiting in the wilderness for the benefit of the parrots and agoutis ; or on huge dark clumps of bamboo, which (probably not indigenous to the island) have in like manner spread themselves along all the streams in the lapse of ages.

Now we scrambled down into the brook, and waded our horses through, amid shoals of the little spotted sardine,[1] who are too fearless, or too unaccustomed to

[1] Hydrocyon.

man, to get out of the way more than a foot or two. But near akin as they are to the trout, they are still nearer to the terrible Pirai,[1] of the Orinocquan waters, the larger of which snap off the legs of swimming ducks and the fingers of unwary boatmen, while the smaller surround the rash bather, and devour him piecemeal till he drowns, torn by a thousand tiny wounds, in water purpled with his own blood. These little fellows prove their kindred with the Pirai by merely nibbling at the bather's skin, making him tingle from head to foot, while he thanks Heaven that his visitors are but two inches, and not a foot in length.

At last we stopped for breakfast. The horses were tethered to a tree, the food got out, and we sat down on a pebbly beach after a bathe in a deep pool, so clear that it looked but four feet deep, though the bathers soon found it to be eight and more. A few dark logs, as usual, were lodged at the bottom, looking suspiciously like alligators or boa-constrictors. The alligator, however, does not come up the mountain streams; and the boa-constrictors are rare, save on the east coast: but it is as well, ere you jump into a pool, to look whether there be not a snake in it, of any length from three to twenty feet.

Over the pool rose a rock, carrying a mass of vegetation, to be seen, doubtless, in every such spot in the island, but of a

[1] Serrasalmo.

richness and variety beyond description. Nearest to the water the primæval garden began with ferns and creeping Selaginella. Next, of course, the common Arum,[1] with snow-white spathe and spadix, mingled with the larger leaves of Balisier, wild Tania, and Seguine, some of the latter upborne on crooked fleshy stalks as thick as a man's leg, and six feet high. Above them was a tangle of twenty different bushes, with leaves of every shape; above them again, the arching shoots of a bamboo clump, forty feet high, threw a deep shade over pool and rock and herbage; while above it again enormous timber trees were packed, one behind the other, up the steep mountain-side. On the more level ground were the usual weeds; Ipomœas with white and purple flowers, Bignonias, Echites and Allamandas, with yellow ones, scrambled and tumbled everywhere; and, if not just there, then often enough elsewhere, might be seen a single Aristolochia scrambling up a low tree, from which hung, amid round leaves, huge flowers shaped like a great helmet with a ladle at the lower lip, a foot or more across, of purplish colour, spotted like a toad, and about as fragrant as a dead dog.

But the plants which would strike a botanist most, I think, the first time he found himself on a tropic burn-side, are the peppers, groves of tall herbs some ten feet high or more, utterly unlike any European plants I have ever seen.

[1] Spathiphyllum cannifolium.

Some[1] have round leaves, peltate, that is, with the footstalk springing from inside the circumference, like a one-sided umbrella. They catch the eye at once, from the great size of their leaves, each a full foot across; but they are hardly as odd and foreign-looking as the more abundant forms of peppers,[2] usually so soft and green that they look as if you might make them into salad, stalks and all, yet with a quaint stiffness and primness, given by the regular jointing of their knotted stalks, and the regular tiling of their pointed, drooping, strong-nerved leaves, which are usually, to add to the odd look of the plant, all crooked, one side of the base (and that in each species always the same side) being much larger than the other, so that the whole head of the bush seems to have got a twist from right to left, or left to right. Nothing can look more unlike than they to the climbing true peppers, or even to the creeping pepper-weeds, which abound in all waste land. But their rat-tails of small green flowers prove them to be peppers nevertheless.

On we went, upward ever, past Cacao and Bois immortelle orchards, and comfortable settlers' hamlets; and now and then through a strip of virgin forest, in which we began to see, for the first time, though not for the last, that "resplendent Calycophyllum" as Dr. Krueger calls it, Chaconia, as it is commonly called here, after poor Alonzo de Chacon,

[1] Pothomorphe. [2] Enckea and Artauthe.

the last Spanish governor of this island. It is indeed the jewel of these woods. A low straggling tree carries, on long pendent branches, leaves like a Spanish chestnut, a foot and more in length; and at the ends of the branches, long corymbs of yellow flowers. But it is not the flowers themselves which make the glory of the tree. As the flower opens, one calyx-lobe, by a rich vagary of nature, grows into a leaf three inches long, of a splendid scarlet; and the whole end of each branch, for two feet or more in length, blazes among the green foliage till you can see it and wonder at it a quarter of a mile away. This is "the resplendent Calycophyllum," elaborated, most probably, by long physical processes of variation and natural selection into a form equally monstrous and beautiful. There are those who will smile at my superstition, if I state my belief that He who makes all things make themselves may have used those very processes of variation and natural selection for a final cause; and that the final cause was, that He might delight Himself in the beauty of one more strange and new creation. Be it so. I can only assume that their minds are, for the present at least, differently constituted from mine.

We reached the head of the glen at last, and outlet from the amphitheatre of wood there seemed none. But now I began to find out what a tropic mountain-path can be, and what a West Indian horse can do. We arrived at the lower end of a narrow ditch full of rocks and mud, which wandered up the face of a hill as steep as the roofs of the Louvre or Château Chambord. Accustomed only to English horses, I confess I paused in dismay: but as men and horses seemed to take the hill as a matter of course, the only thing to be done was to give the stout little cob his head, and not to slip over his tail. So up we went, splashing, clawing, slipping, stumbling, but never falling down; pausing every now and then to get breath for a fresh rush, and then on again, up a place as steep as a Devonshire furze-bank for twenty or thirty feet, till we had risen a thousand feet, as I suppose, and were on a long and more level chine, in the midst of ghastly dead forests, the remains of last year's fires. Much was burnt to tinder and ash; much more was simply killed and scorched, and stood or hung in an infinite tangle of lianes and boughs, all grey and bare. Here and there some huge tree had burnt as it stood, and rose like a soot-grimed tower; here another had fallen right across the path, and we had to cut our way round it step by step, amid a mass of fallen branches sometimes much higher than our heads, or to lead the horses underneath boughs which were too large to cut through, and just high enough to let them pass. An English horse would have lost his nerve, and become restive from confusion and terror; but these wise brutes, like the pack-mule, seemed to understand the matter as well as we; waited patiently till a passage was cut; and then struggled gallantly through, often among logs where I expected to see their leg-bones snapt in two. But my fears were needless; the deft gallant animals got safe through without a scratch. However, for them, as for us, the work was very warm. The burnt forest was utterly without shade; and wood-cutting under a perpendicular noon-day sun would have been trying enough had not our spirits been kept up by the excitement, the sense of freedom and of power, and also by the magnificent scenery which began to break upon us. From one cliff, off which the whole forest had been burnt away, we caught at last a sight westward of Tocuche, from summit to base, rising out of a green sea of wood—for the fire, coming from the eastward, had stopped half-way down the cliff; and to the right of the picture the blue Northern Sea shone through a gap in the hills. What a view that was! To conceive it, the reader must fancy himself at Clovelly, on the north coast of Devon, if he ever has had the good fortune to see that most beautiful of English cliff-woodlands; he must magnify the whole scene four or five times; and then pour down on it a tropic sunshine and a tropic haze.

Soon we felt, and thankful we were to feel it, a rush of air, soft and yet bracing, cool yet not chilly; the "champagne atmosphere," as some one called it, of the trade-wind: and all, even the very horses, plucked up heart;

for that told us that we were at the summit of the pass, and that the worst of our day's work was over. In five minutes more we were aware, between the tree-stems, of a green misty gulf beneath our very feet, which seemed at the first glance boundless, but which gradually resolved itself into mile after mile of forest, rushing down into the sea. The hues of the distant woodlands, twenty miles away, seen through a veil of ultramarine, mingled with the pale greens and blues of the water: and they again with the pale sky, till the eye could hardly discern where land and sea and air parted from each other.

We stopped to gaze, and breathe; and then downward again for nigh two thousand feet toward Blanchisseuse. And so, leading our tired horses, we went cheerily down the mountain side in Indian file, hopping and slipping from ledge to mud and mud to ledge, and calling a halt every five minutes to look at some fresh curiosity: now a tree-fern, now a climbing fern; now some huge tree-trunk, whose name was only to be guessed at; now a fresh armadillo-burrow; now a parasol-ants' warren, which had to be avoided lest horse and man should sink in it knee-deep, and come out sorely bitten; now some glimpse of sea and forest far below; now we cut a water-vine, and had a long cool drink; now a great moth had to be hunted, if not caught; or a toucan or some other strange bird listened to; or an eagle watched as he soared high over the green gulf. Now all stopped together; for the ground was sprinkled thick with great beads, scarlet, with a black eye, which had fallen from some tree high overhead; and we all set to work like schoolboys, filling our pockets with them for the ladies at home. Now the path was lost, having vanished in the six months' growth of weeds; and we had to hunt about for it over fallen logs, through tangles of liane and thickets of the tall Arouma,[1] a cane with a flat tuft of leaves atop, which is plentiful in these dark, damp, northern slopes. Now we struggled and hopped, horse and man, down and round a corner, at the head of a glen, where a few flag-stones fallen across a gully gave an uncertain foothold, and paused, under damp rocks covered with white and pink Begonias and ferns of innumerable forms, to drink the clear mountain water out of cups extemporised from a Calathea leaf; and then struggled up again over roots and ledges, and round the next spur, in cool green darkness, on which it seemed the sun had never shone; and in a silence which, when our own voices ceased, was saddening, all but appalling.

At last, striking into a broader trace which came from the westward, we found ourselves some six or eight hundred feet above the sea, in scenery still like a magnified Clovelly, but amid a vegetation which—how can I describe? Suffice it to say, that right and left of the path, and arching together

[1] Ischnosiphon.

Fillette

overhead, rose a natural avenue of Cocorite palms, beneath whose shade I rode for miles, enjoying the fresh trade-wind, the perfume of the Vanilla flowers, and last, but not least, the conversation of one who used his high post to acquaint himself thoroughly with the beauties, the productions, the capabilities of the island which he governed; and his high culture to make such journeys as this a continuous stream of instruction and pleasure to those who accompanied him. Under his guidance we stopped at one point, silent with delight and awe.

Through an arch of Cocorite boughs—ah that English painters would go to paint such pictures, set in such natural frames—we saw, nearly a thousand feet below us, the little bay of Fillette. The height of the horizon line told us how high we were ourselves; for the blue of the Caribbean Sea rose far above a point which stretched out on our right, covered with noble wood; while the dark olive cliffs along its base were gnawed by snowy surf. On our left, the nearer mountain woods rushed into the sea, cutting off the view; and under our very feet, in the centre of an amphitheatre of wood, as the eye of the whole picture, was a group—such as I cannot hope to see again. Out of a group of scarlet Bois immortelles rose three Palmistes, and close to them a single Balata, whose height I hardly dare to estimate. So tall they were, that though they were perhaps a thousand feet below us, they stood out against the blue sea, far up toward the horizon line; the central palm a hundred and fifty feet at least, the two others, as we guessed, a hundred and twenty feet or more. Their stems were perfectly straight and motionless, while their dark crowns, even at that distance, could be seen to toss and rage impatiently before the rush of the strong trade-wind. The black glossy head of the Balata, almost as high aloft as they, threw off sheets of spangled light, which mingled with the spangles of the waves; and, above the tree-tops, as if poised in a blue hazy sky, one tiny white sail danced before the breeze. The whole scene swam in soft sea-air; and such combined grandeur and delicacy of form and of colour I never beheld before.

We rode on and downward, toward a spot where we expected to find water. Our Negros had lagged behind with the provisions; and, hungry and thirsty, we tethered our horses to the trees at the bottom of a gully, and went down through the bush toward a low cliff. As we went, if I recollect, we found on the ground many curious pods,[1] curled two or three times round, something like those of a Medic, and when they split, bright red inside, setting off prettily enough the bright blue seeds. Some animal or other, however, admired these seeds as much as we; for they had been

[1] Pithecolobium (?).

stripped as soon as they opened, and out of hundreds of pods we only secured one or two beads.

We got to the cliff—a smugglers' crack in the rock, and peered down, with some disgust. There should have been a pole or two there, to get down by: but they were washed away; a canoe also: but it had been carried off, probably out of the way of the surf. To get down the crack, for active men, was easy enough: but to get up again seemed, the longer we looked at it, the more impossible, at least for me. So after scrambling down, holding on by wild pines, as far as we dare—during which process one of us was stung (not bitten) by a great hunting-ant, causing much pain and swelling — we turned away; for the heat of

Avocado Pear.

the little corner was intolerable. But wistful eyes did we cast back at the next point of rock, behind which broke out the tantalizing spring, which we could just not reach.

We rode on, sick and sorry, to find unexpected relief. We entered a clearing, with Bananas and Tanias, Cacao and Bois immortelle, and better still, Avocado pears and orange-tree with fruit. A tall and stately dame was there; her only garment a long cotton-print gown, which covered her tall figure from throat to ankle and wrist, showing brown feet and hands which had once been delicate, and a brown face, half Spanish, half Indian, modest and serious enough. We pointed to a tall orange-tree overhead, laden with fruit of every hue from bright green to gold. She, on being appealed to in Spanish, answered with a courteous smile, and then a piercing scream of—"Candelaria, come hither, and get oranges for the Governor and other señors!" Candelaria, who might have been eighteen or twenty, came sliding down under the Banana-leaves, all modest smiles, and blushes through her whitey-brown skin. But having no more clothes on than her mother, she naturally hesitated at climbing the tree; and after ineffectual attempts to knock down oranges with a bamboo, screamed in her turn for some José or Juan. José or Juan made his appearance, in a ragged shirt. A lanky lad, about seventeen years old, he was evidently the oaf or hobbedehoy of the family, just as he would have been on this side of the sea; was treated as such; and was accustomed to be so treated. In a tone of angry contempt (the poor boy had done and said nothing) the two women hounded him up the tree. He obeyed in meek resignation, and in a couple of minutes we had more oranges than we could eat. And such oranges: golden-green, but rather more green than gold, which cannot be (as at home) bitten or sucked; for so strong is the fragrant essential-oil in the skin, that it would blister the lips and disorder the stomach; and the orange must be carefully stripped of the outer coat before you attack a pulp compared with which, for flavour, the orange of our shops is but bad sugar and water.

As I tethered my horse to a cacao-stem, and sat on a log among hothouse ferns, peeling oranges with a bowie-knife beneath the burning mid-day sun, the quaintest fancy came over me that it was all a dream, a phantasmagoria, a Christmas pantomime got up by my host for my special amusement; and that if I only winked my eyes hard enough, when I opened them again it would be all gone, and I should find myself walking with him on Ascot Heath, while the snow whirled over the heather, and the black fir-trees groaned in the north-east wind.

We soon rode on, with blessings on fair Candelaria and her stately mother, while the noise of the surf grew louder and louder in front of us. We took (if I remember right) a sudden turn to the left, to get our horses to the shore. Our pedestrians held straight on; there was a Mangrove swamp and a lagoon in front, for which they, bold lads, cared nothing.

We passed over a sort of open down, from which all vegetation had been cleared, save the Palmistes—such a wood of them as I had never seen before. A hundred or more, averaging at least a hundred feet in height, stood motionless in the full cut of the strong trade-wind. One would have expected them, when the wood round was felled, to feel the sudden nakedness. One would have expected the inrush of salt air and foam to have injured their foliage. But, seemingly, it was not so. They stood utterly unharmed; save some half-dozen who had had their tops snapped off by a gale—there are no hurricanes in Trinidad—and remained as enormous unmeaning pikes, or posts, fifty to eighty feet high, transformed, by that one blast, from one of the loveliest to one of the ugliest natural objects.

Through the Palmiste pillars; through the usual Black Roseau scrub; then under tangled boughs down a steep stony bank; and we were on a long beach of deep sand and quartz gravel. On our right the Shore-grapes with their green bunches of fruit, the Mahauts[1] with their poplar-like leaves and great yellow flowers, and the ubiquitous Matapalos, fringed the shore. On our left weltered a broad waste of plunging foam; in front green mountains were piled on mountains, blazing in sunlight, yet softened and shrouded by an air saturated with steam and salt. We waded our horses over the mouth of the little Yarra, which hurried down through the sand, brown and foul from the lagoon above. We sat

[1] Paritium and Thespesia.

down on bare polished logs, which floods had carried from the hills above, and ate and drank—for our Negros had by now rejoined us; and then scrambled up the shore back again, and into a trace running along the low cliff, even more beautiful, if possible, than that which we had followed in the morning. Along the cliff tall Balatas and Palmistes, with here and there an equally tall Cedar, and on the inside bank a green wall of Balisiers, with leaves full fifteen feet long and heads of scarlet flowers, marked the richness of the soil. Here and there, too, a Cannon-ball tree rose, grand and strange, among the Balatas; and in one place the ground was strewn with large white flowers, whose peculiar shape told us at once of some other Lecythid tree high overhead. These Lecythids are peculiar to the hottest parts of South America; to the valleys of the Oroonoco and Amazon; to Trinidad, as a fragment of the old Oroonocquan land, and possibly to some of the southern Antilles. So now, as we are in their home, it may be worth our while to pause a little round these strange and noble forms.

Botanists tell us that they are, or rather may have been in old times, akin to myrtles. If so, they have taken a grand and original line of their own, and persevered in it for ages, till they have specialized themselves to a condition far in advance of most myrtles, in size, beauty, and use. They may be known from all other trees by one mark—their large handsome flowers. A group of the innumerable stamens have grown together on one side of the flower into a hood, which bends over the stigma and the other stamens. Tall trees they are, and glorious to behold, when in full flower; but they are notorious mostly for their huge fruits and delicious nuts. One of their finest forms, and the only one which the traveller is likely to see often in Trinidad, is the Cannon-ball tree.[1] There is a grand specimen in the Botanic Garden; and several may be met with in any day's ride through the high woods, and distinguished at once from any other tree. The stem rises, without a fork, for sixty feet or more, and rolls out at the top into a head very like that of an elm trimmed up, and like an elm too in its lateral water-boughs. For the whole of the stem, from the very ground to the forks, and the larger fork-branches likewise, are feathered all over with numberless

Cannon-ball Tree.

[1] Couroupita Guianensis.

short prickly pendent branchlets, which roll outward, and then down, and then up again in graceful curves, and carry large pale crimson flowers, each with a pink hood in the middle, looking like a new-born baby's fist. Those flowers, when torn, turn blue on exposure to the light; and when they fall, leave behind them the cannon-ball, a rough brown globe, as big as a thirty-two-pound shot, which you must get down with a certain caution, lest that befal you which befel a certain gallant officer on the mainland of America. For, fired with a post-prandial ambition to obtain a cannon-ball, he took to himself a long bamboo, and poked at the tree. He succeeded: but not altogether as he had hoped. For the cannon-ball, in coming down, avenged itself by dropping exactly on the bridge of his nose, felling him to the ground, and giving him such a pair of black eyes that he was not seen on parade for a fortnight.

The pulp of this Cannon-ball is, they say, "vinous and pleasant" when fresh; but those who are mindful of what befel our forefather Adam from eating strange fruits, will avoid it, as they will many more fruits eaten in the Tropics, but digestible only by the dura ilia of Indians and Negros. Whatever virtue it may have when fresh, it begins, as soon as stale, to give out an odour too abominable to be even recollected with comfort.

More useful, and the fruit of an even grander tree, are

those "Brazil nuts" which are sold in every sweet-shop at home. They belong to Bertholletia excelsa, a tree which grows sparingly — I have never seen it wild — in the southern part of the island, but plentifully in the forests of Guiana, and which is said to be one of the tallest of all the forest giants. The fruit, round like the cannon-ball, and about the size of a twenty-four pounder, is harder than the hardest wood, and has to be battered to pieces with the back of a hatchet to disclose the nuts, which lie packed close inside. Any one who has hammered at a Bertholletia fruit will be ready to believe the story that the Indians, fond as they are of the nuts, avoid the "totocke" trees till the fruit has all fallen, for fear of fractured skulls; and the older story which Humboldt gives out of old Laet,[1] that the Indians dared not enter the forests, when the trees were fruiting, without having their heads and shoulders covered with bucklers of hard wood. These "Almendras de Peru," Peru almonds, as they were called, were known in Europe as early as the sixteenth century, the seeds being carried up the Maragnon, and by the Cordilleras to Peru, men knew not from whence. To Humboldt himself, I believe, is due the re-discovery of the tree itself and its enormous fruit; and the name of Bertholletia excelsa was given by him. The tree, he says,

[1] "Personal Narrative," vol. v. p. 537.

" is not more than two or three feet in diameter, but attains one hundred or one hundred and twenty feet in height. It does not resemble the Mammee, the star-apple, and several other trees of the Tropics, of which the branches, as in the laurels of the temperate zone, rise straight toward the sky. The branches of the Bertholletia are open, very long, almost entirely bare toward the base, and loaded at their summits with tufts of very close foliage. This disposition of the semi-coriaceous leaves, a little silvery beneath and more than two feet long, makes the branches bend down toward the ground, like the fronds of the palm trees."

"The Capuchin monkeys," he continues, "are singularly fond of these 'chestnuts of Brazil,' and the noise made by the seeds, when the fruit is shaken as it fell from the tree, excites their appetency in the highest degree." He does not, however, believe the "tale, very current on the lower Oroonoko, that the monkeys place themselves in a circle, and by striking the shell with a stone succeed in opening it." That they may try is possible enough; for there is no doubt, I believe, that monkeys—at least the South American—do use stones to crack nuts; and I have seen myself a monkey, untaught, use a stick to rake his food up to him when put beyond the reach of his chain. The impossibility in this case would lie, not in want of wits, but want of strength; and the monkeys must have too often to wait for these feasts till the rainy season, when the woody shell rots of itself, and amuse themselves meanwhile, as Humboldt describes them, in rolling the fruit about, vainly longing to get their paws in through the one little hole at its base. The Agoutis, however, and Pacas, and other rodents, says Humboldt, have teeth and perseverance to gnaw through the shell; and when the seeds are once out "all the animals of the forest, the monkeys, the manaviris, the squirrels, the agoutis, the parrots, the macaws, hasten thither to dispute the prey. They have all strength enough to break the woody covering of the seeds; they get out the kernel and carry it to the tops of the trees. 'It is their festival also,' said the Indians who had returned from the nut-harvest; and on hearing their complaints of the animals you perceive that they think themselves alone the legitimate masters of the forest."

But if nature has played the poor monkeys a somewhat tantalizing trick about Brazil nuts, she has been more generous to them in the case of some other Lecythids,[1] which go by the name of monkey-pots. Huge trees like their kinsfolk, they are clothed in bark layers so delicate that the Indians beat them out till they are as thin as satin-paper, and use them as cigarette wrappers. They carry great urn-shaped fruits, big enough to serve for drinking-vessels, each

[1] Lecythis Ollaris, &c.

kindly provided with a round wooden cover, which becomes loose and lets out the savoury sapucaya nuts inside, to the comfort of all our "poor relations." Ah, when will there arise a Tropic Landseer to draw for us some of the strange fashions of the strange birds and beasts of these lands?—to draw, for instance, the cunning, selfish, greedy grin of delight on the face of some burly, hairy, goitred old red Howler, as he lifts off a "tapa del cacao de monos," a monkey-cacao cover, and looks defiance out of the corners of his winking eyes at his wives and children, cousins and grandchildren, who sit round jabbering and screeching, and, monkey fashion, twisting their heads upside down, as they put their arms round each other's waists to peer over each other's shoulders at the great bully, who must feed himself first as his fee for having roared to them for an hour at sunrise on a treetop, while they sat on the lower branches and looked up, trembling and delighted at the sound and fury of the idiot sermon.

What an untried world is here for the artist of every kind; not merely for the animal painter, for the landscape painter, for the student of human form and attitude, if he chose to live awhile among the still untrained Indians of the Main, or among the graceful Coolies of Trinidad and Demerara; but also for the botanical artist, for the man who should study long and carefully the more striking and beautiful of these wonderful leaves and stems, flowers and fruits, and introduce them into ornamentation, architectural or other.

And so I end my little episode about these Lecythids, only adding that the reader must not confound with their nuts the butter-nuts, Çaryocar, or Souari, which may be bought, I believe, at Fortnum and Mason's, and which are of all nuts the largest and the most delicious. They have not been found as yet in Trinidad, though they abound in Guiana. They are the fruit also of an enormous tree [1]—there is a young one fruiting finely in the Botanic Garden at Port of Spain— of a quite different order; a cousin of the Matapalos and of the Soap-berries. It carries large threefold leaves on pointed stalks; spikes of flowers with innumerable stamens; and here and there a fruit something like the Cannon-ball, though not quite as large. On breaking the soft rind you find it full of white meal, probably eatable, and in the meal three or four great hard wrinkled nuts, rounded on one side, wedge-shaped on the other, which, cracked, are found full of almond-like white jelly, so delicious that one can well believe travellers when they tell us that the Indian tribes wage war against each other for the possession of the trees which bear these precious vagaries of bounteous Nature.

And now we began to near the village, two scattered rows of clay and timber bowers right and left of the trace, each

[1] Çaryocar butyrosum.

half-buried in fruit-trees and vegetables, and fenced in with hedges of scarlet Hibiscus; the wooded mountains shading them to the south, the sea thundering behind them to the north. As we came up we heard a bell, and soon were aware of a brown mob running, with somewhat mysterious in the midst. Was it the Host? or a funeral? or a fight? Soon the mob came up with profound salutations, and smiles of self-satisfaction, evidently thinking that they had done a fine thing; and disclosed, hanging on a long bamboo, their one church-bell. Their old church (a clay and timber thing of their own handywork) had become ruinous; and they dared not leave their bell aloft in it. But now they were going to build themselves a new and larger church, Government giving them the site; and the bell, being on furlough, was put into requisition to ring in His Excellency the Governor and his muddy and quaintly attired—or unattired—suite.

Ah, that I could have given a detailed picture of the scene before the police court-house—the coloured folk, of all hues of skin, all types of feature, and all gay colours of dress, crowding round, the tall stately brown policeman, Thompson, called forward and receiving with a military salute the Governor's commendations for having saved, at the risk of his life, some shipwrecked folk out of the surf close by; and the flash of his eye when he heard that he was to receive the Humane Society's medal from England, and to have his name mentioned, probably to the Queen herself; the greetings, too, of almost filial respect which were bestowed by the coloured people on one who, though still young, had been to them a father; who, indeed, had set the policeman the example of gallantry by saving, in another cove near by, other shipwrecked folk out of a still worse surf, by swimming out beyond a ledge of rock swarming with sharks, at the risk every moment of a hideous death. There, as in other places since, he had worked, like his elder brother at Montserrat, as a true civilizer in every sense of the word; and, when his health broke down from the noxious climate, had moved elsewhere to still harder and more extensive work, belying, like his father and his brothers, the common story that the climate forbids exertion, and that the Creole gentleman cannot or will not, when he has a chance, do as good work as the English gentleman at home. I do not mention these men's names. In England it matters little; in Trinidad there is no need to mention those whom all know; all I shall say is, Heaven send the Queen many more such public servants, and me many more such friends.

Then up hurried the good little priest, and set forth in French—he was very indignant, by the bye, at being taken for a Frenchman, and begged it to be understood that he was Belgian born and bred—setting forth how His Excellency had not been expected till next day, or he would have had ready an address from the loyal inhabitants of Blanchisseuse testifying their delight at the honour of, &c. &c.; which he begged leave to present in due form next day; and all the while the brown crowd surged round and in and out, and the naked brown children got between every one's legs, and every one was in a fume of curiosity and delight—anything being an event in Blanchisseuse—save the one Chinaman, if I recollect right, who stood in his blue jacket and trousers, his hands behind his back, with visage unimpassioned, dolorous, seemingly stolid, a creature of the earth, earthy,—say rather of the dirt, dirty,—but doubtless by no means as stolid as he looked. And all the while the palms and bananas rustled above, and the surf thundered, and long streams of light poured down through the glens in the black northern wall, and flooded the glossy foliage of the mangos and sapodillas, and rose fast up the palm-stems, and to their very heads, and then vanished; for the sun was sinking, and, in half an hour more darkness would have fallen on the most remote little paradise in Her Majesty's dominions.

But where was the warden, who was by office, as well as by courtesy, to have received us? He too had not expected us, and was gone home after his day's work to his new clearing inland: but a man had been sent on to him over the mountain; and over the mountain we must go, and on foot too, for the horses could do no more, and there was no stabling for them further on. How far was the new clearing? Oh, perhaps a couple of miles—perhaps a league. And how high up? Oh, nothing—only a hundred feet or two. One knew what that meant; and, with a sigh, resigned oneself to a four or five miles' mountain walk at the end of a long day, and started up the steep zigzag, through cacao groves, past the loveliest gardens—I recollect in one an agave in flower, nigh thirty feet high, its spike all primrose and golden yellow in the fading sunlight—then up into rastrajo; and then into high wood, and a world of ferns—tree ferns, climbing ferns, and all other ferns which ever delighted the eye in an English hothouse. For along these northern slopes, sheltered from the sun for the greater part of the year, and for ever watered by the steam of the trade-wind, ferns are far more luxuriant and varied than in any other part of the island.

Soon it grew dark, and we strode on up hill and down dale, at one time for a mile or more through burnt forest, with its ghastly spider-work of leafless decaying branches and creepers against the moonlit sky— a sad sight: but music enough we had to cheer us on our way. We did not hear the howl of a monkey, nor the yell of a tiger-cat, common enough on the mountains which lay in front of us: but of harping, fiddling, humming, drumming, croaking, clacking, snoring, screaming, hooting, from cicadas, toads, birds, and what not, there was a concert at every step, which made the glens ring again, as the Brocken might ring on a Walpurgis-night.

At last, pausing on the top of a hill, we could hear voices on the opposite side of the glen. Shouts and "cooeys" soon brought us to the party which were awaiting us. We hurried joyfully down a steep hill-side, across a shallow ford, and then up another hill-side—this time with care, for the felled logs and brushwood lay all about a path full of stumps, and we needed a guide to show us our way in the moonlight up to the hospitable house above. And a right hospitable house it was. Its owner, a French gentleman of ancient Irish family—whose ancestors probably had gone to France as one of the valiant "Irish Brigade;" whose children may have emigrated thence to St. Domingo, and their children or grand-children again to Trinidad—had prepared for us in the wilderness a right sumptuous feast: "nor did any soul lack aught of the equal banquet."

We went to bed: or rather I did. For here, as elsewhere before and after, I was compelled, by the courtesy of the Governor, to occupy the one bed of the house, as being the oldest, least acclimatized, and alas! weakliest of the party; while he, his little suite, and the owner of the house, slept anywhere upon the floor; on which, between fatigue and enjoyment of the wild life, I would have gladly slept myself.

When we turned out before sunrise next morning, I found myself in perhaps the most charming of all the charming "camps" of these forests. Its owner, the warden, fearing the unhealthy air of the sea-coast, had bought some hundreds of acres up here in the hills, cleared them, and built, or rather was building, in the midst. As yet the house was rudimentary. A cottage of precious woods cut off the clearing, standing of course on stilts, contained two rooms, an inner and an outer. There was no glass in the windows, which occupied half the walls. Door or shutters, to be closed if the wind and rain were too violent, are all that is needed in a climate where the temperature changes but little, day or night, throughout the year. A table, unpolished, like the wooden walls, but like them of some precious wood; a few chairs or benches, not forgetting, of course, an American rocking-chair; a shelf or two, with books of law and medicine, and beside them a few good books of devotion; a press; a "perch" for hanging clothes—for they mildew when kept in drawers—just such as would have been seen in a mediæval house in England; a covered four-post bed, with gauze curtains, indispensable for fear of vampires, mosquitos, and other forest plagues; these make up the furniture of such a bachelor's camp as, to the man who lives doing good work all day out of doors, leaves nothing to be desired. Where is the kitchen? It consists of half-a-dozen great stones under yonder shed, where as good meals are cooked as in any London kitchen. Other sheds hold the servants and hangers-on, the horses and mules; and as the establishment grows more will be added, and the house itself will probably expand laterally, like a peripheral Greek temple, by rows of posts, probably of palm-stems thatched over with wooden shingle or with the leaves of the Timit[1] palm. If ladies come to inhabit the camp, fresh rooms will be partitioned off by boardings as high as the eaves, leaving the roof within open and common, for the sake of air. Soon, no regular garden, but beautiful flowering shrubs—Crotons, Dracænas, and Cereuses, will be planted; great bushes of Bauhinia and blue Petræa will roll their long curved shoots over and over each other; Gardenias fill the air with fragrance; and the Bougainvillia or the Clerodendron cover some arbour with lilac or white racemes.

But this camp had not yet arrived at so high a state of civilization. All round it, almost up to the very doors, a tangle of logs, stumps, branches, dead ropes and nets of liane, lay still in the process of clearing; and the ground was seemingly as waste, as it was difficult—often impossible —to cross. A second glance, however, showed that, amongst the stumps and logs, Indian corn was planted everywhere; and that a few months would give a crop which would richly repay the clearing, over and above the fact that the

[1] Manicaria.

whole materials of the house had been cut on the spot, and cost nothing.

As for the situation of the little oasis in the wilderness, it bespoke good sense and good taste. The owner had stumbled, in his forest wanderings, on a spot where two mountain streams, after nearly meeting, parted again, and enclosed in a ring a hill some hundred feet high, before they finally joined each other below. That ring was his estate; which was formally christened on the occasion of our visit, Avoca — the meeting of the waters; a name, as all agreed, full of remembrances of the Old World and the land of his remote ancestors; and yet like enough to one of the graceful and sonorous Indian names of the island not to seem barbarous and out of place. Round the clearing the mountain woods surged up a thousand feet aloft: but so gradually, and so far off, as to allow free circulation of air and a broad sheet of sky overhead; and as the camp stood on the highest point of the rise, it did not give that choking and crushing sensation of being in a ditch, which makes houses in most mountain valleys—to me at least—intolerable. Up one glen, toward the south, we had a full view of the green Cerro of Arima, three thousand feet in height; and down another, to the north-east, was a great gate in the mountains, through which we could hear—though not see—the surf rolling upon the rocks three miles away.

I was woke that morning, as often before and afterwards, by a clacking of stones; and, looking out, saw in the dusk a Negro squatting, and hammering, with a round stone on a flat one, the coffee which we were to drink in a quarter of an hour. It was turned into a tin saucepan; put to boil over a firestick between two more great stones; clarified, by some cunning island trick, with a few drops of cold water; and then served up, bearing, in fragrance and taste, the same relation to average English coffee as fresh things usually do to stale ones, or live to dead. After which "mañana," and a little quinine for fear of fever, we lounged about waiting for breakfast, and for the arrival of the horses from the village.

Then we inspected a Coolie's great toe, which had been severely bitten by a vampire in the night. And here let me say, that the popular disbelief of vampire stories is only owing to English ignorance, and disinclination to believe any of the many quaint things which John Bull has not seen, because he does not care to see them. If he comes to these parts, he must be careful not to leave his feet or hands out of bed without mosquito curtains; if he has good horses, he ought not to leave them exposed at night without wire-gauze round the stable-shed—a plan which, to my surprise I never saw used in the West Indies. Otherwise, he will be but too likely to find in the morning a triangular bit cut out of his own flesh, or even worse, out of his horse's withers or throat, where twisting and lashing cannot shake the tormentor off; and must be content to have himself lamed, or his horses weakened to staggering and thrown out of collar-work for a week, as I have seen happen more than once or twice. The only method of keeping off the vampire yet employed in stables is light; and a lamp is usually kept burning there. But the Negro—not the most careful of men —is apt not to fill and trim it; and if it goes out in the small hours, the horses are pretty sure to be sucked, if there is a forest near. So numerous and troublesome, indeed, are the vampires, that there are pastures in Trinidad in which, at least till the adjoining woods were cleared, the cattle would not fatten, or even thrive; being found, morning after morning, weak and sick from the bleedings which they had endured at night.

After looking at the Coolie's toe, of which he made light, though the bleeding from the triangular hole would not stop, any more than that from the bite of a horse-leech, we feasted our ears on the notes of delicate songsters, and our eyes on the colours and shapes of the forest, which, rising on the opposite side of the streams right and left, could be seen here more thoroughly than at any spot I yet visited. Again and again were the opera-glasses in requisition, to make out, or try to make out, what this or that tree might be. Here and there a Norantea, a mile or two miles off, showed like a whole crimson flower-bed in the tree-tops; or a Poui, just coming into flower, made a spot of golden yellow—" a guinea stuck against the mountain-side," as some one said; or the head of a palm broke the monotony of the broad-leaved foliage with its huge star of green.

Near us we descried several trees covered with pale yellow flowers, conspicuous enough on the hill-side. No one knew what they were; and a couple of Negros (who are admirable woodmen) were sent off to cut one down and see What mattered a tree or two less amid a world of trees? It was a quaint sight,—the two stalwart black figures struggling down over the fallen logs, and with them an Englishman, who thought he discerned which tree the flowers belonged to; while we at the house guided them by our shouts, and scanned the trunks through the glasses to make out in our turn which tree should be felled. From the moment that they entered under the green cloud, they of course could see little or nothing over their heads. Animated were the arguments—almost the bets—as to which tree-top belonged to which tree-trunk. Many were the mistakes made; and had it not been for the head of a certain palm, which served as a fixed point which there was no mistaking, three or four trees would have been cut before the right one was hit upon. At last the right tree came crashing down, and a branch of the flowers was brought up, to be carried home, and verified at Port of Spain; and meanwhile, disturbed by the axe-strokes, pair after pair of birds flew screaming over the tree-tops, which looked like rooks, till, as they turned in the sun, their colour—brilliant even at that distance—showed them to be great green parrots.

After breakfast—which among French and Spanish West Indians means a solid and elaborate luncheon—our party broke up. . . . I must be excused if I am almost prolix over the events of a day memorable to me.

The majority went down, on horse and foot, to Blanchisseuse again on official business. The site of the new church, an address from the inhabitants to the Governor, inspection of roads, examination of disputed claims, squatter questions, enclosure questions, and so forth, would occupy some hours in hard work. But the "pièce de résistance" of the day was to be the examination and probable committal of the Obeah-man of those parts. That worthy, not being satisfied with the official conduct of our host the warden, had advised himself to bribe, with certain dollars, a Coolie servant of his to "put Obeah upon him;" and had, with that intent, entrusted to him a Charm to be buried at his door, consisting, as usual, of a bottle containing toad, spider, rusty nails, dirty water, and other terrible jumbiferous articles. In addition to which attempt on the life and fortunes of the warden, he was said to have promised the Coolie forty dollars if he would do the business thoroughly for him. Now the Coolie well understood what doing the business thoroughly for an Obeah-man involved; namely, the putting Brinvilliers or other bush-poison into his food; or at least administering to him sundry doses of ground glass, in hopes of producing that "dysentery of the country" which proceeds in the West Indies, I am sorry to say, now and then, from other causes than that of climate. But having an affection for his master, and a conscience likewise, though he was but a heathen, he brought the bottle straight to the intended victim; and the Obeah-man was now in durance vile, awaiting further examination, and probably on his way to a felon's cell.

A sort of petition, or testimonial, had been sent up to the Governor, composed apparently by the hapless wizard himself, who seemed to be no mean penman, and signed by a dozen or more of the coloured inhabitants: setting forth how he was known by all to be far too virtuous a personage to dabble in that unlawful practice of Obeah, of which both he and his friends testified the deepest abhorrence. But there was the bottle, safe under lock and key; and as for the testimonial, those who read it said that it was not worth the paper it was written on. Most probably every one of these poor fellows had either employed the Obeah-man themselves to avert thieves or evil eye from a particularly fine fruit-tree, by hanging up thereon a somewhat similar bottle

—such as may be seen, and more than one of them, in any long day's march. It was said again, that if asked by an Obeah-man to swear to his good character, they could not well refuse, under penalty of finding some fine morning a white cock's head—sign of all supernatural plagues—in their garden path, the beak pointing to their door; or an Obeah bottle under their door-step; and either Brinvilliers in their pottage, or such an expectation of it, and of plague and ruin to them and all their worldly belongings, in their foolish souls, as would be likely enough to kill them, in a few months, of simple mortal fear.

Here perhaps I may be allowed to tell what I know about this curious question of Obeah, or Fêtish-worship. It appears to me, on closer examination, that it is not a worship of natural objects; not a primæval worship; scarcely a worship at all: but simply a system of incantation, carried on by a priesthood, or rather a sorcerer class; and this being the case, it seems to me unfortunate that the term Fêtish-worship should have been adopted by so many learned men, as the general name for the supposed primæval Nature-worship. The Negro does not, as the primæval man is supposed to have done, regard as divine (and therefore as Fêtish, or Obeah) any object which excites his imagination; anything peculiarly beautiful, noble, or powerful; anything even which causes curiosity or fear. In fact, a Fêtish is no natural object at all; it is a spirit, an Obeah, Jumby, Duppy, like the "Duvvels" or spirits of the air, which are the only deities of which our Gipsies have a conception left. That spirit belongs to the Obeah, or Fêtish-man; and he puts it, by magic ceremonies, into any object which he chooses. Thus anything may become Obeah, as far as I have ascertained. In a case which happened very lately, an Obeah-man came into the country, put the Obeah into a fresh monkey's jaw-bone, and made the people offer to it fowls and plantains, which of course he himself ate. Such is Obeah now; and such it was, as may be seen by De Bry's plates, when the Portuguese first met with it on the African coast four hundred years ago.

But surely it is an idolatry, and not a nature-worship. Just so does the priest of Southern India, after having made his idol, enchant his God into it by due ceremonial. It may be a very ancient system: but as for its being a primæval one, as neither I, nor any one else, ever had the pleasure of meeting a primæval man, it seems to me somewhat rash to imagine what primæval man's creeds and worships must have been like; more rash still to conclude that they must have been like those of the modern Negro. For if, as is probable, the Negro is one of the most ancient varieties of the human race; if, as is probable, he has remained—to his great misfortune—till the last three hundred years isolated on that vast island of Central Africa, which has probably continued as dry land during ages which have seen the whole of Europe, and Eastern and Southern Asia, sink more than once beneath the sea: then it is possible, and even probable, that during these long ages of the Negro's history, creed after creed, ceremonial after ceremonial, may have grown up and died out among the different tribes; and that any worship, or quasi-worship, which may linger among the Negros now, are likely to be the mere dregs and fragments of those older superstitions.

As a fact, Obeah is rather to be ranked, it seems to me, with those ancient Eastern mysteries, at once magical and profligate, which troubled society and morals in later Rome, when

"In Tiberim defluxit Orontes."

If so, we shall not be surprised to find that a very important, indeed the most practically important element of Obeah, is poisoning. This habit of poisoning has not (as one might well suppose) sprung up among the slaves desirous of revenge against their white masters. It has been imported, like the rest of the system, from Africa. Travellers of late have told us enough—and too much for our comfort of mind—of that prevailing dread of poison as well as of magic which urges the African Negros to deeds of horrible cruelty; and the fact that these African Negros, up to the very latest importations, are the special practisers of Obeah, is notorious through the West Indies. The existence of this trick of poisoning is denied, often enough. Sometimes Europeans, willing to believe the best of their fellow-men—and who shall blame them?—simply disbelieve it because it is unpleasant to believe. Sometimes, again, white West Indians will deny it, and the existence of Obeah beside, simply because they believe in it a little too much, and are afraid of the Negros knowing that they believe in it. Not two generations ago there might be found, up and down the islands, respectable white men and women who had the same half-belief in the powers of an Obeah-man, as our own ancestors, especially in the Highlands and in Devonshire, had in those of witches: while as to poisoning, it was, in some islands, a matter on which the less said the safer. It was but a few years ago that in a West Indian city an old and faithful free servant, in a family well known to me, astonished her master, on her death-bed, by a voluntary confession of more than a dozen murders.

"You remember such and such a party, when every one was ill? Well, I put something in the soup."

As another instance; a woman who died respectable, a Christian and a communicant, told this to her clergyman:—She had lived from youth, for many years, happily and faithfully with a white gentleman who considered her as his wife. She saw him pine away and die from slow poison, administered, she knew, by another woman whom he had wronged. But she dared not speak. She had not courage enough to be poisoned herself likewise.

It is easy to conceive the terrorism, and the exactions in the shape of fowls, plantains, rum, and so forth, which are at the command of an Obeah practitioner, who is believed by the Negro to be invulnerable himself, while he is both able and willing to destroy them. Nothing but the strong arm of English law can put down the sorcerer; and that seldom enough, owing to the poor folks' dread of giving evidence. Thus a woman, Madame Phyllis by name, ruled in a certain forest-hamlet of Trinidad. Like Deborah of old, she sat under her own palm-tree, and judged her little Israel—by the Devil's law instead of God's. Her murders (or supposed murders) were notorious: but no evidence could be obtained; Madame Phyllis dealt in poisons, charms, and philtres; and waxed fat on her trade for many a year. The first shock her reputation received was from a friend of mine, who, in his Government duty, planned out a road which ran somewhat nearer her dwelling than was pleasant or safe for her privacy. She came out denouncing, threatening. The coloured workmen dared not proceed. My friend persevered coolly; and Madame, finding that the Government official considered himself Obeah-proof, tried to bribe him off, with the foolish cunning of a savage, with a present of—bottled beer. To the horror of his workmen, he accepted—for the day was hot, as usual—a single bottle; and drank it there and then. The Negros looked—like the honest Maltese at St. Paul—"when he should have swollen, or fallen down dead suddenly:" but nothing happened; and they went on with their work, secure under a leader whom even Madame Phyllis dared not poison. But he ran a great risk; and knew it.

"I took care," said he, "to see that the cork had not been drawn and put back again; and then, to draw it myself."

At last Madame Phyllis's cup was full, and she fell into the snare which she had set for others. For a certain coloured policeman went off to her one night; and having poured out his love-lorn heart, and the agonies which he endured from the cruelty of a neighbouring fair, he begged for, got, and paid for a philtre to win her affections. On which, saying with Danton—"Que mon nom soit flétri, mais que la patrie soit libre," he carried the philtre to the magistrate; laid his information; and Madame Phyllis and her male accomplice were sent to gaol as rogues and impostors.

Her coloured victims looked on aghast at the audacity of English lawyers. But when they found that Madame was actually going to prison, they rose—just as if they had been French Republicans—deposed their despot after she had been taken prisoner, sacked her magic castle, and levelled it with the ground. Whether they did, or did not, find skeletons of children buried under the floor, or what they found at all, I could not discover; and should be very careful how I believed any statement about the matter. But what they wanted specially to find was, the skeleton of a certain rival Obeah-man, who having, some years before, rashly challenged Madame to a trial of skill, had gone to visit her one night, and never left her cottage again.

The chief centre of this detestable system is St. Vincent, where—so I was told by one who knows that island well—some sort of secret College, or School of the Prophets Diabolic, exists. Its emissaries spread over the islands, fattening themselves at the expense of their dupes, and exercising no small political authority, which has been ere now, and may be again, dangerous to society. In Jamaica, I was assured by a Nonconformist Missionary who had long lived there, Obeah is by no means on the decrease; and in Hayti it is probably on the increase, and taking—at least until the fall and death of Salnave—shapes which, when made public in the civilized world, will excite more than mere disgust. But of Hayti I shall be silent; having heard more of the state of society in that unhappy place than it is prudent, for the sake of the few white residents, to tell at present.

The same Missionary told me that in Sierra Leone, also,

Obeah and poisoning go hand in hand. Arriving home one night, he said, with two friends, he heard hideous screams from the house of a Portuguese Negro, a known Obeah-man. Fearing that murder was being done, they burst open his door, and found that he had tied up his wife hand and foot, and was flogging her horribly. They cut the poor creature down, and placed her in safety.

A day or two after, the Missionary's servant came in at sunrise with a mysterious air.

"You no go out just now, massa."

There was something in the road: but what, he would not tell. My friend went out, of course, in spite of the faithful fellow's entreaties; and found, as he expected, a bottle containing the usual charms, and round it—sight of horror to all Negros of the old school—three white cocks' heads—an old remnant, it is said, of a worship "de quo sileat musa"—pointing their beaks, one to his door, one to the door of each of his friends. He picked them up, laughing, and threw them away, to the horror of his servant.

But the Obeah-man was not so easily beaten. In a few days the servant came in again with a wise visage.

"You no drink a milk to-day, massa."

"Why not?"

"Oh, perhaps something bad in it. You give it a cat."

"But I don't want to poison the cat?"

"Oh, dere a strange cat in a stable; me give it her."

He did so; and the cat was dead in half an hour.

Again the fellow tried, watching when the three white men, as was their custom, should dine together, that he might poison them all. And again the black servant foiled him, though afraid to accuse him openly. This time it was—" You no drink a water in a filter." And when the filter was searched, it was full of poison-leaves.

A third attempt the rascal made with no more success; and then vanished from Sierra Leone; considering—as the Obeah-men in the West Indies are said to hold of the Catholic priests—that "Buccra Padre's Obeah was too strong for his Obeah."

I know not how true the prevailing belief is, that some of these Obeah-men carry a drop of snake's poison under a sharpened finger-nail, a scratch from which is death. A similar story was told to Humboldt of a tribe of Indians on the Orinoco; and the thing is possible enough. One story, which seemingly corroborates it, I heard, so curiously illustrative of Negro manners in Trinidad during the last generation, that I shall give it at length. I owe it —as I do many curious facts—to the kindness of Mr. Lionel Fraser, chief of police of the Port of Spain, to whom it was told, as it here stands, by the late Mr. R——, stipendiary magistrate; himself a Creole and a man of colour:—

"When I was a lad of about seventeen years of age, I was very frequently on a sugar estate belonging to a relation of mine; and during crop-time particularly I took good care to be there.

"Owing to my connection with the owner of the estate, I naturally had some authority with the people; and I did my best to preserve order amongst them, particularly in the boiling-house, where there used to be a good deal of petty theft, especially at night; for we had not then the powerful machinery which enables the planter to commence his grinding late and finish it early.

"There was one African on the estate who was the terror of the Negros, owing to his reputed supernatural powers as an Obeah-man.

"This man, whom I will call Martin, was a tall powerful Negro, who, even apart from the mysterious powers with which he was supposed to be invested, was a formidable opponent from his mere size and strength.

"I very soon found that Martin was determined to try his authority and influence against mine; and I resolved to give him the earliest possible opportunity for doing so.

"I remember the occasion when we first came into contact perfectly well. It was a Saturday night, and we were boiling off. The boiling-house was but very dimly lighted by two murky oil-lamps, the rays from which could scarcely penetrate through the dense atmosphere of steam which rose from the seething coppers. Occasionally a bright glow from the furnace-mouths lighted up the scene for a single instant, only to leave it the next moment darker than ever.

"It was during one of these flashes of light that I distinctly saw Martin deliberately filling a large tin pan with sugar from one of the coolers.

"I called out to him to desist: but he never deigned to take the slightest notice of me. I repeated my order in a louder and more angry tone; whereupon he turned his eyes upon me, and said, in a most contemptuous tone, 'Chut, ti bequé : quitté moué tranquille, ou 'tende sinon malheur ka rivé ou.' (P'shaw, little white boy : leave me alone, or worse will happen to you.)

"It was the tone more than the words themselves that enraged me; and without for one moment reflecting on the great disparity between us, I made a spring from the sort of raised platform on which I stood, and snatching the panful of sugar from his hand, I flung it, sugar and all, into the tache, from which I knew nothing short of a miracle could recover it.

"For a moment only did Martin hesitate; and then, after fumbling for one instant with his right hand in his girdle, he made a rush at me. Fortunately for me, I was prepared ; and springing back to the spot where I had before been standing,

I took up a light cutlass, which I always carried about with me, and stood on the defensive.

"I had, however, no occasion to use the weapon; for, in running towards me, Martin's foot slipped in some molasses which had been spilt on the ground, and he fell heavily to the floor, striking his head against the corner of one of the large wooden sugar-coolers.

"The blow stunned him for the time, and before he recovered I had left the boiling-house.

"The next day, to my surprise, I found him excessively civil, and almost obsequious: but I noticed that he had taken a violent dislike to our head overseer, whom I shall call Jean Marie, and whom he seemed to suspect as the person who had betrayed him to me when stealing the sugar.

"Things went on pretty quietly for some weeks, till the crop was nearly over.

"One afternoon Jean Marie told me there was to be a Jumby-dance amongst the Africans on the estate that very night. Now Jumby-dances were even then becoming less frequent, and I was extremely anxious to see one; and after a good deal of difficulty, I succeeded in persuading Jean Marie to accompany me to the hut wherein it was to be held.

"It was a miserable kind of an ajoupa near the river-side; and we had some difficulty in making our way to it through the tangled dank grass and brushwood which surrounded it. Nor was the journey rendered more pleasant by the constant rustling among this undergrowth, that reminded us that there were such things as snakes and other ugly creatures to be met with on our road.

"Curiosity, however, urged us on; and at length we reached the ajoupa, which was built on a small open space near the river, beneath a gigantic silk-cotton tree.

"Here we found assembled some thirty Africans, men and women, very scantily dressed, and with necklaces of beads, sharks'-teeth, dried frogs, &c., hung round their necks. They were all squatted on their haunches outside the hut, apparently waiting for a signal to go in.

"They did not seem particularly pleased at seeing us; and one of the men said something in African, apparently addressed to some one inside the house; for an instant after the door was flung open, and Martin, almost naked, and with his body painted to represent a skeleton, stalked forth to meet us.

"He asked us very angrily what we wanted there, and seemed particularly annoyed at seeing Jean Marie. However, on my repeated assurances that we only came to see what was going on, he at last consented to our remaining to see the dance; only cautioning us that we must keep perfect silence, and that a word, much more a laugh, would entail most serious consequences.

"As long as I live I shall never forget that scene. The hut was lighted by some eight or ten candles or lamps; and in the centre, dimly visible, was a Fêtish, somewhat of the appearance of a man, but with the head of a cock. Everything that the coarsest fancy could invent had been done to make this image horrible; and yet it appeared to be the object of special adoration to the devotees assembled.

"Jean Marie, to be out of the way, clambered on to one of the cross-beams that supported the roof, whilst I leaned against the side wall, as near as I could get to the aperture that served for a window, to avoid the smells, which were overpowering.

"Martin took his seat astride of an African tom-tom or drum; and I noticed at the time that Jean Marie's naked foot hung down from the cross-beam almost directly over Martin's head.

"Martin now began to chant a monotonous African song, accompanying with the tom-tom.

"Gradually he began to quicken the measure; quicker went the words; quicker beat the drum; and suddenly one of the women sprang into the open space in front of the Fêtish. Round and round she went, keeping admirable time with the music.

"Quicker still went the drum. And now the whole of the woman's body seemed electrified by it; and, as if catching the infection, a man now joined her in the mad dance. Couple after couple entered the arena, and a true sorcerers' sabbath began; while light after light was extinguished, till at last but one remained; by whose dim ray I could just perceive the faint outlines of the remaining persons.

"At this moment, from some cause or other, Jean Marie burst into a loud laugh.

"Instantly the drum stopped; and I distinctly saw Martin raise his right hand, and, as it appeared to me, seize Jean Marie's naked foot between his finger and thumb.

"As he did so, Jean Marie, with a terrible scream, which I shall never forget, fell to the ground in strong convulsions.

"We succeeded in getting him outside. But he never spoke again; and died two hours afterwards, his body having swollen up like that of a drowned man.

"In those days there were no inquests; and but little interest was created by the affair. Martin himself soon after died."

But enough of these abominations, of which I am forced to omit the worst.

That day—to go on with my own story—I left the rest of the party to go down to the court-house, while I stayed at the camp, sorry to lose so curious a scene, but too tired to face a crowded tropic court, and an atmosphere of perspiration and perjury.

Moreover, that had befallen me which might never befall me again—I had a chance of being alone in the forests; and into them I would wander, and meditate on them in silence.

So, when all had departed, I lounged awhile in the rocking-chair, watching two Negros astride on the roof of a shed, on which they were nailing shingles. Their heads were bare; the sun was intense; the roof on which they sat must have been of the temperature of an average frying-pan on an English fire: but the good fellows worked on, steadily and carefully, though not fast, chattering and singing, evidently enjoying the very act of living, and fattening in the genial heat. Lucky dogs: who had probably never known hunger, certainly never known cold; never known, possibly, a single animal want which they could not satisfy. I could not but compare their lot with that of an average English artisan. Ah, well: there is no use in fruitless comparisons; and it is no reason that one should grudge the Negro what he has because others, who deserve it certainly as much as he, have it not. After all, the ancestors of these Negros have been, for centuries past, so hard-worked, ill-fed, ill-used too—sometimes worse than ill-used—that it is hard if the descendants may not have a holiday, and take the world easy for a generation or two.

The perpetual Saturnalia in which the Negro, in Trinidad at least, lives, will surely give physical strength and health to the body, and something of cheerfulness, self-help, independence to the spirit. If the Saturnalia be prolonged too far, and run, as they seem inclined to run, into brutality and licence, those stern laws of Nature which men call political economy will pull the Negro up short, and waken him out of his dream, soon enough and sharply enough—a "judgment" by which the wise will profit and be preserved, while the fools only will be destroyed. And meanwhile, what if in these Saturnalia (as in Rome of old) the new sense of independence manifests itself in somewhat of self-assertion and rudeness, often in insolence, especially disagreeable, because deliberate? What if "You call me black fellow? I mash you white face in," were the first words one heard at St. Thomas's from a Negro, on being asked, civilly enough, by a sailor to cast off from a boat to which he had no right to be holding on? What if a Negro now and then addresses you as simple "Buccra," while he expects you to call him "Sir;" or if a Negro woman, on being begged by an English lady to call to another Negro woman, answers at last, after long pretences not to hear, "You coloured lady! you hear dis white woman a wanting of you?" Let it be. We white people bullied these black people quite enough for three hundred years, to be able to allow them to play (for it is no more) at bullying us. As long as the Negros are decently loyal and peaceable, and do not murder their magistrates and drink their brains mixed with rum, nor send delegates to the President of Hayti to ask if he will assist them, in case of a general rising, to exterminate the whites—tricks which the harmless Negros of Trinidad, to do them justice, never have played, or had a thought of playing—we must remember that we are very seriously in debt to the Negro, and must allow him to take out instalments of his debt, now and then, in his own fashion. After all, we brought him here, and we have no right to complain of our own work. If, like Frankenstein, we have tried to make a man, and made him badly; we must, like Frankenstein, pay the penalty.

So much for the Negro. As for the coloured population—especially the educated and civilized coloured population of the towns—they stand to us in an altogether different relation. They claim to be, and are, our kinsfolk, on another ground than that of common humanity. We are bound to them by a tie more sacred, I had almost said more stern, than we are to the mere Negro. They claim, and justly, to be considered as our kinsfolk and equals; and I believe, from what I have seen of them, that they will prove themselves such, whenever they are treated as they are in Trinidad. What faults some of them have, proceed mainly from a not dishonourable ambition, mixed with uncertainty of their own position. Let them be made to feel that they are now not a class; to forget, if possible, that they ever were one. Let any allusion to the painful past be treated, not merely as an offence against good manners, but as what it practically is, an offence against the British Government; and that Government will find in them, I believe, loyal citizens and able servants.

But to go back to the forest. I sauntered forth with cutlass and collecting-box, careless whither I went, and careless of what I saw; for everything that I could see would be worth seeing. I know not that I found many rare or new things that day. I recollect, amid the endless variety of objects, Film-ferns of various delicate species, some growing in the moss tree-trunks, some clasping the trunk itself by horizontal lateral fronds, while the main rachis climbed straight up many feet, thus embracing the stem in a network of semi-transparent green Guipure lace. I recollect, too, a coarse low fern[1] on stream-gravel which was remarkable, because its stem was set with thick green prickles. I recollect, too, a dead giant tree, the ruins of which struck me with awe. The stump stood some thirty feet high, crumbling into tinder and dust, though its death was so recent that the creepers and parasites had not yet had time to lay hold of it; and around its great spur-roots lay what had been its trunk and head, piled in stacks of rotten wood, over which I scrambled with some

[1] *Pteris podophylla*.

caution, for fear my leg, on breaking through, might be saluted from the inside by some deadly snake. The only sign of animal life, however, I found about the tree, save a few millipedes and land snails, were some lizard-eggs in a crack, about the size of those of a humming-bird.

I scrambled down on gravelly beaches, and gazed up the green avenues of the brooks. I sat amid the Balisiers and Aroumas, above still blue pools, bridged by huge fallen trunks, or with wild Pines of half-a-dozen kinds set in rows: I watched the shoals of fish play in and out of the black logs at the bottom: I gave myself up to the simple enjoyment of looking, careless of what I looked at, or what I thought about it all. There are times when the mind, like the body, had best feed, gorge if you will, and leave the digestion of its food to the unconscious alchemy of nature. It is as unwise to be always saying to oneself, "Into what pigeon-hole of my brain ought I to put this fact, and what conclusion ought I to draw from it?" as to ask your teeth how they intend to chew, and your gastric juice how it intends to convert your three courses and a dessert into chyle. Whether on a Scotch moor or in a Tropic forest, it is well at times to have full faith in Nature; to resign yourself to her, as a child upon a holiday; to be still and let her speak. She knows best what to say.

And yet I could not altogether do it that day. There was

one class of objects in the forest which I had set my heart on examining, with all my eyes and soul; and after a while, I scrambled and hewed my way to them, and was well repaid for a quarter of an hour's very hard work.

I had remarked, from the camp, palms unlike any I had seen before, starring the opposite forest with pale grey-green leaves. Long and earnestly I had scanned them through the glasses. Now was the time to see them close, and from beneath. I soon guessed (and rightly) that I was looking at that Palma de Jagua,[1] which excited—and no wonder—the enthusiasm of the usually unimpassioned Humboldt. Magnificent as the tree is when its radiating leaves are viewed from above, it is even more magnificent when you stand beneath it. The stem, like that of the Coco-nut, usually curves the height of a man ere it rises in a shaft for fifty or sixty feet more. From the summit of that shaft springs a crown—I had rather say, a fountain—of pinnated leaves; only eight or ten of them; but five-and-twenty feet long each. For three-fourths of their length they rise at an angle of 45° or more; for the last fourth they fall over, till the point hangs straight down; and each leaflet, which is about two feet and a half long, falls over in a similar curve, completing the likeness of the whole to a fountain of water, or a gush of rockets. I stood and looked up, watching the innumerable curled leaflets,

[1] Jessenia.

JAGÚAS AND PIRIAJOS.

pale green above and silver-grey below, shiver and rattle amid the denser foliage of the broad-leaved trees; and then went on to another and to another, to stare up again, and enjoy the mere shape of the most beautiful plant I had ever beheld, excepting always the Musa Ensete, from Abyssinia, in the Palm-house at Kew. Truly spoke Humboldt, of this or a closely allied species, " Nature has lavished every beauty of form on the Jagua Palm."

But here, as elsewhere to my great regret, I looked in vain for that famous and beautiful tree, the Piriajo,[1] or "Peach Palm," which is described in Mr. Bates's book, vol. ii. p. 218, under the name of Pupunha. It grows here and there in the island, and always marks the site of an ancient Indian settlement. This is probable enough, for " it grows," says Mr. Bates, "wild nowhere on the Amazons. It is one of those few vegetable productions (including three kinds of Manioc and the American species of Banana) which the Indians have cultivated from time immemorial, and brought with them in their original migration to Brazil." From whence? It has never yet been found wild; "its native home may possibly," Mr. Bates thinks, "be in some still unexplored tract on the eastern slopes of the Æquatorial Andes." Possibly so: and possibly, again, on tracts long sunk beneath the sea. He describes the tree as "a noble ornament,

[a] Gulielma speciosa.

from fifty to sixty feet in height, and often as straight as a scaffold-pole. The taste of the fruit may be compared to a mixture of chestnuts and cheese. Vultures devour it greedily, and come in quarrelsome flocks to the trees when it is ripe. Dogs will also eat it. I do not recollect seeing cats do the same, though they will go into the woods to eat Tucuma, another kind of palm fruit."

"It is only the more advanced tribes," says Mr. Bates, "who have kept up the cultivation. .... Bunches of sterile or seedless fruits"—a mark of very long cultivation, as in the case of the Plantain—" occur. .... It is one of the principal articles of food at Ega when in season, and is boiled and eaten with treacle or salt. A dozen of the seedless fruits make a good nourishing meal for a full-grown person. It is the general belief that there is more nutriment in Pupunha than in fish, or Vacca Marina (Manati)."

My friend Mr. Bates will, I am sure, excuse my borrowing so much from him about a tree which must be as significant in his eyes as it is in mine.

So passed many hours, till I began to be tired of—I may almost say, pained by—the appalling silence and loneliness; and I was glad to get back to a point where I could hear the click of the axes in the clearing. I welcomed it just as, after a long night on a calm sea, when one nears the harbour again, one welcomes the sound of the children's voices and the stir of life about the quay, as a relief from the utter blank, and feels oneself no longer a bubble afloat on an infinity which knows one not, and cares nothing for one's existence. For in the dead stillness of mid-day, when not only the deer, and the agoutis, and the armadillos, but the birds and insects likewise, are all asleep, the crack of a falling branch was all that struck my ear, as I tried in vain to verify the truth of that beautiful passage of Humboldt's— true, doubtless, in other forests, or for ears more acute than mine. "In the mid-day," he says,[1] "the larger animals seek shelter in the recesses of the forest, and the birds hide themselves under the thick foliage of the trees, or in the clefts of the rocks: but if, in this apparent entire stillness of nature, one listens for the faintest tones which an attentive ear can seize, there is perceived an all-pervading rustling sound, a humming and fluttering of insects close to the ground, and in the lower strata of the atmosphere. Everything announces a world of organic activity and life. In every bush, in the cracked bark of the trees, in the earth undermined by hymenopterous insects, life stirs audibly. It is, as it were, one of the many voices of Nature, and can only be heard by the sensitive and reverent ear of her true votaries."

Be not too severe, great master. A man's ear may be

[1] "Aspects of Nature," vol. ii. p. 272.

reverent enough: but you must forgive its not being sensitive while it is recovering from that most deafening of plagues, a tropic cold in the head.

Would that I had space to tell at length of our long and delightful journey back the next day, which lay for several miles along the path by which we came, and then, after we had looked down once more on the exquisite bay of Fillette, kept along the northern wall of the mountains, instead of turning up to the slope which we came over out of Caura. For miles we paced a mule-path, narrow, but well-kept—as it had need to be; for a fall would have involved a roll into green abysses, from which we should probably not have re-ascended. Again the surf rolled softly far below; and here and there a vista through the trees showed us some view of the sea and woodlands almost as beautiful as that at Fillette. Ever and anon some fresh valuable tree or plant, wasting in the wilderness, was pointed out. More than once we became aware of a keen and dreadful scent, as of a concentrated essence of unwashed tropic humanity, which proceeded from that strange animal, the porcupine with a prehensile tail,[1] who prowls in the tree-tops all night, and sleeps in them all day, spending his idle hours in making this hideous smell. Probably he or his ancestors have found

[1] Synetheres.

it pay as a protection; for no jaguar or tiger-cat, it is to be presumed, would care to meddle with anything so exquisitely nasty, especially when it is all over sharp prickles.

Once—I should know the spot again among a thousand—where we scrambled over a stony brook just like one in a Devonshire wood, the boulders and the little pools between them swarmed with things like scarlet and orange fingers, or sticks of sealing-wax, which we recognized, and, looking up, saw a magnificent Bois Châtaigne,[1]—Pachira, as the Indians call it,—like a great horse-chestnut, spreading its heavy boughs overhead. And these were the fallen petals of its last-night's crop of flowers, which had opened there, under the moonlight, unseen and alone. Unseen and alone? How do we know that?

Then we emerged upon a beach, the very perfection of typical tropic shore, with little rocky coves, from one to another of which we had to ride through rolling surf, beneath the welcome shade of low shrub-fringed cliffs; while over the little mangrove-swamp at the mouth of the glen, Tocuche rose sheer, like McGilbicuddy's Reeks transfigured into one huge emerald.

We turned inland again, and stopped for luncheon at a clear brook, running through a grove of Cacao and Bois Immortelles. We sat beneath the shade of a huge

[1] Carolinea insignis.

Bamboo clump; cut ourselves pint-stoups out of the joints; and then, like great boys, got, some of us at least, very wet in fruitless attempts to catch a huge cray-fish nigh eighteen inches long, blue and grey, and of a shape something between a gnat and a spider, who, with a wife and child, had taken up his abode in a pool among the spurs of a great Bois Immortelle. However, he was too nimble for us; and we went on, and inland once more, luckily not leaving our bamboo stoups behind.

We descended, I remember, to the sea-shore again, at a certain Maraccas bay, and had a long ride along bright sands, between surf and scrub; in which ride, by the bye, the civilizer of Montserrat and I, to avoid the blinding glare of the sand, rode along the firm sand between the sea and the lagoon, through the low wood of Shore Grape and Mahaut, Pinguin and Swamp Seguine[1]—which last is an Arum with a knotted stem, from three to twelve feet high. We brushed our way along with our cutlasses, as we sat on our saddles, enjoying the cool shade; till my companion's mule found herself jammed tight in scrub, and unable to forge either ahead or astern. Her rider was jammed too, and unable to get off; and the two had to be cut out of the bush by fair hewing, amid much laughter, while the wise old mule, as the cutlasses flashed close to her nose, never moved a

[1] Montrichardia.

A Tropic Beach.

muscle, perfectly well aware of what had happened, and how she was to be got out of the scrape, as she had been probably fifty times before.

We stopped at the end of the long beach, thoroughly tired and hungry, for we had been on the march many hours; and discovered for the first time that we had nothing left to eat. Luckily, a certain little pot of "Ramornie" essence of soup was recollected and brought out. The kettle was boiling in five minutes, and half a teaspoonful per man of the essence put on a knife's point, and stirred with a cutlass, to the astonishment of the grinning and unbelieving Negros, who were told that we were going to make Obeah soup, and were more than half of that opinion themselves. Meanwhile, I saw the wise mule led up into the bush; and, on asking its owner why, was told that she was to be fed—on what, I could not see. But, much to my amusement, he cut down a quantity of the young leaves of the Cocorite palm; and she began to eat them greedily, as did my police-horse. And, when the bamboo stoups were brought out, and three-quarters of a pint of good soup was served round—not forgetting the Negros, one of whom, after sucking it down, rubbed his stomach, and declared, with a grin, that it was very good Obeah—the oddness of the scene came over me. The blazing beach, the misty mountains, the hot trade-wind, the fantastic leaves overhead, the black limbs and faces, the horses eating palm-leaves, and we sitting on logs among the strange ungainly Montrichardias, drinking " Ramornie " out of bamboo, and washing it down with milk from green coco-nuts—was this, too, a scene in a pantomime? Would it, too vanish if one only shut one's eyes and shook one's head?

We turned up into the loveliest green trace, where, I know not how, the mountain vegetation had, some of it, come down to the sea-level. Nowhere did I see the Melastomas more luxuriant; and among them, arching over our heads like parasols of green lace, between us and the sky, were tall tree-ferns, as fine as those on the mountain-slopes.

In front of us opened a flat meadow of a few acres; and beyond it, spur upon spur, rose a noble mountain, in so steep a wall that it was difficult to see how we were to ascend.

Ere we got to the mountain foot, some of our party had nigh come to grief. For across the Savanna wandered a deep lagoon-brook. The only bridge had been washed away by rains; and we had to get the horses through as we could, all but swimming them, two men on each horse; and then to drive the poor creatures back for a fresh double load, with fallings, splashings, much laughter, and a qualm or two at the recollection that there might be unpleasant animals in the water. Electric eels, happily, were not invented at the time when Trinidad parted from the Main, or at least had not spread so far east: but alligators had been by that time fully developed, and had arrived here in plenty; and to be laid hold of by one, would have been undesirable: though our party was strong enough to have made very short work with the monster.

So over we got, and through much mud, and up mountains some fifteen hundred feet high, on which the vegetation was even richer than any we had seen before; and down the other side, with the great lowland and the Gulf of Paria opening before us. We rested at a police-station—always a pleasant sight in Trinidad, for the sake of the stalwart soldier-like brown policemen and their buxom wives, and neat houses and gardens, a focus of discipline and civilization amid what would otherwise relapse too soon into anarchy and barbarism; we whiled away the time by inspecting the ward police-reports, which were kept as neatly, and worded as well, as they would have been in England; and then rolled comfortably in the carriage down to Port of Spain, tired and happy, after three such days as had made old blood and old brains young again.

CHAPTER XII.

THE SAVANNA OF ARIPO.

THE last of my pleasant rides, and one which would have been perhaps the pleasantest of all, had I had (as on other occasions) the company of my host, was to the Cocal, or Coco-palm grove, of the east coast, taking on my way the Savanna of Aripo. It had been our wish to go up the Oroonoco, as far as Ciudad Bolivar (the Angostura of Humboldt's travels), to see the new capital of Southern Venezuela, fast rising into wealth and importance under the wise and pacific policy of its president, Señor Dalla Costa, a man said to possess a genius and an integrity far superior to the average of South American republicans—of which latter the less said the better; to push back, if possible, across those Llanos which Humboldt describes in his "Personal Narrative," vol. iv. p. 295; it may be to visit the Falls of the Caroni. But that had to be done by others, after we were gone. My days in the island were growing short; and the most I could do was to see at Aripo a small specimen of that peculiar Savanna vegetation, which occupies thousands of square miles on the mainland.

If therefore the reader cares nothing for botanical and geological speculations, he will be wise to skip this chapter. But those who are interested in the vast changes of level and distribution of land which have taken place all over the world since the present forms of animals and vegetables were established on it, may possibly find a valuable fact or two in what I thought I saw at the Savanna of Aripo.

My first point was, of course, the little city of San Josef. To an Englishman, the place will be always interesting as the scene of Raleigh's exploit, and the capture of Berreos; and, to one who has received the kindness which I have received from the Spanish gentlemen of the neighbourhood, a spot full of most grateful memories. It lies pleasantly enough, on a rise at the southern foot of the mountains, and at the mouth of a torrent which comes down from the famous "Chorro," or waterfall, of Maraccas. In going up to that waterfall, just at the back of the town, I found buried, in several feet of earth, a great number of seemingly recent but very ancient shells. Whether they be remnants of an elevated sea-beach, or of some Indian "kitchen-midden," I dare not decide. But the question is well worth the attention of any geologist who may go that way. The waterfall, and the road up to it, are best described by one who, after fourteen years of hard scientific work in the island, now lies lonely in San Fernando churchyard, far from his beloved Fatherland—he, or at least all of him that could die. I wonder whether that of him which can never die, knows what his Fatherland is doing now? But to the waterfall of Maraccas, or rather to poor Dr. Krueger's description of it :—

"The northern chain of mountains, covered nearly everywhere with dense forests, is intersected at various angles by numbers of valleys presenting the most lovely character. Generally each valley is watered by a silvery stream, tumbling here and there over rocks and natural dams, ministering in a continuous rain to the strange-looking river-canes, dumb-canes, and balisiers, that voluptuously bend their heads to the drizzly shower which plays incessantly on their glistening leaves, off which the globules roll in a thousand pearls, as from the glossy plumage of a stately swan.

"One of these falls deserves particular notice—the Cascade of Maraccas—in the valley of that name. The high road leads up the valley a few miles, over hills, and along the windings of the river, exhibiting the varying scenery of our mountain district in the fairest style. There, on the river side, you may admire the gigantic pepper-trees, or the silvery leaves of the Calathea, the lofty bamboo, or the fragrant

Pothos, the curious Cyclanthus, or frowning nettles, some of the latter from ten to twelve feet high. But how to describe the numberless treasures which everywhere strike the eye of the wandering naturalist?

"To reach the Chorro, or Cascade, you strike to the right into a 'path' that brings you first to a cacao plantation, through a few rice or maize fields, and then you enter the shade of the virgin forest. Thousands of interesting objects now attract your attention: here, the wonderful Norantea or the resplendent Calycophyllum, a Tabernæmontana or a Faramea filling the air afar off with the fragrance of their blossoms; there, a graceful Heliconia winking at you from out some dark ravine. That shrubbery above is composed of a species of Bœhmeria or Ardisia, and that scarlet flower belongs to our native Aphelandra. In the rear are one or two Philodendrons—disagreeable guests, for their smell is bad enough, and they blister when imprudently touched. There also you may see a tree-fern, though a small one. Nearer to us, and low down beneath our feet, that rich panicle of flowers belongs to a Begonia; and here also is an assemblage of ferns of the genera Asplenium, Hymenophyllum, and Trichomanes, as well as of Hepaticæ and Mosses. But what are those yellow and purple flowers hanging above our heads? They are Bignonias and Mucunas—creepers straying from afar, which have selected this spot, where they may, under the influence of the sun's beams, propagate their race. Those chain-like, fantastic, strange-looking lianes, resembling a family of boas, are Bauhinias; and beyond, through the opening you see, in the abandoned ground of some squatter's garden, the trumpet-tree (Cecropia) and the groo-groo, the characteristic plants of the rastrajo.

"Now, let us proceed on our walk; we mean the cascade: —Here it is, opposite to you, a grand spectacle indeed! From a perpendicular wall of solid rock, of more than three hundred feet, down rushes a stream of water, splitting in the air and producing a constant shower, which renders this lovely spot singularly and deliciously cool. Nearly the whole extent of this natural wall is covered with plants, among which you can easily discern numbers of ferns and mosses, two species of Pitcairnia with beautiful red flowers, some Aroids, various nettles, and here and there a Begonia. How different such a spot would look in cold Europe! Below, in the midst of a never-failing drizzle, grow luxuriant Ardisias, Aroids, Ferns, Costas, Heliconias, Centropogons, Hydrocotyles, Cyperoids, and Grasses of various genera, Tradescantias and Commelynas, Billbergias, and, occasionally, a few small Rubiaceæ and Melastomaceæ."

The cascade, when I saw it, was somewhat disfigured above and below. Above, the forest-fires of last year had swept the edge of the cliff, and had even crawled half-way down, leaving blackened rocks and grey stems; and below, loyal zeal had cut away only too much of the rich vegetation, to make a shed, or stable, in anticipation of a visit from the Duke of Edinburgh, who did not come. A year or two, however, in this climate, will heal these temporary scars, and all will be as luxuriant as ever. Indeed such scars heal only too fast here. For the paths become impassable from brush and weeds every six months, and have to be cutlassed out afresh; and when it was known that we were going up to the waterfall, a gang had to be set to work to save the lady of the party being wetted through by leaf-dew up to her shoulders, as she sat upon her horse. Pretty it was—a bit out of an older and more simple world—to see the yeoman-gentleman who had contracted for the mending of the road, and who counts among his ancestors the famous Ponce de Leon, meeting us half-way on our return; dressed more simply, and probably much poorer, than an average English yeoman: but keeping untainted the stately Castilian courtesy, as with hat in hand—I hope I need not say that my hat was at my saddle-bow all the while—he inquired whether La Señorita had found the path free from all obstructions, and so forth.

> "The old order changes, giving place to the new:
> Lest one good custom should corrupt the world."

But when, two hundred years hence, there are no more

such gentlemen of the old school left in the world, what higher form of true civilization shall we have invented to put in its place? None as yet. All our best civilization, in every class, is derived from that; from the true self-respect which is founded on respect for others.

From San Josef, I was taken on in the carriage of a Spanish gentleman through Arima, a large village where an Indian colony makes those baskets and other wares from the Arouma leaf for which Trinidad is noted; and on to his estate at Guanapo, a pleasant lowland place, with wide plantations of Cacao, only fourteen years old, but in full and most profitable bearing; rich meadows with huge clumps of bamboo; and a roomy timber-house, beautifully thatched with palm, which serves as a retreat, in the dry season, for him and his ladies, when baked out of dusty San Josef. On my way there, by the bye, I espied, and gathered for the first and last time, a flower very dear to me—a crimson Passion-flower, rambling wild over the bush.

When we arrived, the sun was still so high in heaven that the kind owner offered to push on that very afternoon to the Savanna of Aripo, some five miles off. Police-horses had arrived from Arima, in one of which I recognized my trusty old brown cob of the Northern Mountains, and laid hands on him at once; and away three or four of us went, the squire leading the way on his mule, with cutlass and umbrella, both needful enough.

We went along a sandy high road, bordered by a vegetation new to me. Low trees, with wiry branches and shining ever-green leaves, which belonged, I was told, principally to the myrtle tribe, were overtopped by Jagua palms, and packed below with Pinguins; with wild pine-apples, whose rose and purple flower-heads were very beautiful; and with a species of palm of which I had often heard, but which I had never seen before, at least in any abundance, namely, the Timit,[1] the leaves of which are used as thatch. A low tree, seldom rising more than twenty or thirty feet, it throws out wedge-shaped leaves some ten or twelve feet long, sometimes all but entire, sometimes irregularly pinnate, because the space between the straight and parallel side nerves has not been filled up. These flat wedge-shaped sheets, often six feet across, and the oblong pinnæ, some three feet long by six inches to a foot in breadth, make admirable thatch; and on emergency, as we often saw that day, good umbrellas. Bundles of them lay along the road-side, tied up, ready for carrying away, and each Negro or Negress whom we passed carried a Timit leaf, and hooked it on to his head when a gush of rain came down.

[1] Manicaria.

After a while we turned off the high road into a forest path, which was sound enough, the soil being one sheet of poor sand and white quartz gravel, which would in Scotland, or even Devonshire, have carried nothing taller than heath, but was here covered with impenetrable jungle. The luxuriance of this jungle, be it remembered, must not delude a stranger, as it has too many ere now, into fancying that the land would be profitable under cultivation. As long as the soil is shaded and kept damp, it will bear an abundant crop of woody fibre, which, composed almost entirely of carbon and water, drains hardly any mineral constituents from the soil. But if that jungle be once cleared off, the slow and careful work of ages has been undone in a moment. The burning sun bakes up everything; and the soil, having no mineral staple wherewith to support a fresh crop if planted, is reduced to aridity and sterility for years to come. Timber, therefore, I believe, and timber only, is the proper crop for these poor soils, unless medicinal or otherwise useful trees should be discovered hereafter worth the planting. To thin out the useless timbers—but cautiously, for fear of letting in the sun's rays—and to replace them by young plants of useful timbers, is all that Government can do with the poorer bits of these Crown lands, beyond protecting (as it does now to the best of its power) the natural crop of Timit-leaves from waste and destruction.

So much it ought to do; and so much it can and will do in Trinidad, which—happily for it—possesses a Government which governs, instead of leaving every man, as in the Irishman's paradise, to "do what is right in the sight of his own eyes, and what is wrong too, av he likes." Without such wise regulation, and even restraint, of the ignorant greediness of human toil, intent only (as in the too exclusive cultivation of the sugar-cane and of the cotton-plant) on present profits, without foresight or care for the future, the lands of warmer climates will surely fall under that curse, so well described by the venerable Elias Fries, of Lund.[1]

"A broad belt of waste land follows gradually in the steps of cultivation. If it expands, its centre and its cradle dies, and on the outer borders only do we find green shoots. But it is not impossible, only difficult, for man, without renouncing the advantage of culture itself, one day to make reparation for the injury which he has inflicted; he is the appointed lord of creation. True it is that thorns and thistles, ill-favoured and poisonous plants, well named by botanists 'rubbish-plants,' mark the track which man has proudly traversed through the earth. Before him lay original Nature in her wild but sublime beauty. Behind him he leaves the desert, a deformed and ruined land; for childish desire of

[1] Schleiden's "Plant: a Biography." End of Lecture xi.

destruction or thoughtless squandering of vegetable treasures have destroyed the character of Nature; and, terrified, man himself flies from the arena of his actions, leaving the impoverished earth to barbarous races or to animals, so long as yet another spot in virgin beauty smiles before him. Here, again, in selfish pursuit of profit, and, consciously or unconsciously, following the abominable principle of the great moral vileness which one man has expressed—'Après nous le déluge,' he begins anew the work of destruction. Thus did cultivation, driven out, leave the East, and perhaps the Deserts formerly robbed of their coverings: like the wild hordes of old over beautiful Greece, thus rolls the conquest with fearful rapidity from east to west through America; and the planter now often leaves the already exhausted land, the eastern climate becomes infertile through the demolition of the forests, to introduce a similar revolution into the far West."

For a couple of miles or more we trotted on through this jungle, till suddenly we saw light ahead; and in five minutes the forest ended, and a scene opened before us which made me understand the admiration which Humboldt and other travellers have expressed at the far vaster Savannas of the Oroonoco.

A large sheet of grey-green grass, bordered by the forest wall, as far as the eye could see, and dotted with low bushes, weltered in mirage; while stretching out into it, some half a mile off, a grey promontory into a green sea, was an object which filled me with more awe and admiration than anything which I had seen in the island.

It was a wood of Moriche palms; like a Greek temple, many hundred yards in length, and, as I guessed, nearly a hundred feet in height; and, like a Greek temple, ending abruptly at its full height. The grey columns, perfectly straight and parallel, supported a dark roof of leaves, grey underneath, and reflecting above, from their broad fans, sheets of pale glittering light. Such serenity of grandeur I never saw in any group of trees; and when we rode up to it, and tethered our horses in its shade, it seemed to me almost irreverent not to kneel and worship in that temple not made with hands.

When we had gazed our fill, we set hastily to work to collect plants, as many as the lateness of the hour and the scalding heat would allow. A glance showed the truth of Dr. Krueger's words:—

"It is impossible to describe the feelings of the botanist when arriving at a field like this, so much unlike anything he has seen before. Here are full-blowing large Orchids, with red, white, and yellow flowers; and among the grasses, smaller ones of great variety, and as great scientific interest— Melastomaceous plants of various genera; Utricularias, Droseras, rare and various grasses, and Cyperoids of small sizes and fine kinds, with a species of Cassytha; in the water, Ceratophyllum (the well-known hornwort of the English ponds) and bog-mosses. Such a variety of forms and colours is nowhere else to be met with in the island."

Of the Orchids, we only found one in flower; and of the rest, of course, we had time only to gather a very few of the more remarkable, among which was that lovely cousin of the Clerodendrons, the crimson Amasonia, which ought to be in all hothouses. The low bushes, I found, were that curious tree the Chaparro,[1] but not the Chaparro[2] so often mentioned by Humboldt as abounding on the Llanos. This Chaparro is remarkable, first, for the queer little Natural Order to which it belongs; secondly, for its tanning properties; thirdly, for the very nasty smell of its flowers; fourthly, for the roughness of its leaves, which make one's flesh creep, and are used, I believe, for polishing steel; and lastly, for its wide geographical range, from Isla de Pinos, near Cuba—where Columbus, to his surprise, saw true pines growing in the Tropics—all over the Llanos, and down to Brazil; an ancient, ugly, sturdy form of vegetation, able to get a scanty living out of the poorest soils, and consequently triumphant, as yet, in the battle of life.

The soil of the Savanna was a poor sandy clay, treacherous,

[1] Curatella Americana.   [2] Rhopala.

and often impassable for horses, being half dried above and wet beneath. The vegetation grew, not over the whole, but in innumerable tussocks, which made walking very difficult. The type of the rushes and grasses was very English: but among them grew, here and there, plants which excited my astonishment; above all, certain Bladder-worts,[1] which I had expected to find, but which, when found, were so utterly unlike any English ones, that I did not recognize at first what they were. Our English Bladder-worts, as everybody knows, float in stagnant water on tangles of hair-like leaves, something like those of the Water-Ranunculus, but furnished with innumerable tiny bladders; and this raft supports the little scape of yellow snapdragon-like flowers. There are in Trinidad and other parts of South America Bladder-worts of this type. But those which we found to-day, growing out of the damp clay, were more like in habit to a delicate stalk of flax, or even a bent of grass, upright, leafless or all but leafless, with heads of small blue or yellow flowers, and carrying, in one species, a few very minute bladders about the roots, in another none at all. A strange variation from the normal type of the family; yet not so strange, after all, as that of another variety in the high mountain woods, which, finding neither ponds to float in or swamp to root in, has taken to lodging as a parasite among

[1] Utricularia.

the wet moss on tree-trunks; not so strange, either, as that of yet another, which floats, but in the most unexpected spots, namely, in the water which lodges between the leaf-sheaths of the wild pines, perched on the tree-boughs, a parasite on parasites; and sends out long runners, as it grows, along the bough, in search of the next wild pine and its tiny reservoirs.

In the face of such strange facts, is it very absurd to guess that these Utricularias, so like each other in their singular and highly specialized flowers, so unlike each other in the habit of the rest of the plant, have started from some one original type, perhaps long since extinct; and that, carried by birds into quite new situations, they have adapted themselves, by natural selection, to new circumstances, changing the parts which required change—the leaves and stalks; but keeping comparatively unchanged those which needed no change—the flowers?

But I was not prepared, as I should have been had I studied my "Griesbach's West Indian Flora" carefully enough beforehand, for the next proof of the wide distribution of water-plants. For as I scratched and stumbled among the tussocks, "larding the lean earth as I stalked along," my kind guide put into my hand, with something of an air of triumph, a little plant, which was—there was no denying it—none other than the long-leaved Sundew,[1]

[1] Drosera longifolia.

with its clammy-haired paws full of dead flies, just as they would have been in any bog in Devonshire or in Hampshire, in Wales or in Scotland. But how came it here? And more, how has it spread, not only over the whole of Northern Europe, Canada, and the United States, but even as far south as Brazil? Its being common to North America and Europe is not surprising. It may belong to that comparatively ancient Flora which existed when there was landway between the two continents by way of Greenland, and the bison ranged from Russia to the Rocky Mountains. But its presence within the Tropics is more probably explained by supposing that it, like the Bladder-worts, has been carried on the feet or in the crop of birds.

The Savanna itself, like those of Caroni and Piarco, offers, I suspect, a fresh proof that a branch of the Oroonoco once ran along the foot of the northern mountains of Trinidad.

"It is impossible," says Humboldt,[1] "to cross the burning plains" (of the Oroonocquan Savannas) "without inquiring whether they have always been in the same state; or whether they have been stripped of their vegetation by some revolution of nature. The stratum of mould now found on them is very thin. . . . . . The plains were, doubtless, less

[1] "Personal Narrative," vol. iv. p. 336 of H. M. Williams's translation.

bare in the fifteenth century than they are now; yet the first Conquistadores, who came from Coro, described them then as Savannas, where nothing could be perceived save the sky and the turf; which were generally destitute of trees, and difficult to traverse on account of the reverberation of heat from the soil. Why does not the great forest of the Oroonoco extend to the north, or the left bank of that river? Why does it not fill that vast space that reaches as far as the Cordillera of the coast, and which is fertilized by various rivers? This question is connected with all that relates to the history of our planet. If, indulging in geological reveries, we suppose that the Steppes of America and the desert of Sahara have been stripped of their vegetation by an irruption of the ocean, or that they formed the bottom of an inland lake"—(the Sahara, as is now well known, is the quite recently elevated bed of a great sea continuous with the Atlantic)—" we may conceive that thousands of years have not sufficed for the trees and shrubs to advance toward the centre from the borders of the forests, from the skirts of the plains either naked or covered with turf, and darken so vast a space with their shade. It is more difficult to explain the origin of bare savannas enclosed in forests, than to recognize the causes which maintain forests and savannas within their ancient limits like continents and seas."

With these words in my mind, I could not but look on the

Savanna of Aripo as one of the last-made bits of dry land in Trinidad, still unfurnished with the common vegetation of the island. The two invading armies of tropical plants—one advancing from the north, off the now almost destroyed land which connected Trinidad and the Cordillera with the Antilles; the other from the south-west, off the utterly destroyed land which connected Trinidad with Guiana—met, as I fancy, ages since, on the opposite banks of a mighty river, or estuary, by which the Oroonoco entered the ocean along the foot of the northern mountains. As that river-bed rose and became dry land, the two Floras crossed and intermingled. Only here and there, as at Aripo, are left patches, as it were, of a third Flora, which once spread uninterruptedly along the southern base of the Cordillera and over the lowland which is now the Gulf of Paria, along the alluvial flats of the mighty stream; and the Moriche palms of Aripo may be the lineal descendants of those which now inhabit the Llanos of the main; as those again may be the lineal descendants of the Moriches which Schomburgk found forming forests among the mountains of Guiana, up to 4,000 feet above the sea. Age after age the Moriche apples floated down the stream, settling themselves on every damp spot not yet occupied by the richer vegetation of the forests, and ennobled, with their solitary grandeur, what without them would have been a dreary waste of mud and sand.

These Savannas of Trinidad stand, it must be remembered, in the very line where, on such a theory, they might be expected to stand, along the newest deposit; the great band of sand, gravel, and clay rubbish which stretches across the island at the mountain-foot, its highest point in thirty-six miles being only 220 feet—an elevation far less than the corresponding depression of the Bocas, which has parted Trinidad from the main Cordillera. That the rubbish on this line was deposited by a river or estuary is as clear to me as that the river was either a very rapid one, or subject to violent and lofty floods, as the Oroonoco is now. For so are best explained not merely the sheets of gravel, but the huge piles of boulder which have accumulated at the mouth of the mountain gorges on the northern side.

As for the southern shore of this supposed channel of the Oroonoco, it at once catches the eye of any one standing on the northern range. He must see that he is on one shore of a vast channel, the other shore of which is formed by the Montserrat, Tamana, and Manzanilla hills; far lower now than the northern range, Tamana only being over a thousand feet, but doubtless, in past ages, far higher than now. No one can doubt this who has seen the extraordinary degradation going on still about the summits, or who remembers that the strata, whether tertiary or lower chalk, have been, over the greater part of the island, upheaved, faulted, set on end, by the convulsions seemingly so common during the Miocene epoch, and since then sawn away by water and air into one rolling outline, quite independent of the dip of the strata. The whole southern two-thirds of Trinidad represent a wear and tear which is not to be counted by thousands, or hundreds of thousands, of years; and yet which, I verily believe, has taken place since the average plants, trees, and animals of the island dwelt therein.

This elevation may have well coincided with the depression of the neighbouring Gulf of Paria. That the southern portion of that gulf was once dry land; that the Serpent's Mouth did not exist when the present varieties of plants and animals were created, is matter of fact, proven by the identity of the majority of plants and animals on both shores. How else—to give a few instances out of hundreds—did the Mora, the Brazil-nut, the Cannon-ball tree; how else did the Ant-eater, the Coendou, the two Cuencos, the Guazupita deer, enter Trinidad? Humboldt—though, unfortunately, he never visited the island—saw this at a glance. While he perceived that the Indian story, how the Boca Drago to the north had been only lately broken through, had a foundation of truth, " It cannot be doubted," he says, " that the Gulf of Paria was once an inland basin, and the Punta Icacque (its south-western extremity) united to the Punta Toleto, east of the Boca de

Pedernales."[1] In which case there may well have been—one may almost say there must have been—an outlet for that vast body of water which pours, often in tremendous floods, from the Pedernales' mouth of the Oroonoco, as well as from those of the Tigre, Guanipa, Caroli, and other streams between it and the Cordillera on the north; and this outlet probably lay along the line now occupied by the northern Savannas of Trinidad.

So much this little natural park of Aripo taught, or seemed to teach me. But I did not learn the whole of the lesson that afternoon, or indeed till long after. There was no time then to work out such theories. The sun was getting low, and more intolerable as he sank; and to escape a sunstroke on the spot, or at least a dark ride home, we hurried off into the forest shade, after one last look at the never-to-be-forgotten Morichal, and trotted home to luxury and sleep.

[1] "Personal Narrative," vol. v. p. 725.

CHAPTER XIII.

THE COCAL.

NEXT day, like the "Young Muleteers of Grenada," a good song which often haunted me in those days,

"With morning's earliest twinkle
Again we are up and gone,"

with two horses, two mules, and a Negro and a Coolie carrying our scanty luggage in Arima baskets: but not without an expression of pity from the Negro who cleaned my boots. "Where were we going?" To the east coast. Cuffy turned up what little nose he had. He plainly considered the east coast, and indeed Trinidad itself, as not worth looking at. "Ah! you should go Barbados, sa. Dat de country to see. I Barbadian, sa." No doubt. It is very quaint, this self-satisfaction of the Barbadian Negro. Whether or not he belonged originally to some higher race—for there are as great differences of race among Negros as among any white men—he looks down on the Negros, and indeed on the white men, of other islands, as beings of an inferior grade; and takes care to inform you in the first five minutes that he is "neider C'rab nor Creole, but true Barbadian barn." This self-conceit of his, meanwhile, is apt to make him unruly, and the cause of unruliness in others when he emigrates. The Barbadian Negros are, I believe, the only ones who give, or ever have given, any trouble in Trinidad; and in Barbados itself, though the agricultural Negros work hard and well, who that knows the West Indies knows not the insubordination of the Bridgetown boatmen, among whose hands a traveller and his luggage are, it is said, likely enough to be pulled in pieces? However, they are rather more quiet just now; for not a thousand years ago a certain steamer's captain, utterly unable to clear his quarter of the fleet of fighting jabbering brown people, turned the steam-pipe on them. At which quite unexpected artillery they fled precipitately; and have had some rational respect for a steamer's quarter ever since. After all, I do not deny that this man's being a Barbadian opened my heart to him at once, for old sakes' sake.

Another specimen of Negro character I was to have analysed, or tried to analyse, at the estate where I had slept. M. F—— had lately caught a black servant at the brook-side busily washing something in a calabash, and asked him what was he doing there? The conversation would have been held, of course,

NEGRO SILLINESS.

in French-Spanish-African—Creole patois, a language which is becoming fixed, with its own grammar and declensions, &c. A curious book on it has lately been published in Trinidad by Mr. Thomas, a coloured gentleman, who seems to be at once no mean philologer and no mean humorist. The substance of the Negro's answer was, "Why, sir, you sent me to the town to buy a packet of sugar and a packet of salt; and coming back it rained so hard, the packets burst, and the salt was all washed into the sugar. And so—I am washing it out again." . . . .

This worthy was to have been brought to me, that I might discover, if possible, by what processes of "that which he was pleased to call his mind" he had arrived at the conclusion that such a thing could be done. Clearly, he could not plead unavoidable ignorance of the subject-matter, as might the old cook at San Josef, who, the first time her master brought home Wenham Lake ice from Port of Spain, was scandalized at the dirtiness of the "American water;" washed off the sawdust, and dried the ice in the sun. His was a case of Handy-Andy-ism, as that intellectual disease may be named, after Mr. Lever's hero; like that of the Obeah-woman, when she tried to bribe the white gentleman with half-a-dozen of bottled beer; a case of muddle-headed craft and elaborate silliness, which keeps no proportion between the means and the end; so common in insane persons; frequent, too, among the lower Irish, such as Handy Andy; and very frequent, I am afraid, among the Negros. But—as might have been expected—the poor boy's moral sense had proved as shaky as his intellectual powers. He had just taken a fancy to some goods of his master's; and had retreated, to enjoy them the more securely, into the southern forests, with a couple of brown policemen on his track. So he was likely to undergo a more simple investigation than that which was submitted to my analysis, viz. how he proposed to wash the salt out of the sugar.

We arrived after a while at Valencia, a scattered hamlet in the woods, with a good shop or "store" upon a village green, under the verandah whereof lay, side by side with bottled ale and biscuit tins, bags of Carapo[1] nuts; trapezoidal brown nuts—enclosed originally in a round fruit—which ought some day to form a valuable article of export. Their bitter anthelminthic oil is said to have medicinal uses; but it will be still more useful for machinery, as it has—like that curious flat gourd the Sequa[2]—the property of keeping iron from rust. The tree itself, common here and in Guiana, is one of the true Forest Giants; we saw many a noble specimen of it in our rides. Its timber is tough, not over heavy, and extensively used already in the island; while its bark is a febrifuge and tonic. In fact, it possesses all those qualities which

[1] Carapa Guianensis. [2] Feuillea cordifolia.

make its brethren, the Meliaceæ, valuable throughout the Tropics. But it is not the only tree of South America whose bark may be used as a substitute for quinine. They may be counted possibly by dozens. A glance at the excellent enumerations of the uses of vegetable products to be found in Lindley's "Vegetable Kingdom" (a monument of learning), will show how God provides, how man neglects and wastes. As a single instance, the Laurels alone are known already to contain several valuable febrifuges, among which the Demerara Greenheart, or Bibiri,[1] claims perhaps the highest rank. "Dr. Maclagan has shown," says Dr. Lindley, "that sulphate of Bibiri acts with rapid and complete success in arresting ague." This tree spreads from Jamaica to the Spanish Main. It is plentiful in Trinidad; still more plentiful in Guiana; and yet all of it which reaches Europe is a little of its hard beautiful wood for the use of cabinet makers; while in Demerara, I am assured by an eye-witness, many tons of this precious Greenheart bark are thrown away year by year. So goes the world; and man meanwhile at once boasts of his civilization, and complains of the niggardliness of Nature.

But if I once begin on this subject I shall not know where to end.

Our way lay now for miles along a path which justified all

[1] Nectandra Rodiæi.

that I had fancied about the magnificent possibilities of landscape gardening in the Tropics. A grass drive, as we should call it in England—a "trace," as it is called in the West Indies—some sixty feet in width, and generally carpeted with short turf, led up hill and down dale; for the land, though low, is much ridged and gullied, and there has been as yet no time to cut down the hills, or to metal the centre of the road. It led, as the land became richer, through a natural avenue even grander than those which I had already seen. The light and air, entering the trace, had called into life the undergrowth and lower boughs, till from the very turf to a hundred and fifty feet in height rose one solid green wall, spangled here and there with flowers. Below was Mamure, Roseau, Timit, Aroumas, and Tulumas,[1] mixed with Myrtles and Melastomas; then the copper Bois Mulatres among the Cocorite and Jagua palms; above them the heads of enormous broad-leaved trees of I know not how many species; and the lianes festooning all from cope to base. The crimson masses of Norantea on the highest tree-tops were here most gorgeous; but we had to beware of staring aloft too long, for fear of riding into mud-holes; for the wet season would not end as yet, though dry weather was due—or, even worse, into the great Parasol-ant warrens, which threatened, besides a heavy fall, stings innumerable. At one point, I

[1] Canna.

recollect, a gold-green Jacamar sat on a log and looked at me, till I was within five yards of her. At another, we heard the screams of Parrots; at another the double note of the Toucan; at another the metallic clank of the Bell-bird, or what was said to be the Bell-bird. But this note was not that solemn and sonorous toll of the Campanese of the mainland which is described by Waterton and others. It resembled rather the less poetical sound of a woman beating a saucepan to make a swarm of bees settle.

At one point we met a gang of Negros felling timber to widen the road. Fresh fallen trees, tied together with lianes, lay everywhere. What a harvest for the botanist was among them! I longed to stay there a week to examine and collect. But time pressed; and, indeed, collecting plants in the wet season is a difficult and disappointing work. In an air saturated with moisture specimens turn black and mouldy, and drop to pieces; and unless turned over and exposed to every chance burst of sunshine, the labour of weeks is lost, if indeed meanwhile the ants, and other creeping things, have not eaten the whole into rags.

Among these Negros was one who excited my astonishment; not merely for his size, though he was perhaps the tallest man whom I saw among the usually tall Negros of Trinidad; but for his features, which were altogether European of the highest type; the forehead high and broad, the cheek-bones flat, the masque long and oval, and the nose aquiline and thin enough for any prince. Conscious of his own beauty and strength, he stood up among the rest as an old Macedonian might have stood up among the Egyptians he had conquered. We tried to find out his parentage. My companions presumed he was an "African," *i.e.* imported during the times of slavery. He said, No: that he was a Creole, island born; but his father, it appeared, had been in one of our Negro regiments, and had been settled afterwards on a Government grant of land. Whether his beauty was the result of 'atavism'—of the reappearance, under the black skin and woolly hair, of some old stain of white blood; or whether, which is more probable, he came of some higher African race; one could not look at him without hopeful surmises as to the possible rise of the Negro, and as to the way in which it will come about,—the only way in which any race has permanently risen, as far as I can ascertain; namely, by the appearance among them of sudden sports of nature; individuals of an altogether higher type; such a man as that terrible Dâaga, whose story has been told. If I am any judge of physiognomy, such a man as that, having— what the Negro has not yet had—"la carrière ouverte aux talents," might raise, not himself merely, but a whole tribe, to an altogether new level in culture and ability.

Just after passing this gang we found, lying by the road,

two large snakes, just killed, which I would gladly have preserved had it been possible. They were, the Negros told us, "Dormillons," or "Mangrove Cascabel," a species as yet, I believe, undescribed; and, of course, here considered as very poisonous, owing to their likeness to the true Cascabel,[1] whose deadly fangs are justly dreaded by the Lapo hunter. For the Cascabel has a fancy for living in the Lapo's burrow, as does the rattle-snake in that of the prairie dog in the Western United States, and in the same friendly and harmless fashion; and is apt, when dug out, to avenge himself and his host by a bite which is fatal in a few hours. But these did not seem to me to have the heads of poisonous snakes; and, in spite of the entreaties of the terrified Negros, I opened their mouths to judge for myself, and found them, as I expected, utterly fangless and harmless. I was not aware then that Dr. De Verteuil had stated the same fact in print; but I am glad to corroborate it, for the benefit of at least the rational people in Trinidad: for snakes, even poisonous ones, should be killed as seldom as possible. They feed on rats and vermin, and are the farmer's good friend, whether in the Tropics or in England; and to kill a snake, or even an adder —who never bites any one if he is allowed to run away—is, in nineteen cases out of twenty, mere wanton mischief.

The way was beguiled, if I recollect rightly, for some miles

[1] Trigonocephalus Jararaca.

on, by stories about Cuba and Cuban slavery from one of our
party. He described the political morality of Cuba as utterly
dissolute; told stories of great sums of money voted for roads
which are not made to this day, while the money had found
its way into the pockets of Government officials; and, on the
whole, said enough to explain the determination of the Cubans
to shake off Spanish misrule, and try what they could do for
themselves on this earth. He described Cuban slavery as,
on the whole, mild; corporal punishment being restricted
by law to a few blows, and very seldom employed: but the
mildness seemed dictated rather by self-interest than by
humanity. "Ill-use our slaves?" said a Cuban to him. "We
cannot afford it. You take good care of your four-legged
mules: we of our two-legged ones." The children, it seems,
are taken away from the mothers, not merely because the
mothers are needed for work, but because they neglect their
offspring so much that the children have more chance of
living—and therefore of paying—if brought up by hand.
So each estate has, or had, its crèche, as the French would
call it—a great nursery, in which the little black things are
reared, kindly enough, by the elder ladies of the estate. To
one old lady, who wearied herself all day long in washing,
doctoring, and cramming the babies, my friend expressed pity
for all the trouble she took about her human brood. "Oh
dear no," answered she; "they are a great deal easier to rear

than chickens." The system, however, is nearly at an end. Already the Cuban Revolution has produced measures of half-emancipation; and in seven years' time probably there will not be a slave in Cuba.

We waded stream after stream under the bamboo clumps, and in one of them we saw swimming a green rigoise, or whip-snake, which must have been nearly ten feet long. It swam with its head and the first two feet of its body curved aloft like a swan, while the rest of the body lay along the surface of the water in many curves—a most graceful object as it glided away into dark shadow along an oily pool. At last we reached an outlying camp, belonging to one of our party who was superintending the making of new roads in that quarter, and there rested our weary limbs, some in hammock, some on the tables, some, again, on the clay floor. Here I saw, as I saw every ten minutes, something new— that quaint vegetable plaything described by Humboldt and others; namely, the spathe of the Timit palm. It encloses, as in most palms, a branched spadix covered with innumerable round buds, most like a head of millet, two feet and a half long: but the spathe, instead of splitting and forming a hood over the flowers, as in the Cocorite and most palms, remains entire, and slips off like the finger of a glove. When slipt off, it is found to be made of two transverse layers of fibre—a bit of veritable natural lace, similar to, though far less delicate than, the famous lace-bark of the Lagetta-tree, peculiar, I believe, to one district in the Jamaica mountains. And as it is elastic and easily stretched, what hinders the brown child from pulling it out till it makes an admirable fool's-cap, some two feet high, and exactly the colour of his own skin, and dancing about therein, the fat oily little Cupidon, without a particle of clothing beside? And what wonder if we grown-up whites made fools' caps too, for children on the other side of the Atlantic? During which process we found—what all said they had never seen before—that one of the spadices carried two caps, one inside the other, and one exactly like the other; a wanton superfluity of Nature, which I should like to hear explained by some morphologist.

We rode away from that hospitable group of huts, whither we were to return in two or three days; and along the green trace once more. As we rode, M—— the civilizer of Montserrat and I side by side, talking of Cuba, and staring at the Noranteas overhead, a dull sound was heard, as if the earth had opened; as indeed it had, engulfing in the mud the whole forehand of M——'s mule; and there he knelt, his beard outspread upon the clay, while the mule's visage looked patiently out from under his left arm. However, it was soft falling there. The mule was hauled out by main force. As for cleaning either her or the rider, that was not thought of in a country where they were sure to be as dirty as ever in an hour; and so we rode on, after taking a note of the spot, and, as it happened, forgetting it again—one of us at least.

On again, along the green trace, which rose now to a ridge, with charming glimpses of wooded hills and glens to right and left; past comfortable squatters' cottages, with cacao drying on sheets at the doors or under sheds; with hedges of dwarf Erythrina, dotted with red jumby beads, and here and there that pretty climbing vetch, the Overlook.[1] I forgot, by the bye, to ask whether it is planted here, as in Jamaica, to keep off the evil eye, or "overlook;" whence its name. Nor can I guess what peculiarity about the plant can have first made the Negro fix on it as a fetish. The genesis of folly is as difficult to analyse as the genesis of most other things.

All this while the dull thunder of the surf was growing louder and louder; till, not as in England over a bare down, but through thickest foliage down to the high-tide mark, we rode out upon the shore, and saw before us a right noble sight; a flat, sandy, surf-beaten shore, along which stretched, in one grand curve, lost at last in the haze of spray, fourteen miles of Coco palms.

This was the Cocal; and it was worth coming all the way

[1] Canavalia.

from England to see it alone. I at once felt the truth of my host's saying, that if I went to the Cocal I should find myself transported suddenly from the West Indies to the East. Just such must be the shore of a Coral island in the Pacific.

Young Coco-palm.

These Cocos, be it understood, are probably not indigenous. They spread, it is said, from an East Indian vessel which was wrecked here. Be that as it may, they have thoroughly naturalized themselves. Every nut which falls and lies, throws out, during the wet season, its roots into the sand; and is ready to take the place of its parent when the old tree dies down.

About thirty to fifty feet is the average height of these Coco palms, which have all, without exception, a peculiarity which I have noticed to a less degree in another sand- and shore-growing tree, the Pinaster of the French Landes. They never spring upright from the ground. The butt curves, indeed lies almost horizontal in some cases, for the lowest two or three yards; and the whole stem, up to the top, is inclined to lean; it matters not toward which quarter, for they lean as often toward the wind as from it, crossing each other very gracefully. I am not mechanician enough to say how this curve of the stem increases their security amid loose sands and furious winds. But that it does so I can hardly doubt, when I see a similar habit in the Pinaster. Another peculiarity was noteworthy: their innumerable roots, long, fleshy, about the thickness of a large string, piercing the sand in every direction, and running down to high-tide mark, apparently enjoying the salt water, and often piercing through bivalve shells, which remained strung upon the roots. Have they a fondness for carbonate of lime, as well as for salt?

The most remarkable, and to me unexpected, peculiarity of a Cocal, is one which I am not aware whether any writer has mentioned; namely, the prevalence of that amber hue which we remarked in the very first specimens seen at St. Thomas's. But this is, certainly, the mark which distinguishes the Coco palm not merely from the cold dark green of the Palmiste, or the silvery grey of the Jagua, but from any other tree which I have ever seen.

When inside the Cocal, the air is full of this amber light. Gradually the eye analyses the cause of it, and finds it to be the resultant of many other hues, from bright vermilion to bright green. Above, the latticed light which breaks between and over the innumerable leaflets of the fruit fronds comes down in warmest green. It passes not over merely, but through, the semi-transparent straw and amber of the older leaves. It falls on yellow spadices and flowers, and rich brown spathes, and on great bunches of green nuts, to acquire from them more yellow yet; for each fruit-stalk and each flower-scale at the base of the nut is veined and tipped with bright orange. It pours down the stems, semi-grey on one side, then yellow, and then, on the opposite side, covered with a powdery lichen varying in colour from orange up to clear vermilion, and spreads itself over a floor of yellow sand and brown fallen nuts, and the only vegetation of which, in general, is a long crawling Echites, with pairs of large cream-white flowers. Thus the transparent shade is flooded with gold. One looks out through it at the chequer-work of blue sky, all the more intense from its contrast; or at a long whirl

The Cocal.

of white surf and grey spray; or, turning the eyes inland toward the lagoon, at dark masses of mangrove, above which rise, black and awful, the dying balatas, stag-headed, blasted, tottering to their fall; and all as through an atmosphere of Rhine wine, or from the inside of a topaz.

We rode along, mile after mile, wondering at many things. First, the innumerable dry fruits of Timit palm, which lay everywhere; mostly single, some double, a few treble, from coalition, I suppose, of the three carpels which every female palm flower ought to have, but of which it usually develops only one. They may have been brought down the lagoon from inland by floods; but the common belief is, that most of them come from the Oroonoco itself, as do also the mighty logs which lie about the beach in every stage of wear and tear; and which, as fast as they are cut up and carried away, are replaced by fresh ones. Some of these trees may actually come from the mainland, and, drifting into this curving bay, be driven on shore by the incessant trade-wind. But I suspect that many of them are the produce of the island itself; and more, that they have grown, some of them, on the very spot where they now lie. For there are, I think, evidences of subsidence going on along this coast. Inside the Cocal, two hundred yards to the westward, stretches inland a labyrinth of lagoons and mangrove swamps, impassable to most creatures save alligators and boa-constrictors.

But amid this labyrinth grow everywhere mighty trees—balatas in plenty among them, in every stage of decay; dying, seemingly, by gradual submergence of their roots, and giving a ghastly and ragged appearance to the forest. At the mouth of the little river Nariva, a few miles down, is proof positive, unless I am much mistaken, of similar subsidence. For there I found trees of all sizes—roseau scrub among them—standing rooted below high-tide mark; and killed where they grew.

So we rode on, stopping now and then to pick up shells; chip-chips,[1] which are said to be excellent eating; a beautiful purple bivalve,[2] to which, in almost every case, a coralline[3] had attached itself, of a form quite new to me. A lash some eighteen inches long, single or forked; purplish as long as its coat of lime—holding the polypes—still remained, but when that was rubbed off a mere round strip of dark horn; and in both cases flexible and elastic, so that it can be coiled up and tied in knots; a very curious and graceful piece of Nature's workmanship. Among them were curious flat cake-urchins, with oval holes punched in them, so brittle that, in spite of all our care, they resolved themselves into the loose sand of which they had been originally compact; and I could therefore verify neither their genus nor their species.

[1] Trigonia. [2] Tellina rosea.
[3] Xiphogorgia setacea (Milne-Edwards).

These were all, if I recollect, that we found that day. The next day we came on hundreds of a most beautiful bivalve,[1] their purple colour quite fresh, their long spines often quite uninjured. Some change of the sandy bottom had unearthed a whole warren of the lovely things; and mixed with chip-chips innumerable, and with a great bivalve[2] with a thin wing along the anterior line of the shell, they strewed the shore for a quarter of a mile and more.

We came at last to a little river, or rather tideway, leading from the lagoon to the sea, which goes by the name of Doubloon River. Some adventurous Spaniard, the story goes, contracted to make a cutting which would let off the lagoon water in time of flood for the sum of one doubloon—some three-pound five—spent six times the money on it; and found his cutting, when once the sea had entered, enlarge into a roaring tideway, dangerous, often impassable, and eating away the Cocal rapidly toward the south; Mother Earth, in this case at least, having known her own business better than the Spaniard.

How we took off our saddles, sat down on the sand, hallooed, waited; how a black policeman—whose house was just being carried away by the sea—appeared at last with a canoe; how we and our baggage got over one by one in the hollow log without—by seeming miracle—being swept

[1] Cytherea Dione.   [2] Mactrella alata.

out to sea or upset; how some horses would swim, and others would not; how the Negros held on by the horses till they all went head-over-ears under the surf; and how, at last, breathless with laughter and anxiety for our scanty wardrobes, we scrambled ashore one by one into prickly roseau, re-saddled our horses in an atmosphere of long thorns, and then cut our way and theirs out through scrub into the Cocal;—all this should not be written in these pages, but drawn for the benefit of "Punch," by him who drew the egg-stealing frog—whose pencil I longed for again and again amid the delightful mishaps of those forest rambles, in all of which I never heard a single grumble, or saw temper lost for a moment. We should have been rather more serious, though, than we were, had we been aware that the river-god, or presiding Jumby, of the Doubloon, was probably watching us the whole time, with the intention of eating any one whom he could catch, and only kept in wholesome awe by our noise and splashing.

At last, after the sun had gone down, and it was ill picking our way among logs and ground-creepers, we were aware of lights; and soon found ourselves again in civilization, and that of no mean kind. A large and comfortable house, only just rebuilt after a fire, stood among the palm-trees, between the sea and the lagoon; and behind it the barns, sheds, and engine-houses of the coco-works; and inside it a hearty welcome from a most agreeable German gentleman and his German engineer. A lady's hand—I am sorry to say the lady was not at home—was evident enough in the arrangements of the central room. Pretty things, a piano, and good books, especially Longfellow and Tennyson, told of cultivation and taste in that remotest wilderness. The material hospitality was what it always is in the West Indies; and we sat up long into the night around the open door, while the surf roared, and the palm-trees sighed, and the fireflies twinkled, talking of dear old Germany, and German unity, and the possibility of many things which have since proved themselves unexpectedly most possible. I went to bed, and to somewhat intermittent sleep. First, my comrades, going to bed romping, like English schoolboys, and not in the least like the effeminate and luxurious Creoles who figure in the English imagination, broke a four-post bedstead down among them with hideous roar and ruin; and had to be picked up and called to order by their elders. Next, the wind, which ranged freely through the open roof, blew my bedclothes off. Then the dogs exploded outside, probably at some henroost-robbing opossum, and had a chevy through the cocos till they tree'd their game, and bayed it to their hearts' content. Then something else exploded—and I do not deny it set me more aghast than I had been for many a day—exploded, I say, under the window, with a shriek of Hut-hut-tut-tut, hut-tut, such as I hope never to hear again. After which, dead silence; save of the surf to the east and the toads to the west. I fell asleep, wondering what animal could own so detestable a voice; and in half an hour was awoke again by another explosion; after which, happily, the thing, I suppose, went its wicked way, for I heard it no more.

I found out the next morning that the obnoxious bird was not an owl, but a large goat-sucker, a Nycteribius, I believe, who goes by the name of jumby-bird among the English Negros: and no wonder; for most ghostly and horrible is his cry. But worse: he has but one eye, and a glance from that glaring eye, as from the basilisk of old, is certain death: and worse still, he can turn off its light as a policeman does his lantern, and become instantly invisible: opinions which, if verified by experiment, are not always found to be in accordance with facts. But that is no reason why they should not be believed.

In St. Vincent, for instance, the Negros one evening rushed shrieking out of a boiling-house, "Oh! Massa Robert, we all killed. Dar one great jumby-bird come in a hole a-top a roof. Oh! Massa Robert, you no go in; you killed, we killed:" &c. &c. Massa Robert went in, and could see no bird. "Ah, Massa Robert, him darky him eye, but him see you all da same. You killed, we killed," &c. *Da capo.*

Massa Robert was not killed: but lives still, to the great benefit of his fellow-creatures, Negros especially. Nevertheless, the Negros held to their opinion. He might, could, would, or should have been killed; and was not that clear proof that they were right?

After this, who can deny that the Negro is a man and a brother, possessing the same reasoning faculties, and exercising them in exactly the same way, as three out of four white persons?

But if the night was disturbed, pleasant was the waking next morning; pleasant the surprise at finding that the whistling and howling air-bath of the night had not given one a severe cold, or any cold at all: pleasant to slip on flannel shirt and trousers—shoes and stockings were needless—and hurry down through a stampede of kicking squealing mules, who were being watered ere their day's work began, under the palms to the sea; pleasant to bathe in warm surf, into which the four-eyes squattered in shoals as one ran down, and the moment they saw one safe in the water, ran up with the next wave to lie staring at the sky: pleasant to sit and read one's book upon a log, and listen to the soft rush of the breeze in the palm-leaves, and look at a sunrise of green and gold, pink and orange, and away over the great ocean, and to recollect, with a feeling of mingled nearness and loneliness, that there was nothing save that watery void between oneself and England, and all that England held; and then, when driven in to breakfast by the morning shower, to begin a new day of seeing, and seeing, and seeing, certain that one would learn more in it than in a whole week of book-reading at home.

We spent the next morning in inspecting the works. We watched the Negros splitting the coco-nuts with a single blow of that all-useful cutlass, which they handle with surprising dexterity and force, throwing the thick husk on one side, the fruit on the other. We saw the husk carded out by machinery into its component fibres, for coco-rope matting, coir-rope, saddle-stuffing, brushes, and a dozen other uses; while the fruit was crushed down for the sake of its oil; and could but wish all success to an industry which would be most profitable, both to the projectors and to the island itself, were it not for the uncertainty, rather than the scarcity, of labour. Almost everything is done, of course, by piece-work. The Negro has the price of his labour almost at his own command; and when, by working really hard and well for a while, he has earned a little money, he throws up his job and goes off, careless whether the whole works stand still or not. However, all prosperity to the coco-works of Messrs. Uhrich and Gerold; and may the day soon come when the English of Trinidad, like the Ceylonese and the Dutch of Java, shall count by millions the coco-palms which they have planted along their shores, and by thousands of pounds, the profit which accrues from them.

After breakfast—call it luncheon rather—we started for the lagoon. We had set our hearts on seeing Manatis—"sea-cows"—which are still not uncommon on the east coast of this island, though they have been exterminated through the rest of the West Indies since the days of Père Labat. That good Missionary speaks of them in his delightful journal as already rare in the year 1695; and now, as far as I am aware, none are to be found north of Trinidad and the Spanish Main, save a few round Cuba and Jamaica. We were anxious, too, to see, if not to get, a boa-constrictor of one kind or other. For there are two kinds in the island, which may be seen alive at the Zoological Gardens in the same cage. The true Boa,[1] which is here called Mahajuel, is striped as well as spotted with two patterns, one over the other. The Huillia, Anaconda, or Water-boa,[2] bears only a few large round spots. Both are fond of the water, the Huillia living almost entirely in it; both grow to a very large size; and both are dangerous, at least to children and small animals. That there were Huillias about the place, possibly within fifty yards of the house, there was no doubt. One of our party had seen with his own eyes one of seven-and-twenty feet long killed, with a whole kid inside it, only a

[1] Boa constrictor.   [2] Eunectes murinus.

few miles off. The brown policeman, crossing an arm of the Guanapo only a month or two before, had been frightened by meeting one in the ford, which his excited imagination magnified so much that its head was on the one bank while its tail was on the other,—a measurement which must, I think, be divided at least by three. But in the very spot in which we stood, some four years since happened what might have been a painful tragedy. Four young ladies, whose names were mentioned to me, preferred, not wisely, a bathe in the still lagoon to one in the surf outside; and as they disported themselves, one of them felt herself seized from behind. Fancying that one of her sisters was playing tricks, she called out to her to let her alone; and looking up, saw, to her astonishment, her three sisters sitting on the bank, and herself alone. She looked back, and shrieked for help: and only just in time; for the Huillia had her. The other three girls, to their honour, dashed in to her assistance. The brute had luckily got hold, not of her poor little body, but of her bathing-dress; and held on stupidly. The girls pulled; the bathing dress, which was luckily of thin cotton, was torn off; the Huillia slid back again with it in his mouth into the dark labyrinth of the mangrove-roots; and the girl was saved. Two minutes' delay, and his coils would have been round her; and all would have been over.

The sudden daring of these lazy and stupid animals is very

great. Their brain seems to act like that of the alligator or the pike, paroxysmally, and by rare fits and starts, after lying for hours motionless as if asleep. But when excited, they will attempt great deeds. Dr. De Verteuil tells a story—and if he tells it, it must be believed—of some hunters who wounded a deer. The deer ran for the stream down a bank: but the hunters had no sooner heard it splash into the water than they heard it scream. They leapt down to the place, and found it in the coils of a Huillia, which they killed with the deer. And yet this snake, which had dared to seize a full-grown deer, could have had no hope of eating her; for it was only seven feet long.

We set out down a foul porter-coloured creek, which soon opened out into a river, reminding us, in spite of all differences, of certain alder and willow-fringed reaches of the Thames. But here the wood which hid the margin was altogether of mangrove; the common Rhizophoras, or black mangroves, being, of course, the most abundant. Over them, however, rose the statelier Avicennias, or white mangroves, to a height of fifty or sixty feet, and poured down from their upper branches whole streams of air-roots, which waved and creaked dolefully in the breeze overhead. But on the water was no breeze at all. The lagoon was still as glass; the sun was sickening; and we were glad to put up our umbrellas and look out from under them for Manatis and Boas. But the

Manatis usually only come in at night, to put their heads out of water and browse on the lowest mangrove leaves; and the Boas hide themselves so cunningly, either altogether under water, or with only the head above, that we might have passed half-a-dozen without seeing them. The only chance, indeed, of coming across them, is when they are travelling from lagoon to lagoon, or basking on the mud at low tide.

So all the game which we saw was a lovely white Egret,[1] its back covered with those stiff pinnated plumes which young ladies—when they can obtain them—are only too happy to wear in their hats. He, after being civil enough to wait on a bough till one of us got a sitting shot at him, heard the cap snap, thought it as well not to wait till a fresh one was put on, and flapped away. He need not have troubled himself. The Negros—but too apt to forget something or other—had forgotten to bring a spare supply; and the gun was useless.

As we descended, the left bank of the river was entirely occupied with cocos; and the contrast between them and the mangroves on the right was made all the more striking by the afternoon sun, which, as it sank behind the forest, left the mangrove wall in black shadow, while it bathed the palm-groves opposite with yellow light. In one of these palm-

[1] Ardea Garzetta.

groves we landed, for we were right thirsty; and to drink lagoon water would be to drink cholera or fever. But there was plenty of pure water in the coco-trees, and we soon had our fill. A Negro walked—not climbed—up a stem like a four-footed animal, his legs and arms straight, his feet pressed flat against it, his hands clinging round it—a feat impossible, as far as I have seen, to an European—tossed us down plenty of green nuts; and our feast began.

Two or three blows with the cutlass, at the small end of the nut, cut off not only the pith-coat, but the point of the shell; and disclose—the nut being held carefully upright meanwhile—a cavity full of perfectly clear water, slightly sweet, and so cold (the pith-coat being a good non-conductor of heat) that you are advised, for fear of cholera, to flavour it with a little brandy. After draining this natural cup, you are presented with a natural spoon of rind, green outside and white within, and told to scoop out and eat the cream which lines the inside of the shell, a very delicious food in the opinion of Creoles. After which, if you are as curious as some of us were, you will sit down under the amber shade, and examine at leisure the construction and germination of these famous and royal nuts. Let me explain it, even at the risk of prolixity. The coat of white pith outside, with its green skin, will gradually develop and harden into that brown fibre of which matting is made. The clear water inside will gradually harden into that sweetmeat which little boys eat off stalls and barrows in the street; the first delicate deposit of which is the cream in the green nut. This is albumen, intended to nourish the young palm till it has grown leaves enough to feed on the air, and roots enough to feed on the soil; and the birth of that young palm is in itself a mystery and a miracle, well worth considering. Much has been written on it, of which I, unfortunately, have read very little: but I can at least tell what I have seen with my own eyes.

If you search among the cream-layer at the larger end of the nut, you will find, gradually separating itself from the mass, a little white lump, like the stalk of a very young mushroom. That is the ovule. In that lies the life, the "forma formativa," of the future tree. How that life works, according to its kind, who can tell? What it does, is this: it is locked up inside a hard woody shell, and outside that shell are several inches of tough tangled fibre. How can it get out, as soft and seemingly helpless as a baby's finger?

All know that there are three eyes in the monkey's face, as the children call it, at the butt of the nut. Two of these eyes are blind, and filled up with hard wood. They are rudiments—hints—that the nut ought to have, perhaps had uncounted ages since, not one ovule, but three, the type-number in palms. One ovule alone is left; and that is opposite the one eye which is less blind than the rest; the eye which a schoolboy feels for with his knife, when he wants to get out the milk.

As the nut lies upon the sand, in shade, and rain, and heat, that baby's finger begins boring its way, with unerring aim, out of the weakest eye. Soft itself, yet with immense wedging power, from the gradual accretion of tiny cells, it pierces the wood, and then rends right and left the tough fibrous coat. Just so may be seen—I have seen—a large flagstone lifted in a night by a crop of tiny soft toadstools which have suddenly blossomed up beneath it. The baby's finger protrudes at last, and curves upward toward the light, to commence the campaign of life: but it has meanwhile established, like a good strategist, a safe base of operations in its rear, from which it intends to draw supplies. Into the albuminous cream which lines the shell, and into the cavity where the milk once was, it throws out white fibrous vessels, which eat up the albumen for it, and at last line the whole inside of the shell with a white pith. The albumen gives it food wherewith to grow, upward and downward. Upward, the white plumule hardens into what will be a stem; the one white cotyledon which sheaths it develops into a flat, ribbed, forked, green leaf, sheathing it still; and above it fresh leaves, sheathing always at their bases, begin to form a tiny crown; and assume each, more and more, the pinnate form of the usual coco-leaf. But long ere this, from the butt of the white plumule, just outside the nut, white threads of root have struck down into the sand; and so the nut lies, chained to the ground by a bridge-like chord, which drains its albumen, through the monkey's eye, into the young plant. After a while—a few months, I believe—the draining of the nut is complete; the chord dries up—I know not how, for I had neither microscope nor time wherewith to examine—and parts; and the little plant, having got all it can out of its poor wet-nurse, casts her ungratefully off to wither on the sand; while it grows up into a stately tree, which will begin to bear fruit in six or seven years, and thenceforth continue, flowering and fruiting the whole year round without a pause, for sixty years and more.

I think I have described this—to me—"miraculum" simply enough to be understood by the non-scientific reader, if only he or she have first learned the undoubted fact—known, I find, to very few "educated" English people—that the coco-palm which produces coir-rope, and coco-nuts, and a hundred other useful things, is not the same plant as the cacao-bush which produces chocolate, nor anything like it. I am sorry to have to insist upon this fact: but till Professor Huxley's dream—and mine—is fulfilled; and our schools deign to teach, in the intervals of Latin and Greek, some slight knowledge of this planet, and of those of its productions which are most commonly in use, even this fact may need to be re-stated more than once.

We re-embarked again, and rowed down to the river-mouth to pick up shells, and drink in the rich roaring trade breeze, after the choking atmosphere of the lagoon; and then rowed up home, tired, and infinitely amused, though neither Manati or Boa-constrictor had been seen; and then we fell to siesta; during which — with Mr. Tennyson's forgiveness — I read myself to sleep with one of his best poems; and then went to dinner, not without a little anxiety.

For M—— (the civilizer of Montserrat) had gone off early, with mule, cutlass, and haversack, back over the Doubloon and into the wilds of Manzanilla, to settle certain disputed squatter claims, and otherwise enforce the law; and now the night had fallen, and he was not yet home. However, he rode up at last, dead beat, with a strong touch of his old swamp-fever, and having had an adventure, which had like to have proved his last. For as he rode through the Doubloon at low tide in the morning, he espied in the surf that river-god, or Jumby, of which I spoke just now; namely, the grey back-fin of a shark; and his mule espied it too, and laid back her ears, knowing well what it was. M—— rode close up to the brute. He seemed full seven feet long, and eyed him surlily, disinclined to move off; so they parted, and M—— went on his way. But his business detained him longer than he expected; when he got back to the river-mouth it was quite dark, and the tide was full high. He must either sleep on the sands, which with fever upon him would not have been over safe, or try the passage. So he stripped, swam the mule over, tied her up, and then went back, up to his shoulders in surf; and cutlass in hand too, for that same shark might be within two yards of him. But on his second journey he had to pile on his head first his saddle, and then his clothes and other goods; few indeed, but enough to require both hands to steady them: and so walked helpless through the surf, expecting every moment to be accosted by a set of teeth, from which he would hardly have escaped with life.

To have faced such a danger, alone and in the dark, and thoroughly well aware, as an experienced man, of its extremity, was good proof (if any had been needed) of the indomitable Scots' courage of the man. Nevertheless, he said, he never felt so cold down his back as he did during that last wade. By God's blessing the shark was not there, or did not see him; and he got safe home, thankful for dinner and quinine.

Going back the next morning at low tide, we kept a good look-out for M———'s shark, spreading out, walkers and riders, in hopes of surrounding him and cutting him up. There were half-a-dozen weapons among us, of which my heavy bowie-knife was not the worst; and we should have given good account of him had we met him, and got between him and the deep water. But our valour was superfluous. The enemy was nowhere to be seen; and we rode on, looking back wistfully, but in vain, for a grey fin among the ripples.

So we rode back, along the Cocal and along that wonderful green glade, where I, staring at Noranteas in tree-tops, instead of at the ground beneath my horse's feet, had the pleasure of being swallowed up—my horse's hind-quarters at least—in the very same slough which had engulfed M——'s mule three days before, and got a roll in much soft mud. Then up to ——'s camp, where we expected breakfast, not with greediness, though we had been nigh six hours in the saddle, but with curiosity. For he had promised to send out the hunters for all game that could be found, and give us a true forest meal; and we were curious to taste what lapo, quenco, guazupita-deer, and other strange meats might be like. Nay, some of us agreed, that if the hunters had but brought in a tender young red monkey,[1] we would surely eat him too, if it were but to say that we had done it. But the hunters had had no luck. They had brought in only a Pajui,[2] an excellent game bird; an Ant-eater,[3] and a great Cachicame, or nine-banded Armadillo. The ant-eater the foolish fellows had eaten themselves—I

[1] Mycetes ursinus.   [2] Penelope.   [3] Myrmecophaga tridactyla.

would have given them what they asked for his skeleton; but the Armadillo was cut up and hashed for us, and was eaten to the last scrap, being about the best game I ever tasted. I fear he is a foul feeder at times, who by no means confines himself to roots, or even worms. If what I was told be true, there is but too much probability for Captain Mayne Reid's statement, that he will eat his way into the soft parts of a dead horse, and stay there until he has eaten his way out again. But, to do him justice, I never heard him accused, like the giant Armadillo[1] of the Main, of digging dead bodies out of their graves, as he is doing in a very clever drawing in Mr. Wood's "Homes without Hands." Be that as it may, the Armadillo, whatever he feeds on, has the power of transmuting it into most delicate and wholesome flesh.

Meanwhile—and hereby hangs a tale—I was interested, not merely in the Armadillo, but in the excellent taste with which it, and everything else, was cooked, in a little open shed over a few stones and firesticks. And complimenting my host thereon, I found that he had, there in the primæval forest, an admirable French cook, to whom I begged to be introduced at once. Poor fellow! A little lithe Parisian, not thirty years old, he had got thither by a wild road. Cook to some good bourgeois family in Paris, he had fallen in love with his master's daughter, and she with him. And when

[1] Priodonta gigas.

their love was hopeless, and discovered, the two young foolish things, not having—as is too common in France—the fear of God before their eyes, could think of no better resource than to shut themselves up with a pan of lighted charcoal, and so go they knew not whither. The poor girl went—and was found dead. But the boy recovered; and was punished with twenty years of Cayenne; and here he was now, on a sort of ticket-of-leave, cooking for his livelihood. I talked a while with him, cheered him with some compliments about the Parisians, and so forth, dear to the Frenchman's heart—what else was there to say?—and so left him, not without the fancy that, if he had had but such an education as the middle classes in Paris have not, there were the makings of a man in that keen eye, large jaw, sharp chin. "The very fellow," said some one, "to have been a first-rate Zouave." Well: perhaps he was a better man, even as he was, than as a Zouave.

And so we rode away again, and through Valencia, and through San Josef, weary and happy, back to Port of Spain.

I would gladly, had I been able, have gone further due westward, into the forests which hide the river Oropuche, that I might have visited the scene of a certain two years' Idyll, which was enacted in them some forty years and more ago.

In 1827, cacao fell to so low a price (two dollars per cwt.) that it was no longer worth cultivating; and the head of the

F—— family, leaving his slaves to live at ease on his estates, retreated, with a household of twelve persons, to a small property of his own, which was buried in the primæval forests of Oropuche. With them went his second son, Monsignor F——, then and afterwards curé of San Josef, who died shortly before my visit to the island. I always heard him spoken of as a gentleman and a scholar, a saintly and cultivated priest of the old French School, respected and beloved by men of all denominations. His church of San Josef, though still unfinished, had been taxed, as well as all the Roman Catholic churches of the island, to build the Roman Catholic Cathedral at Port of Spain; and he, refusing to obey an order which he considered unjust, threw up his cure, and retreated with the rest of the family to the palm-leaf ajoupas in the forest.

M. F—— chose three of his finest Negros as companions. Melchior was to go out every day to shoot wild pigeons, coming every morning to ask how many were needed, so as not to squander powder and shot. The number ordered were always punctually brought in, besides sometimes a wild turkey—Pajui—or other fine birds. Alejos, who is now a cacao proprietor, and owner of a house in Arima, was chosen to go out every day, except Sundays, with the dogs; and scarcely ever failed to bring in a lapo or quenco. Aristobal was chosen for the fishing, and brought in good loads of river fish, some sixteen pounds weight: and thus the little party of cultivated gentlemen and ladies were able to live, though in poverty, yet sumptuously.

The Bishop had given Monsignor F—— permission to perform service on any of his father's estates. So a little chapel was built; the family and servants attended every Sunday, and many days in the week; and the country folk from great distances found their way through the woods to hear Mass in the palm-thatched sanctuary of "El Riposo."

So did that happy family live "the gentle life" for some two years; till cacao rose again in price, the tax on the churches was taken off, and the F——s returned again to the world: but not to civilization and Christianity. Those they had carried with them into the wilderness; and those they brought back with them unstained.

CHAPTER XIV.

THE "EDUCATION QUESTION" IN TRINIDAD.

When I arrived in Trinidad, the little island was somewhat excited about changes in the system of education, which ended in a compromise like that at home, though starting from almost the opposite point.

Among the many good deeds which Lord Harris did for the colony was the establishment throughout it of secular elementary ward schools, helped by Government grants, on a system which had, I think, but two defects. First, that attendance was not compulsory; and next, that it was too advanced for the state of society in the island.

In an ideal system, secular and religious education ought, I believe, to be strictly separate, and given, as far as possible, by different classes of men. The first is the business of scientific men and their pupils; the second, of the clergy and their pupils: and the less either invades the domain of the other, the better for the community. But, like all ideals, it requires not only first-rate workmen, but first-rate material to work on; an intelligent and high-minded populace, who can and will think for themselves upon religious questions; and who have, moreover, a thirst for truth and knowledge of every kind. With such a populace, secular and religious education can be safely parted. But can they be safely parted in the case of a populace either degraded or still savage; given up to the "lusts of the flesh;" with no desire for improvement, and ignorant of that "moral ideal," without the influence of which, as my friend Professor Huxley well says, there can be no true education? It is well if such a people can be made to submit to one system of education. Is it wise to try to burden them with two at once? But if one system is to give way to the other, which is most important: to teach them the elements of reading, writing, and arithmetic; or the elements of duty and morals? And how these latter can be taught without religion is a problem as yet unsolved.

So argued some of the Protestant, and the whole of the Roman Catholic clergy of Trinidad, and withdrew their support from the Government schools, to such an extent that at least three-fourths of the children, I understand, went to no school at all.

The Roman Catholic clergy had, certainly, much to urge on their own behalf. The great majority of the coloured population of the island, besides a large proportion of the white, belonged to their creed. Their influence was the chief (I had almost said the only) civilizing and Christianizing influence at work on the lower orders of their own coloured people. They knew, none so well, how much the Negro required, not merely to be instructed, but to be reclaimed from gross and ruinous vices. It was not a question in Port of Spain, any more than it is in Martinique, of whether the Negros should be able to read and write, but of whether they should exist on the earth at all for a few generations longer. I say this openly and deliberately; and clergymen and police magistrates know but too well what I mean. The Priesthood were, and are, doing their best to save the Negro; and they naturally wished to do their work, on behalf of society and of the colony, in their own way; and to subordinate all teaching to that of Religion, which includes, with them, morality and decency. They therefore opposed the Government schools; because they tended, it was thought, to withdraw the Negro from his Priest's influence.

I am not likely, I presume, to be suspected of any leaning toward Romanism. But I think a Roman Catholic priest would have a right to a fair and respectful hearing, if he said :—

"You have set these people free, without letting them go through that intermediate stage of feudalism, by which, and by which alone, the white races of Europe were educated into true freedom. I do not blame you. You could do no otherwise. But will you hinder their passing through that process of religious education under a priesthood, by which, and by which alone, the white races of Europe were educated up to something like obedience, virtue, and purity?

"These last, you know, we teach in the interest of the State, as well as of the Negro: and if we should ask the State for aid, in order that we may teach them, over and above a little reading and writing—which will not be taught save by us, for we only shall be listened to—are we asking too much, or anything which the State will not be wise in granting us? We can have no temptation to abuse our power for political purposes. It would not suit us—to put the matter on its lowest ground —to become demagogues. For our congregations include persons of every rank and occupation; and therefore it is our interest, as much as that of the British Government, that all classes should be loyal, peaceable, and wealthy.

"As for our peculiar creed, with its vivid appeals to the senses: is it not a question whether the utterly unimaginative and illogical Negro can be taught the facts of Christianity, or indeed any religion at all, save through his senses? Is it not a question whether we do not, on the whole, give him a juster and clearer notion of the very truths which you hold in common with us, than an average Protestant Missionary does?

"Your Church of England"—it must be understood that the relations between the Anglican and the Romish clergy in Trinidad are, as far as I have seen, friendly and tolerant—"does good work among its coloured members. But it does so by speaking, as we speak, with authority. It, too, finds it prudent to keep up in its services somewhat at least of that dignity, even pomp, which is as necessary for the Negro as it was for the half-savage European of the early Middle Age, if he is to be raised above his mere natural dread of spells, witches, and other harmful powers, to somewhat of admiration and reverence.

"As for the merely dogmatic teaching of the Dissenters: we do not believe that the mere Negro really comprehends one of those propositions, whether true or false, Catholic or Calvinist, which have been elaborated by the intellect and the emotions of races who have gone through a training unknown to the Negro. With all respect for those who disseminate such books, we think that the Negro can no more conceive the true meaning of an average Dissenting Hymnbook, than a Sclavonian of the German Marches a thousand years ago could have conceived the meaning of St. Augustine's Confessions. For what we see is this—that when the personal influence of the white Missionary is withdrawn, and the Negro left to perpetuate his sect on democratic principles, his creed merely feeds his inordinate natural vanity with the notion that everybody who differs from him is going to hell, while he is going to heaven whatever his morals may be."

If a Roman Catholic priest should say all this, he would at least have a right, I believe, to a respectful hearing.

Nay, more. If he were to say, "You are afraid of our having too much to do with the education of the Negro, because we use the Confessional as an instrument of education. Now how far the Confessional is needful, or useful, or prudent, in a highly civilized and generally virtuous community, may be an open matter. But in spite of all your English dislike of it, hear our side of the question, as far as Negros and races in a similar condition are concerned. Do you know why and how the Confessional arose? Have you looked, for instance, into the old middle-age Penitentials? If so, you must be aware that it arose in an age of coarseness, which seems now inconceivable; in those barbarous times when the lower classes of Europe, slaves or serfs, especially in remote country districts, lived lives little better than those of the monkeys in the forest, and committed habitually the most fearful crimes, without any clear notion that they were doing wrong: while the upper classes, to judge from the literature which they have left, were so coarse, and often so profligate, in spite of nobler instincts and a higher sense of duty, that the purest and justest spirits among them had again and again to flee from their own class into the cloister or the hermit's cell.

"In those days, it was found necessary to ask Christian people perpetually—Have you been doing this, or that? For if you have, you are not only unfit to be called a Christian; you are unfit to be called a decent human being. And this, because there was every reason to suppose that they had been doing it; and that they would not tell of themselves, if they could possibly avoid it. So the Confessional arose, as a necessary element for educating savages into common morality and decency. And for the same reasons we employ it among the Negros of Trinidad. Have no fears lest we should corrupt the minds of the young. They see and hear more harm daily than we could ever teach them, were we so devilishly minded. There is vice now, rampant and notorious, in Port of Spain, which eludes even our Confessional. Let us alone to do our best. God knows we are trying to do it, according to our light."

If any Roman Catholic clergyman in Port of Spain spoke thus to me—and I have been spoken to in words not unlike these—I could only answer, "God's blessing on you, and all your efforts, whether I agree with you in detail or not."

The Roman Catholic inhabitants of the island are to the

Protestant as about 2½ to 1.[1] The whole of the more educated portion of them, as far as I could ascertain, are willing to entrust the education of their children to the clergy. The Archbishop of Trinidad, Monsignor Gonin, who has jurisdiction also in St. Lucia, St. Vincent, Grenada, and Tobago, is a man not only of great energy and devotion, but of cultivation and knowledge of the world; having, I was told, attained distinction as a barrister elsewhere before he took Holy Orders. A group of clergy is working under him—among them a personal friend of mine—able and ready to do their best to mend a state of things in which most of the children in the island, born nominal Roman Catholics, but the majority illegitimate, were growing up not only in ignorance, but in heathendom and brutality. Meanwhile, the clergy were in want of funds. There were no funds at all, indeed, which would enable them to set up in remote forest districts a religious school side by side with the secular ward school; and

[1] In 1858 they were computed as :—
   Roman Catholics 44,576
   Church of England 16,350
   Presbyterians 2,570
   Baptists 449
   Independents, &c. 239

From "Trinidad, its Geography, &c." by L. A. De Verteuil, M.D.P., a very able and interesting book. I regret much that its accomplished author resists the solicitations of his friends, and declines to bring out a fresh edition of one of the most complete monographs of a colony which I have yet seen.

the colony could not well be asked for Government grants to two sets of schools at once. In face of these circumstances, the late Governor thought fit to take action on the very able and interesting report of Mr. J. P. Keenan, one of the chiefs of inspection of the Irish National Board of Education, who had been sent out as special commissioner to inquire into the state of education in the island; to modify Lord Harris's plan, however excellent in itself; and to pass an Ordinance by which Government aid was extended to private elementary schools, of whatever denomination, provided they had duly certificated teachers; were accessible to all children of the neighbourhood without distinction of religion or race; and "offered solid guarantees for abstinence from proselytism and intolerance, by subjecting their rules and course of teaching to the Board of Education, and empowering that Board at any moment to cancel the certificate of the teacher." In the wards in which such schools were founded, and proved to be working satisfactorily, the secular ward schools were to be discontinued. But the Government reserved to itself the power of re-opening a secular school in the ward, in case the private school turned out a failure.

Such is a short sketch of an Ordinance which seems, to me at least, a rational and fair compromise, identical, mutatis mutandis, with that embodied in Mr. Forster's new Education

Act; and the only one by which the lower orders of Trinidad were likely to get any education whatever. It was received, of course, with applause by the Roman Catholics, and by a great number of the Protestants of the colony. But, as was to be expected, it met with strong expressions of dissent from some of the Protestant gentry and clergy; especially from one gentleman, who attacked the new scheme with an acuteness and humour which made even those who differed from him regret that such remarkable talents had no wider sphere than a little island of 45 miles by 60. An accession of power to the Roman Catholic clergy was, of course, dreaded; and all the more because it was known that the scheme met with the approval of the Archbishop; that it was, indeed, a compromise with the requests made in a petition which that prelate had lately sent in to the Governor; a petition which seems to me most rational and temperate. It was argued, too, that though the existing Act—that of 1851—had more or less failed, it might still succeed, if Lord Harris's plan was fully carried out, and the choice of the ward schoolmaster, the selection of ward school-books, and the direction of the course of instruction, was vested in local committees. The simple answer was, that eighteen years had elapsed, and the colony had done nothing in that direction; that the great majority of children in the island did not go to school at all, while those who did attended most irregularly, and learnt little or nothing;[1] that the secular system of education had not attracted, as it was hoped, the children of the Hindoo immigrants, of whom scarcely one was to be found in a ward school; that the ward schoolmasters were generally inefficient, and the Central Board of Education inactive; that there was no rigorous local supervision, and no local interest felt in the schools; that there were fewer children in the ward schools in 1868 than there had been in 1863, in spite of the rapid increase of population: and all this for the simple reason which the Archbishop had pointed out—the want of religious instruction. As was to be expected, the good people of the island, being most of them religious people also, felt no enthusiasm about schools where little was likely to be taught beyond the three royal R's.

I believe they were wrong. Any teaching which involves moral discipline is better than mere anarchy and idleness. But they had a right to their opinion; and a right too, being the great majority of the islanders, to have that opinion respected by the Governor. Even now, it will be but too likely, I think, that the establishment and superintendence of schools in remote districts will devolve—as it did in Europe during the Middle Age—entirely on the different clergies, simply by default of laymen of sufficient zeal for

[1] See Mr. Keenan's Report, and other papers, printed by order of the House of Commons, 10th August, 1870.

the welfare of the coloured people. Be that as it may, the Ordinance has become Law; and I have faith enough in the loyalty of the good folk of Trinidad to believe that they will do their best to make it work.

If indeed the present Ordinance does not work, it is difficult to conceive any that will. It seems exactly fitted for the needs of Trinidad. I do not say that it is fitted for the needs of any and every country. In Ireland, for instance, such a system would be, in my opinion, simply retrograde. The Irishman, to his honour, has passed, centuries since, beyond the stage at which he requires to be educated by a priesthood in the primary laws of religion and morality. His morality is—on certain important points—superior to that of almost any people. What he needs is to be trained to loyalty and order; to be brought more in contact with the secular science and civilization of the rest of Europe: and that must be done by a secular, and not by an ecclesiastical system of education.

The higher education, in Trinidad, seems in a more satisfactory state than the elementary. The young ladies, many of them, go "home"—*i.e.* to England or France—for their schooling; and some of the young men to Oxford, Cambridge, London, or Edinburgh. The Gilchrist Trust of the University of London has lately offered annually a Scholarship of 100*l.* a year for three years, to lads from the West India colonies, the examinations for it to be held in Jamaica, Barbados,

Trinidad, and Demerara; and in Trinidad itself two Exhibitions of 150*l.* a year each, tenable for three years, are attainable by lads of the Queen's Collegiate School, to help them toward their studies at a British University.

The Collegiate School received aid from the State to the amount of 3,000*l.* per annum—less by the students' fees; and was open to all denominations. But in it, again, the secular system would not work. The great majority of Roman Catholic lads were educated at St. Mary's College, which received no State aid at all. 417 Catholic pupils at the former school, as against 111 at the latter, were—as Mr. Keenan says—"a poor expression of confidence or favour on the part of the colonists." The Roman Catholic religion was the creed of the great majority of the islanders, and especially of the wealthier and better educated of the coloured families. Justice seemed to demand that if State aid were given, it should be given to all creeds alike; and prudence certainly demanded that the respectable young men of Trinidad should not be arrayed in two alien camps, in which the differences of creed were intensified by those of race, and—in one camp at least—by a sense of something very like injustice on the part of a Protestant, and, it must always be remembered, originally conquering, Government. To give the lads as much as possible the same interests, the same views; to make them all alike feel that they were growing up not merely English subjects, but English men, was one of the most important social problems in Trinidad. And the simplest way of solving it was, to educate them as much as possible side by side in the same school, on terms of perfect equality.

The late Governor, therefore, with the advice and consent of his Council, determined to develop the Queen's Collegiate School into a new Royal College, which was to be open to all creeds and races without distinction: but upon such terms as will, it is hoped, secure the willing attendance of Roman Catholic scholars.[1] Not only it, but schools duly affiliated to it, are to receive Government aid; and four Exhibitions of 150*l.* a year each, instead of two, are granted to young men going home to a British University. The College was inaugurated—I am sorry to say after I had left the island —in June 1870, by the Governor, in the presence of (to quote the Port of Spain Gazette) the Council, consisting of

The Honourable the Chief Judge Needham.

J. Scott Bushe (Colonial Secretary).

Charles W. Warner, C.B.

E. J. Eagles.

F. Warner.

Dr. L. A. A. Verteuil.

Henry Court.

[1] See Papers on the State of Education in Trinidad, p. 137 et seq.

M. Maxwell Philip.

His Honour Mr. Justice Fitzgerald.

André Bernard, Esq.

The last five of these gentlemen being, I believe, Roman Catholics. Most of the Board of Education were also present; the Principal and Masters of the Collegiate School, the Superiors and Reverend Professors of St. Mary's College, the Clergy of the Church of England in the island; the leading professional men, and merchants, &c., and especially a large number of the Roman Catholic gentry of the island; "MM. Ambard, O'Connor, Giuseppi, Laney, Farfan, Gillineau, Rat, Pantin, Léotaud, Besson, Fraser, Paüll, Hobson, Garcia, Dr. Padron," &c. I quote their names from the Gazette, in the order in which they occur. Many of them I have not the honour of knowing: but judging of those whom I do not know by those whom I do, I should say that their presence at the inauguration was a solid proof that the foundation of the new College was a just and politic measure, opening, as the Gazette well says, a great future to the youth of all creeds in the colony.

The late Governor's speech on the occasion I shall print entire. It will explain the circumstances of the case far better than I can do; and it may possibly meet with interest and approval from those who like to hear sound spoken, even in a small colony.

"We are met here to-day to inaugurate the Royal College, an institution in which the benefits of a sound education, I trust, will be secured to Protestants and Roman Catholics alike, without the slightest compromise of their respective principles.

"The Queen's Collegiate School, of which this College is, in some sort, an out-growth and development, was founded with the same object: but, successful as it has been in other respects, it cannot be said to have altogether attained this.

"St. Mary's College was founded by private enterprise with a different view, and to meet the wants of those who objected to the Collegiate School.

"It has long been felt the existence of two Colleges—one, the smaller, almost entirely supported by the State, the other, the larger, wholly without State aid—was objectionable; and that the whole question of secondary education presented a most difficult problem.

"Some saw its solution in the withdrawal of all State aid from higher education; others in the establishment by the State of two distinct Denominational Colleges.

"I have elsewhere explained the reason why I consider both these suggestions faulty, and their probable effect bad; the one being certain to check and discourage superior education altogether, the other likely to substitute inefficient for efficient teaching, and small exclusive schools for a wide national institution.

"I knew that, whilst insuperable objections existed to a combined education in all subjects, that objection had its limits: that in America and in Germany I had seen Protestants and Catholics learning side by side; that in Mauritius, a College numbering 700 pupils, partly Protestants, partly Roman Catholics, existed; and that similar establishments were not uncommon elsewhere.

"I therefore determined to endeavour to effect the establishment of a College where combined study might be carried on in those branches of education with respect to which no objection to such a course was felt, and to support with Government aid, and bring under Government supervision, those establishments where those branches in which a separate education was deemed necessary were taught.

"I had, when last at home, some anxious conferences with the highest ecclesiastical authority of the Roman Catholic Church in England on the subject, and came to a complete understanding with him in respect to it. That distinguished prelate, himself a man of the highest University eminence, is not one to be indifferent to the interests of learning. His position, his known opinions, afford a guarantee that nothing sanctioned by him could, even by the most scrupulous, be considered in the least degree inconsistent with the interests of his church or his religion.

"He expressed a strong preference for a totally separate education: but candidly admitted the objections to such a course in a small and not very wealthy island, and drew a wide distinction between combination for all purposes, and for some only.

"There were certain courses of instruction in which combined instruction could not possibly be given consistently with due regard to the faith of the pupils; there were others where it was difficult to decide whether it could or could not properly be given; there were others again where it might be certainly given without objection.

"On this understanding the plan carried into effect is based: but the Legislature have gone far beyond what was then agreed; and whilst Archbishop Manning would have assented to an arrangement which would have excluded certain branches only of education from the common course, the law, as now in force, allows exemption from attendance on all, provided competent instruction is given to the pupils in the same branches elsewhere; till, in fact, all that remains obligatory is attendance at examinations, and at the course of instruction in one or more of four given branches of education, if it should so happen that no adequate teaching in that particular branch is given in the pupil's own school.

VOL. II.   R

"A scheme more liberal—a bond more elastic—could hardly have been devised, capable of effecting, if desired, the closest union—capable of being stretched to almost any degree of slight connection; and even if some Catholics would still prefer a wholly separate system, they must, if candid men, admit that the Protestant population here have a right to demand that they should not be called on to surrender, in order to satisfy a mere preference, the great advantages they derive from a united College under State control, with its efficient staff and national character.

"If religious difficulties are met, and conscientious scruples are not wounded, a sacrifice of preferences must often be made. Private wishes must often yield to the public good.

"In the first instance, all the boys of the former Collegiate School have become students of the College: but probably a school of a similar character, but affiliated to the College, will shortly be formed, in which a large number of those boys will be included.

"That the headship of the College should be entrusted to the Principal of the Queen's Collegiate School will, I am sure, be universally felt to be only a just tribute to the zeal, efficiency, and success with which he has hitherto laboured in his office, whilst, in addition to these qualifications, he possesses the no less important one for the post he is about to fill, of a mind singularly impartial, just, liberal and candid.

"I hope that the other Professors of the College may be taken from affiliated schools indiscriminately, the lectures being given as may be most convenient, and as may be arranged by the College Council.

"It is intended by the College Council that the fees charged for attendance at the Royal College should be much lower than those heretofore charged at the Queen's Collegiate School. I do not believe that the mere financial loss will be great, whilst I believe a good education will, by this means, be placed within the reach of many who cannot now afford it.

"I hope—but I express only my own personal wish, not that of the Council, which, as yet, has pronounced no opinion—that some of the changes introduced in most states of modern education will be made here, and that especial attention will be given to the teaching of some of the Eastern languages.

"It is almost impossible to overrate the importance of this both to the Government and the community;—to the Government, as enabling it to avail itself of the services of honest, competent, and trustworthy interpreters; and to the general community, as relieving both employer and employed from the necessity of depending on the interpretation of men not always very competent, nor always very scrupulous, whose mistakes or errors, whether wilful or accidental, may often effect much injustice, and on whose fidelity life may not unfrequently depend.

"I thank the members of the College Council for having accepted a task which will, at first, involve much delicate tact, forbearance, caution, and firmness, and the exercise of talents I know them to possess, and which I am confident will be freely bestowed in working out the success of the institution committed to their care.

"I thank the Principal and his staff for their past exertions, and I count with confidence on their future labours.

"I thank the parents who, by their presence, have manifested their interest in our undertaking and their wishes for its success, and I especially thank the ladies who have been drawn within these walls by graver attractions than those which generally bring us together at this building.

"I rejoice to see here the Superior of St. Mary's College, and the goodly array of those under his charge, and I do so for many reasons.

"I rejoice, because being not as yet affiliated or in any way officially connected with the Royal College, their presence is a spontaneous evidence of their goodwill and kindly feeling, and of the spirit in which they have been disposed to meet the efforts made to consult their feelings in the arrangements of this institution; a spirit yet further evinced by the fact that the Superior has informed me that he is about voluntarily to alter the course of study pursued in St. Mary's College, so as more nearly to assimilate it to that pursued here.

"I rejoice, because in their presence I hail a sign that the affiliation which is, I believe, desired by the great body of the Roman Catholic community in this island, and to which it has been shown no insuperable religious obstacle exists, will take place at no more distant day than is necessary to secure the approval, the naturally requisite approval, of ecclesiastical authority elsewhere.

"I rejoice at their presence, because it enables me before this company to express my high sense of the courage and liberality which have maintained their College for years past without any aid whatever from the State, and, in spite of manifold obstacles and discouragements, have caused it to increase in numbers and efficiency.

"I rejoice at their presence, because I desire to see the youth of Trinidad of every race, without indifference to their respective creeds, brought together on all possible occasions, whether for recreation or for work: because I wish to see them engaged in friendly rivalry in their studies now, as they will hereafter be in the world, which I desire to see them enter, not as strangers to each other, but as friends and fellow-citizens.

"I rejoice, because their presence enables me to take a

personal farewell of so many of those who will in the next generation be the planters, the merchants, the official and professional men of Trinidad. By the time that you are men all the petty jealousies, all the mean resentments of this our day, will have faded into the oblivion which is their proper bourn. But the work now accomplished will not, I trust, so fade. They will melt and perish as the snow of the north would before our tropical sun: but the College will, I trust, remain as the rock on which the snow rests, and which remains uninjured by the heat, unmoved by the passing storm. May it endure and strengthen as it passes from the first feeble beginnings of this its infancy to a vigorous youth and maturity. You will sometimes in days to come recall the inauguration of your College, and perhaps not forget that its founder prayed you to bear in mind the truth that you will find, even now, the truest satisfaction in the strict discharge of duty; that he urged you to form high and unselfish aims—to seek noble and worthy objects; and as you enter on the world and all its tossing sea of jealousies, strife, division and distrust, to heed the lesson which an Apostle, whose words we all alike revere, has taught us, 'If ye bite and devour one another, take ye heed that ye be not consumed one of another.'

"Here, we hope, a point of union has been found which may last through life, and that whilst every man cherishes a love for his own peculiar School, all alike will have an interest in their common College, all alike be proud of a national institution, jealous of its honour, and eager to advance its welfare.

"It is a common thing to hear the bitterness of religious discord here deplored. I for one, looking back on the history of past years, cannot think, as some seem to do, that it has increased. On the contrary, it seems to me that it has greatly diminished in violence when displayed, and that its displays are far less frequent. Such, I believe, will be more and more the case; and that whilst religious distinctions will remain the same, and conscientious convictions unaltered, social and party differences consequent on those distinctions and convictions will daily diminish; that all alike will more and more feel in how many things they can think and act together for the benefit of their common country, and of the community of which they all are members; how they can be glad together in her prosperity, and be sad together in the day of her distress; and work together at all times to promote her good. That this College is calculated to aid in a great degree in effecting this happy result, I for one cannot entertain the shadow of a doubt. 'Esto perpetua!'"

"Esto perpetua." But there remains, I believe, more yet to be done for education in the West Indies; and that is to carry out Mr. Keenan's scheme for a Central University for the whole of the West Indian Colonies,[1] as a focus of higher education; and a focus, also, of cultivated public opinion, round which all that is shrewdest and noblest in the islands shall rally, and find strength in moral and intellectual union. I earnestly recommend all West Indians to ponder Mr. Keenan's weighty words on this matter; believing that, as they do so, even stronger reasons than he has given for establishing such an institution will suggest themselves to West Indian minds.

I am not aware, nor would the reader care much to know, what schools there may be in Port of Spain for Protestant young ladies. I can only say that, to judge from the young ladies themselves, the schools must be excellent. But one school in Port of Spain I am bound in honour, as a clergyman of the Church of England, not to pass by without earnest approval; namely, "The Convent," as it is usually called. It was established in 1836, under the patronage of the Roman Catholic Bishop, the Right Rev. Dr. Macdonnel, and was founded by the ladies of St. Joseph, a religious Sisterhood which originated in France a few years since, for the special purpose of diffusing instruction through the colonies.[2] This institution, which Dr. De Verteuil says is "unique in the West Indies," besides keeping up two large girls' schools for poor

[1] Mr. Keenan's Report, pp. 63—67.
[2] Dr. De Verteuil's "Trinidad."

children, gave in 1857 a higher education to 120 girls of the middle and upper classes, and the number has much increased since then. It is impossible to doubt that this Convent has been "a blessing to the colony." At the very time when, just after slavery was abolished, society throughout the island was in the greatest peril, these good ladies came to supply a want which, under the peculiar circumstances of Trinidad, could only have been supplied by the self-sacrifice of devoted women. The Convent has not only spread instruction and religion among the wealthier coloured class: but it has done more; it has been a centre of true civilization, purity, virtue, where one was but too much needed; and has preserved, doubtless, hundreds of young creatures from serious harm; and that without interfering in any wise, I should think, with their duty to their parents. On the contrary, many a mother in Port of Spain must have found in the Convent a protection for her daughters, better than she herself could give, against influences to which she herself had been but too much exposed during the evil days of slavery; influences which are not yet, alas! extinct in Port of Spain. Creoles will understand my words; and will understand too, why I, Protestant though I am, bid heartily God speed to the good ladies of St. Joseph.

To the Anglican clergy, meanwhile, whom I met in the West Indies, I am bound to offer my thanks, not for courtesies shown to me—that is a slight matter—but for the worthy fashion in which they seem to be upholding the honour of the good old Church in the colonies. In Port of Spain I heard and saw enough of their work to believe that they are in nowise less active—more active they cannot be—than if they were sea-port clergymen in England. The services were performed thoroughly well; with a certain stateliness, which is not only allowable but necessary, in a colony where the majority of the congregation are coloured; but without the least foppery or extravagance. The very best sermon, perhaps, for matter and manner, which I ever heard preached to unlettered folk, was preached by a young clergyman—a West Indian born—in the Great Church of Port of Spain; and he had no lack of hearers, and those attentive ones. The Great Church was always a pleasant sight, with its crowded congregation of every hue, all well dressed, and with the universal West Indian look of comfort; and it's noble span of roof overhead, all cut from island timber—another proof of what the wood-carver may effect in the island hereafter. Certainly distractions were frequent and troublesome, at least to a new-comer. A large centipede would come out and take a hurried turn round the Governor's seat; or a bat would settle in broad daylight in the curate's hood; or one had to turn away one's eyes lest they should behold—not vanity, but—the magnificent head of a Cabbage-palm just outside the opposite window, with the black vultures trying to sit on the footstalks in a high wind, and slipping down, and flopping up again, half the service through. But one soon got accustomed to the strange sights; though it was, to say the least, somewhat startling to find, on Christmas Day, the altar and pulpit decked with exquisite tropic flowers; and each doorway arched over with a single pair of coco-nut leaves, fifteen feet high.

The Christmas Day Communion, too, was one not easily to be forgotten. At least 250 persons, mostly coloured, many as black as jet, attended; and were, I must say for them, most devout in manner. Pleasant it was to see the large proportion of men among them, many young white men of the middle and upper class; and still more pleasant, too, to see that all hues and ranks knelt side by side without the least distinction. One trio touched me deeply. An old lady —I know not who she was—with the unmistakeable long, delicate, once beautiful features of a high-bred West Indian of the "Ancien Régime," came and knelt reverently, feebly, sadly, between two old Negro women. One of them seemed her maid. Both of them might have been once her slaves. Here at least they were equals. True Equality—the consecration of humility, not the consecration of envy—first appeared on earth in the house of God, and at the altar of Christ: and I question much whether it will linger long in any spot on earth where that house and that altar are despised. It is easy to propose an equality without Christianity; as easy as to propose to kick down the ladder by which you have climbed, or to saw off the bough on which you sit. As easy; and as safe.

But I must not forget, while speaking of education in Trinidad, one truly "educational" establishment which I visited at Tacarigua; namely, a Coolie Orphan Home, assisted by the State, but set up and kept up almost entirely by the zeal of one man,—the Rev. —— Richards, brother of the excellent Rector of Trinity Church, Port of Spain. This good man, having no children of his own, has taken for his children the little brown immigrants, who, losing father and mother, are but too apt to be neglected by their own folk. At the foot of the mountains, beside a clear swift stream, amid scenery and vegetation which an European millionaire might envy, he has built a smart little quadrangle, with a long low house, on one side for the girls, on the other for the boys; a schoolroom, which was as well supplied with books, maps, and pictures as any average National School in England; and, adjoining the buildings, a garden where the boys are taught to work. A matron—who seemed thoroughly worthy of her post—conducts the whole; and comfort, cleanliness, and order were visible everywhere. A pleasant sight: but the pleasantest sight of all was to see the little bright-eyed brown darlings clustering round him who was indeed their father in God; who had delivered them from misery and loneliness, and—in the case of the girls—too probably vice likewise; and drawn them, by love, to civilization and Christianity. The children, as fast as they grow up, are put out to domestic service, and the great majority of the boys at least turn out well. The girls, I was told, are curiously inferior to the boys in intellect and force of character; an inferiority which is certainly not to be found in Negros, among whom the two sexes are more on a par, not only intellectually, but physically also, than among any race which I have seen. One instance, indeed, we saw of the success of the school. A young creature, brought up there, and well married near by, came in during our visit to show off her first baby to the matron and the children; as pretty a mother and babe as one could well see. Only we regretted, that, in obedience to the supposed demands of civilization, and of a rise in life, she had discarded the graceful and modest Hindoo dress of her ancestresses, for a French bonnet and all that accompanies it. The transfiguration added, one must charitably suppose, to her self-respect; if so, it must be condoned on moral grounds: but in an æsthetic view, she had made a great mistake.

In remembrance of our visit, a little brown child, some three or four years old, who had been christened that day, was named after me; and I was glad to have my name connected, even in so minute an item, with an institution which at all events delivers children from the fancy that they can, without being good or doing good, conciliate the upper powers by hanging garlands on a trident inside a hut, or putting red dust on a stump of wood outside it, while they stare in and mumble prayers to they know not what of gilded wood.

The Coolie temples are curious places to those who have never before been face to face with real heathendom. Their mark is, generally, a long bamboo with a pennon atop, outside a low dark hut, with a broad flat verandah, or rather shed, outside the door. Under the latter, opposite each door, if I recollect rightly, is a stone or small stump, on which offerings are made of red dust and flowers. From it the worshippers can see the images within. The white man, stooping, enters the temple. The attendant priest, so far from forbidding him, seems highly honoured, especially if the visitor give him a shilling; and points out, in the darkness—for there is no light save through the low doors—three or four squatting abominations, usually gilded. Sometimes these have been carved in the island. Sometimes the poor folk have taken the trouble to bring them all the way from India on board ship. Hung beside them on the walls are little pictures, often very well executed in the miniature-like Hindoo style, by native artists in the island.

Large brass pots, which have some sacred meaning, stand about, and with them a curious trident-shaped stand, about four feet high, on the horns of which garlands of flowers are hung as offerings. The visitor is told that the male figures are Mahadeva, and the female Kali: we could hear of no other deities. I leave it to those who know Indian mythology better than I do, to interpret the meaning—or rather the past meaning, for I suspect it means very little now—of all this trumpery and nonsense, on which the poor folk seem to spend much money. It was impossible, of course, even if one had understood their language, to find out what notions they attached to it all; and all I could do, on looking at these heathen idol chapels, in the midst of a Christian and civilized land, was to ponder, in sadness and astonishment, over a puzzle as yet to me inexplicable: namely, how human beings first got into their heads the vagary of worshipping images. I fully allow the cleverness and apparent reasonableness of M. Comte's now famous theory of the development of religions. I blame no one for holding it. But I cannot agree with it. The more of a "saine appréciation," as M. Comte calls it, I bring to bear on the known facts; the more I "let my thought play freely around them," the more it is inconceivable to me, according to any laws of the human intellect which I have seen at work, that savage or half-savage folk should have invented idolatries. I do

not believe that Fêtishism is the parent of idolatry; but rather
—as I have said elsewhere—that it is the dregs and remnants
of idolatry. The idolatrous nations now, as always, are not
the savage nations: but those who profess a very ancient and
decaying civilization. The Hebrew Scriptures uniformly
represent the non-idolatrous and monotheistic peoples, from
Abraham to Cyrus, as lower in what we now call the scale
of civilization, than the idolatrous and polytheistic peoples
about them. May not the contrast between the Patriarchs
and the Pharaohs, David and the Philistines, the Persians
and the Babylonians, mark a law of history of wider application than we are wont to suspect? But if so, what was the
parent of idolatry? For a natural genesis it must have had,
whether it be a healthy and necessary development of the
human mind—as some hold, not without weighty arguments
on their side; or whether it be a diseased and merely
fungoid growth, as I believe it to be. I cannot hold that it
originated in Nature-worship, simply because I can find no
evidence of such an origin. There is rather evidence, if the
statements of the idolaters themselves are to be taken, that it
originated in the worship of superior races by inferior races;
possibly also in the worship of works of art which those
races, dying out, had left behind them, and which the lower
race, while unable to copy them, believed to be possessed of
magical powers derived from a civilization which they

had lost. After a while the priesthood, which has usually, in all ages and countries, proclaimed itself the depository of a knowledge and a civilization lost to the mass of the people, may

Coolie sacrificing.

have gained courage to imitate these old works of art, with proper improvements for the worse, and have persuaded the people that the new idols would do as well as the old ones.

Would that some truly learned man would "let his thoughts play freely" round this view of the mystery, and see what can be made out of it. But whatever is made out, on either view, it will still remain a mystery—to me at least, as much as to Isaiah of old—how this utterly abnormal and astonishing animal called man first got into his foolish head that he could cut a thing out of wood or stone which would listen to him and answer his prayers. Yet so it is; so it has been for unnumbered ages. Man may be defined as a speaking animal, or a cooking animal. He is best, I fear, defined as an idolatrous animal; and so much the worse for him. But what if that very fact, diseased as it is, should be a sure proof that he is more than an animal?

CHAPTER XV.

THE RACES—A LETTER.

DEAR ——,

I have been to the races: not to bet, nor to see the horses run: not even to see the fair ladies on the Grand Stand, in all the newest fashions of Paris *viâ* New York: but to wander en mufti among the crowd outside, and behold the humours of men. And I must say that their humours were very good humours; far better, it seemed to me, than those of an English race-ground. Not that I have set foot on one for thirty years: but at railway stations, and elsewhere, one cannot help seeing what manner of folk, beside mere holiday folk, rich or poor, affect English races; or help pronouncing them, if physiognomy be any test of character, the most degraded beings, even some of those smart-dressed men who carry bags with their names on them, which our pseudo-civilization has yet done itself the dishonour of producing. Now, of that class I saw absolutely none. I do not suppose that the brown fellows who hung about the horses, whether Barbadians or Trinidad men, were of very angelic morals: but they looked like heroes compared with the bloated hangdog roughs and quasi-grooms of English races. As for the sporting gentlemen, not having the honour to know them, I can only say that they looked like gentlemen, and that I wish, in all courtesy, that they had been more wisely employed.

But the Negro, or the coloured man of the lower class, was in his glory. He was smart, clean, shiny, happy, according to his light. He got up into trees, and clustered there, grinning from ear to ear. He bawled about island horses and Barbadian horses—for the Barbadians mustered strong, and a fight was expected, which, however, never came off; he sang songs, possibly some of them extempore, like that which amused one's childhood concerning a once notable event in a certain island—

> "I went to da Place
> To see da horse-race,
> I see Mr. Barton
> A-wipin' ob his face.
>
> Run, Allwright,
> Run for your life;
> See Mr. Barton
> A-comin' wid a knife.
>
> Oh, Mr. Barton,
> I sarry for your loss:
> If you no believe me,
> I tie my head across."

Waiting for the Races.

That is—go into mourning. But no one seemed inclined to tie their heads across that day. The Coolies seemed as merry as the Negros; even about the face of the Chinese there flickered, at times, a feeble ray of interest.

The coloured women wandered about, in showy prints, great crinolines, and gorgeous turbans. The Coolie women sat in groups on the grass—ah Isle of the Blest, where people can sit on the grass in January—like live flower-beds of the most splendid and yet harmonious hues. As for jewels, of gold as well as silver, there were many there, on arms, ankles, necks and noses, which made white ladies fresh from England break the tenth commandment.

I wandered about, looking at the live flower-beds, and giving passing glances into booths, which I longed to enter, and hear what sort of human speech might be going on therein: but I was deterred, first by the thought that much of the speech might not be over-edifying, and next by the smells, especially by that most hideous of all smells—new rum.

At last I came to a crowd; and in the midst of it, one of those great French merry-go-rounds, turned by machinery, with pictures of languishing ladies round the central column. All the way from the Champs Elysées the huge piece of fools' tackle had lumbered and creaked hither across the sea to Martinique, and was now making the round of the islands; and a very profitable round, to judge from the number of its customers. The hobby-horses swarmed with Negresses and Hindoos of the lower order. The Negresses, I am sorry to say, forgot themselves, kicked up their legs, shouted to the bystanders, and were altogether incondite. The Hindoo women, though showing much more of their limbs than the Negresses, kept them gracefully together, drew their veils round their heads, and sat coyly, half frightened, half amused, to the delight of their "papas," or husbands, who had in some cases to urge them to get up and ride, while they stood by, as on guard, with the long hardwood quarter-staff in hand.

As I looked on, considered what a strange creature man is, and wondered what possible pleasure these women could derive from being whirled round till they were giddy and stupid, I saw an old gentleman seemingly absorbed in the very same reflection. He was dressed in dark blue, with a straw hat. He stood with his hands behind his back, his knees a little bent, and a sort of wise, half-sad, half-humorous smile upon his aquiline high-cheek-boned features. I took him for an old Scot; a canny, austere man—a man, too, who had known sorrow, and profited thereby; and I drew near to him. But as he turned his head deliberately round to me, I beheld to my astonishment the unmistakeable features of a Chinese. He and I looked each other full in the face, without a word; and I fancied that we understood each other about the merry-go-round, and many things besides. And then we both walked off different ways, as having seen enough, and more than enough. Was he, after all, an honest man and true? Or had he, like Ah Sin, in Mr. Bret Harte's delectable ballad, with "the smile that was child-like and bland"—

> " In his sleeves, which were large,
> Twenty-four packs of cards,
> And—On his nails, which were taper,
> What's common in tapers—that's wax?"

I know not; for the Chinese visage is unfathomable. But I incline to this day to the more charitable judgment; for the man's face haunted me, and haunts me still; and I am weak enough to believe that I should know the man and like him, if I met him in another planet, a thousand years hence.

Then I walked back under the blazing sun across the Savanna, over the sensitive plants and the mole-crickets' nests, while the great locusts whirred up before me at every step; toward the archway between the bamboo-clumps, and the red sentry shining like a spark of fire beneath its deep shadow; and found on my way a dying racehorse, with a group of coloured men round him, whom I advised in vain to do the one thing needful—put a blanket over him to keep off the sun, for the poor thing had fallen from sunstroke; so I left them to jabber and do nothing: asking myself—Is the human race, in the matter of amusements, as civilized as it was—say three thousand years ago? People have, certainly

—quite of late years—given up going to see cocks fight, or heretics burnt: but that is mainly because the heretics just now make the laws—in favour of themselves and the cocks. But are our amusements to be compared with those of the old Greeks, with the one exception of liking to hear really good music? Yet that fruit of civilization is barely twenty years old; and we owe its introduction, be it always remembered, to the Germans. French civilization signifies practically, certainly in the New World, little save ballet-girls, billiard-tables, and thin boots: English civilization, little save horse-racing and cricket. The latter sport is certainly blameless; nay, in the West Indies, laudable and even heroic, when played, as on the Savanna here, under a noon-day sun which feels hot enough to cook a mutton-chop. But with all respect for cricket, one cannot help looking back at the old games of Greece, and questioning whether man has advanced much in the art of amusing himself rationally and wholesomely.

I had reason to ask the same question that evening, as we sat in the cool verandah, watching the fire-flies flicker about the tree-tops, and listening to the weary din of the tom-toms which came from all sides of the Savanna save our own, drowning the screeching and snoring of the toads, and even, at times, the screams of an European band, which was playing a "combination tune," near the Grand Stand, half a mile off.

To the music of tom-tom and chac-chac, the coloured folk would dance perpetually till ten o'clock, after which time the rites of Mylitta are silenced by the policeman, for the sake of quiet folk in bed. They are but too apt, however, to break out again with fresh din about one in the morning, under the excuse—"Dis am not last night, Policeman. Dis am 'nother day."

Well: but is the nightly tom-tom dance so much more absurd than the nightly ball, which is now considered an integral element of white civilization? A few centuries hence may not both of them be looked back on as equally sheer barbarisms?

These tom-tom dances are not easily seen. The only glance I ever had of them was from the steep slope of once beautiful Belmont. "Sitting on a hill apart," my host and I were discoursing, not "of fate, free-will, free-knowledge absolute," but of a question almost as mysterious—the doings of the Parasol-ants who marched up and down their trackways past us, and whether these doings were guided by an intellect differing from ours, only in degree, but not in kind. A hundred yards below we espied a dance in a Negro garden; a few couples, mostly of women, pousetting to each other with violent and ungainly stampings, to the music of tom-tom and chac-chac, if music it can be called. Some power over the emotions it must have; for the Negros are said to be gradually maddened by it; and white people have told me that its very monotony, if listened to long, is strangely exciting, like the monotony of a bagpipe drone, or of a drum. What more went on at the dance we could not see; and if we had tried, we should probably not have been allowed to see. ' The Negro is chary of admitting white men to his amusements; and no wonder. If a London ball-room were suddenly invaded by Phœbus, Ares, and Hermes, such as Homer drew them, they would probably be unwelcome guests; at least in the eyes of the gentlemen. The latter would, I suspect, thoroughly sympathise with the Negro in the old story, intelligible enough to those who know what is the favourite food of a West Indian chicken.

"Well, John, so they gave a dignity ball on the estate last night?"

"Yes, massa, very nice ball. Plenty of pretty ladies, massa."

"Why did you not ask me, John? I like to look at pretty ladies as well as you."

"Ah, massa: when cockroach give a ball, him no ask da fowls."

Great and worthy exertions are made, every London Season, for the conversion of the Negro and the Heathen, and the abolition of their barbarous customs and dances. It is to be hoped that the Negro and the Heathen will some day show their gratitude to us, by sending Missionaries hither to convert the London Season itself, dances and all; and assist it to take the beam out of its own eye, in return for having taken the mote out of theirs.

CHAPTER XVI.

A PROVISION GROUND.

The "provision grounds" of the Negros were very interesting. I had longed to behold, alive and growing, fruits and plants which I had heard so often named, and seen so often figured, that I had expected to recognize many of them at first sight; and found, in nine cases out of ten, that I could not. Again, I had longed to gather some hints as to the possibility of carrying out in the West Indian islands that system of "Petite Culture"—of small spade farming—which I have long regarded, with Mr. John Stuart Mill and others, as not only the ideal form of agriculture, but perhaps the basis of any ideal rustic civilization. And what scanty and imperfect facts I could collect I set down here.

It was a pleasant sensation to have, day after day, old names translated for me into new facts. Pleasant, at least to me: not so pleasant, I fear, to my kind companions, whose courtesy I taxed to the uttermost by stopping to look over

The Last of the Giants.

BEAUTY OF FRUIT-TREES.

every fence, and ask, "What is that? And that?" Let the reader who has a taste for the beautiful as well as the useful in horticulture, do the same, and look in fancy over the hedge of the nearest provision ground.

There are orange-trees laden with fruit: who knows not them? and that awkward-boughed tree, with huge green fruit, and deeply-cut leaves a foot or more across—leaves so grand that, as one of our party often suggested, their form ought to be introduced into architectural ornamentation, and to take the place of the Greek acanthus, which they surpass in beauty—that is, of course, a Bread-fruit tree.

That round-headed tree, with dark rich Portugal laurel foliage, arranged in stars at the end of each twig, is the Mango, always a beautiful object, whether in orchard or in open park.

Bread fruit.

In the West Indies, as far as I have seen, the Mango has not yet reached the huge size of its ancestors in Hindostan. There—to judge, at least, from photographs—the Mango must be indeed the queen of trees; growing to the size of the largest English oak, and keeping always the round oak-like form. Rich in resplendent foliage, and still more rich in fruit, the tree easily became encircled with an atmosphere of myth in the fancy of the imaginative Hindoo.

That tree with upright branches, and large, dark, glossy leaves tiled upwards along them, is the Mammee Sapota,[1] beautiful likewise. And what is the next, like an evergreen peach, shedding from the underside of every leaf a golden light —call it not shade? A Star-apple;[2] and that young thing which you may often see grown into a great timber-tree, with leaves like a Spanish chestnut, is the Avocado,[3] or, as some call it, alligator, pear. This with the glossy leaves, somewhat like the Mammee Sapota, is a Sapodilla,[4] and that with leaves like a great myrtle, and bright flesh-coloured fruit, a Malacca-apple, or perhaps a Rose-apple.[5] Its neighbour, with large leaves, grey and rough underneath, flowers as big as your two hands, with greenish petals and a purple eye, followed by fat scaly yellow apples, is the Sweet-sop;[6] and that privet-like bush with little flowers and green berries a Guava,[7] of which you may eat if you will, as you may of the rest.

The truth, however, must be told. These West Indian fruits are, most of them, still so little improved by careful culture and selection of kinds, that not one of them (as far

[1] Lucuma mammosa.
[2] Chrysophyllum cainito.
[3] Persea gratissima.
[4] Sapota achras.
[5] Jambosa malaccensis and vulgaris.
[6] Anona squamosa.
[7] Psidium Guava.

as we have tried them) is to be compared with an average strawberry, plum, or pear.

But how beautiful they are all and each, after their kinds! What a joy for a man to stand at his door and simply look at them growing, leafing, blossoming, fruiting, without pause, through the perpetual summer, in his little garden of the Hesperides, where, as in those of the Phœnicians of old, "pear grows ripe on pear, and fig on fig," for ever and for ever!

Now look at the vegetables. At the Bananas and Plantains first of all. A stranger's eye would not distinguish them. The practical difference between them is, that the Plantain[1] bears large fruits which require cooking; the Banana[2] smaller and sweeter fruits, which are eaten raw. As for the plant on which they grow, no mere words can picture the simple grandeur and grace of a form which startles me whenever I look steadily at it. For however common it is—none commoner here—it is so unlike aught else, so perfect in itself, that, like a palm, it might well have become, in early ages, an object of worship.

And who knows that it has not? Who knows that there have not been races who looked on it as the Red Indians looked on Mondamin, the maize-plant; as a gift of a god—perhaps the incarnation of a god? Who knows? Whence

[1] Musa paradisiaca.   [2] M. sapientum.

did the ancestors of that plant come? What was its wild stock like ages ago? It is wild nowhere now on earth. It stands alone and unique in the vegetable kingdom, with distant cousins, but no brother kinds. It has been cultivated so long that though it flowers and fruits, it seldom or never seeds, and is propagated entirely by cuttings. The only spot, as far as I am aware, in which it seeds regularly and plentifully, is the remote, and till of late barbarous Andaman Islands in the Bay of Bengal.[1]

There it regularly springs up in the second growth, after the forest is cleared, and bears fruits full of seed as close together as they can be pressed. How did the plant get there? Was it once cultivated there by a race superior to the now utterly savage islanders, and at an epoch so remote that it had not yet lost the power of seeding? Are the Andamans its original home? or rather, was its original home that great southern continent of which the Andamans are perhaps a remnant? Does not this fact, as well as the broader fact that different varieties of the Plantain and Banana girdle the earth round at the Tropics, and have girdled it as long as records go back, hint at a time when there was a tropic continent or archipelago round the whole equator, and at a civilization and a horticulture to which

[1] I owe these curious facts, and specimens of the seeds, to the courtesy of Dr. King, of the Bengal army. The seeds are now in the hands of Dr. Hooker, at Kew.

those of old Egypt are upstarts of yesterday? There are those who never can look at the Banana without a feeling of awe, as at a token of how ancient the race of man may be, and how little we know of his history.

Most beautiful it is. The lush fat green stem; the crown of huge leaves, falling over in curves like those of human limbs; and below, the whorls of green or golden fruit, with the purple heart of flowers dangling below them; and all so full of life, that this splendid object is the product of a few months. I am told that if you cut the stem off at certain seasons, you may see the young leaf—remember that it is an endogen, and grows from within, like a palm, or a lily, or a grass—actually move upward from within and grow before your eyes; and that each stem of Plantain will bear from thirty to sixty pounds of rich food during the year of its short life.

But, beside the grand Plantains and Bananas, there are other interesting plants, whose names you have often heard. The tall plant with stem unbranched, but knotty and zigzag, and leaves atop like hemp, but of a cold purplish tinge, is the famous Cassava,[1] or Manioc, the old food of the Indians, poisonous till its juice is squeezed out in a curious spiral grass basket. The young Laburnums (as they seem), with purple flowers, are Pigeon-peas,[2] right good to eat. The

[1] Janipha Manihot.   [2] Cajanus Indicus.

creeping vines, like our Tamus, or Black Bryony, are Yams,[1]—best of all roots.

The branching broad-leaved canes, with strange white flowers, is Arrow-root.[2] The tall mallow-like shrub, with large pale yellowish-white flowers, Cotton. The huge grass with beads on it[3] is covered with the Job's tears which are precious in children's eyes, and will be used as beads for necklaces. The castor-oil plants, and the maize—that last always beautiful—are of course well known. The arrow leaves, three feet long, on stalks three feet high, like gigantic Arums, are Tanias,[4] whose roots are excellent. The plot of creeping convolvulus-like plants, with purple flowers, is the Sweet, or true, Potato.[5]

Yam.

And we must not overlook the French Physic-nut,[6] with its hemp-like leaves, and a little bunch of red coral in the midst, with which the Negro loves to adorn his garden, and uses it also as medicine; or the Indian Shot,[7] which may be seen planted out now in summer gardens in England.

| Dioscorea. | [2] Maranta. | [3] Coix lacryma. | [4] Xanthosoma. |
| Ipomœa Batatas. | [6] Jatropha multifida. | | [7] Canna. |

THE VEGETABLES.

The Negro grows it, not for its pretty crimson flowers, but because its hard seed put into a bladder furnishes him with that detestable musical instrument the chac-chac, wherewith he accompanies nightly that equally detestable instrument the tom-tom.

The list of vegetables is already long: but there are a few more to be added to it. For there, in a corner, creep some plants of the Earth-nut,[1] a little vetch which buries its pods in the earth. The owner will roast and eat their oily seeds. There is also a tall bunch of Ochro[2]—a purple-stemmed mallow-flowered plant—whose mucilaginous seeds

Sweet Potato.

will thicken his soup. Up a tree, and round the house-eaves, scramble a large coarse Pumpkin, and a more delicate Granadilla,[3] whose large yellow fruits hang ready to be plucked, and eaten principally for a few seeds of the shape and colour of young cockroaches. If he be a prudent man (especially if he lives in Jamaica), he will have a plant of the pretty Overlook pea,[4] trailing aloft somewhere, to prevent his garden

[1] Arachis hypogæa. [2] Abelmoschus esculentus. [3] Passiflora. [4] Canavalia.

being "overlooked," *i.e.* bewitched by an evil eye, in case the Obeah-bottle which hangs from the Mango-tree, charged with toad and spider, dirty water, and so forth, has no terrors for his secret enemy. He will have a Libidibi[1] tree, too, for astringent medicine; and his hedge will be composed, if he be a man of taste—as he often seems to be—of Hibiscus bushes, whose magnificent crimson flowers contrast with the bright yellow bunches of the common Cassia, and the scarlet flowers of the Jumby-bead bush,[2] and blue and white and pink Convolvuluses. The sulphur and purple Neerembergia of our hothouses, which is here one mass of flower at Christmas, and the creeping Crab's-eye Vine,[3] will scramble over the fence; while, as a finish to his little Paradise, he will have planted at each of its four corners an upright Dragon's-blood[4] bush, whose violet and red leaves bedeck our dinner-tables in winter; and are here used, from their unlikeness to any other plant in the island, to mark boundaries.

I have not dared—for fear of prolixity—to make this catalogue as complete as I could have done. But it must be remembered that, over and above all this, every hedge and wood furnishes wild fruit more or less eatable; the high forests plenty of oily seeds, in which the tropic

[1] Libidibia coriacea, now largely imported into Liverpool for tanning.
[2] Erythrina corallodendron.   [3] Abrus precatorius.
[4] Dracæna terminalis.

man delights; and woods, forests, and fields medicinal plants uncounted. "There is more medicine in the bush, and better, than in all the shops in Port of Spain," said a wise medical man to me; and to the Exhibition of 1862 Mr. M'Clintock alone contributed, from British Guiana, 140 species of barks used as medicine by the Indians. There is therefore no fear that the tropical small farmer should suffer, either from want, or from monotony of food; and equally small fear lest, when his children have eaten themselves sick—as they are likely to do if, like the Negro children, they are eating all day long—he should be unable to find something in the hedge which will set them all right again.

At the amount of food which a man can get off this little patch I dare not guess. Well says Humboldt, that an European lately arrived in the torrid zone is struck with nothing so much as the extreme smallness of the spots under cultivation round a cabin which contains a numerous family. The plantains alone ought, according to Humboldt, to give 133 times as much food as the same space of ground sown with wheat, and 44 times as much as if it grew potatoes. True, the plantain is by no means as nourishing as wheat: which reduces the actual difference between their value per acre to twenty-five to one. But under his plantains he can grow other vegetables.

He has no winter, and therefore some crop or other is always coming forward. From whence it comes, that, as I just hinted, his wife and children seem to have always something to eat in their mouths, if it be only the berries and nuts which abound in every hedge and wood. Neither dare I guess at the profit which he might make, and I hope will some day make, out of his land, if he would cultivate somewhat more for exportation, and not merely for home consumption. If any one wishes to know more on this matter, let him consult the catalogue of contributions from British Guiana to the London Exhibition of 1862; especially the pages from lix. to lxviii. on the starch-producing plants of the West Indies.

Beyond the facts which I have given as to the Plantain, I have no statistics of the amount of produce which is usually raised on a West Indian provision ground. Nor would any be of use; for a glance shows that the limit of production has not been nearly reached. Were the fork used instead of the hoe; were the weeds kept down; were the manure returned to the soil, instead of festering about everywhere in sun and rain: in a word, were even as much done for the land as an English labourer does for his garden; still more, if as much were done for it as for a suburban market-garden, the produce might be doubled or trebled, and that without exhausting the soil.

The West Indian peasant can, if he will, carry "la petite culture" to a perfection and a wealth which it has not yet attained even in China, Japan, and Hindostan, and make every rood of ground not merely maintain its man, but its civilized man. This, however, will require a skill and a thoughtfulness which the Negro does not as yet possess. If he ever had them, he lost them under slavery, from the brutalizing effects of a rough and unscientific "grande culture;" and it will need several generations of training ere he recovers them. Garden-tillage and spade-farming are not learnt in a day, especially when they depend—as they always must in temperate climates—for their main profit on some article which requires skilled labour to prepare it for the market—on flax, for instance, silk, wine, or fruits. An average English labourer, I fear, if put in possession of half a dozen acres of land, would fare as badly as the poor Chartists who, some twenty years ago, joined in Feargus O'Connor's land scheme, unless he knew half-a-dozen ways of eking out a livelihood which even our squatters around Windsor and the New Forest are, alas! forgetting, under the money-making and man-unmaking influences of the "division of labour." He is vanishing fast, the old bee-keeping, apple-growing, basket-making, copse-cutting, many-counselled Ulysses of our youth, as handy as a sailor: and we know too well what he leaves behind him; grand-children better fed, better clothed, better taught than he, but his inferiors in intellect and in manhood, because—whatever they may be taught—they cannot be taught by schooling to use their fingers and their wits. I fear, therefore, that the average English labourer would not prosper here. He has not stamina enough for the hard work of the sugar plantation. He has not wit and handiness enough for the more delicate work of a little spade-farm: and he would sink, as the Negro seems inclined to sink, into a mere grower of food for himself; or take to drink—as too many of the white immigrants to certain West Indian colonies did thirty years ago—and burn the life out of himself with new rum. The Hindoo immigrant, on the other hand, has been trained by long ages to a somewhat scientific agriculture, and civilized into the want of many luxuries for which the Negro cares nothing; and it is to him that we must look, I think, for a "petite culture" which will do justice to the inexhaustible wealth of the West Indian soil and climate.

As for the house, which is embowered in the little Paradise which I have been describing, I am sorry to say that it is, in general, the merest wooden hut on stilts; the front half altogether open and unwalled; the back half boarded up to form a single room, a passing glance into which will not make the stranger wish to enter, if he has any nose, or any dislike of vermin. The group at the door, meanwhile, will do anything but invite him to enter; and he will ride on, with something like a sigh at what man might be, and what he is.

Doubtless, there are great excuses for the inmates. A house in this climate is only needed for a sleeping or lounging place. The cooking is carried on between a few stones in the garden; the washing at the neighbouring brook. No store-rooms are needed, where there is no winter, and everything grows fresh and fresh, save the saltfish, which can be easily kept—and I understand usually is kept—underneath the bed. As for separate bedrooms for boys and girls, and all those decencies and moralities for which those who build model cottages strive, and with good cause—of such things none dream. But it is not so very long ago that the British Isles were not perfect in such matters; some think that they are not quite perfect yet. So we will take the beam out of our own eye, before we try to take the mote from the Negro's. The latter, however, no man can do. For the Negro, being a freeholder and the owner of his own cottage, must take the mote out of his own eye, having no landlord to build cottages for him; in the meanwhile, however, the less said about his lodging the better.

In the villages, however, in Maraval, for instance, y

houses of a far better stamp, belonging, I believe, to coloured people employed in trades; long and low wooden buildings with jalousies instead of windows—for no glass is needed here; divided into rooms, and smart with paint, which is not as pretty as the native wood. You catch sight as you pass of prints, usually devotional, on the walls, comfortable furniture, looking-glasses, and sideboards, and other pleasant signs that a civilization of the middle classes is springing up; and springing, to judge from the number of new houses building everywhere, very rapidly, as befits a colony whose revenue has risen, since 1855, from 72,300*l.* to 240,000*l.*, beside the local taxation of the wards, some 30,000*l.* or 40,000*l.* more.

What will be the future of agriculture in the West Indian colonies I of course dare not guess. The profits of sugar-growing, in spite of all drawbacks, have been of late very great. They will be greater still under the improved methods of manufacture which will be employed now that the sugar duties have been at least rationally reformed by Mr. Lowe. And therefore, for some time to come, capital will naturally flow towards sugar-planting; and great sheets of the forest will be, too probably, ruthlessly and wastefully swept away to make room for canes. And yet one must ask, regretfully, are there no other cultures save that of cane which will yield a fair, even an ample, return, to men of small capital and energetic habits? What of the culture of bamboo for paper-fibre, of which I have spoken already? It has been, I understand, taken up successfully in Jamaica, to supply the United States' paper market. Why should it not be taken up in Trinidad? Why should not Plantain-meal[1] be hereafter largely exported for the use of the English working classes? Why should not Trinidad, and other islands, export fruits—preserved fruits especially? Surely such a trade might be profitable, if only a quarter as much care were taken in the West Indies as is taken in England to improve the varieties by selection and culture; and care taken also not to spoil the preserves, as now, for the English market, by swamping them with sugar or sling. Can nothing be done in growing the oil-producing seeds with which the Tropics abound, and for which a demand is rising in England, if it be only for use about machinery? Nothing, too, toward growing drugs for the home market? Nothing toward using the treasures of gutta-percha which are now wasting in the Balatas? Above all, can nothing be done to increase the yield of the cacao-farms, and the quality of Trinidad cacao?

For this latter industry, at least, I have hope. My friend— if he will allow me to call him so— Mr. John Law, has shown what extraordinary returns may be obtained from improved

[1] Directions for preparing it may be found in the catalogue of contributions from British Guiana to the International Exhibition of 1862. Preface, pp. lix. lxiii.

cacao-growing; at least, so far to his own satisfaction that he is himself trying the experiment. He calculates [1] that 200 acres, at a maximum outlay of about 11,000 dollars spread over six years, and diminishing from that time till the end of the tenth year, should give, for fifty years after that, a net income of 6,800 dollars; and then "the industrious planter may sit down," as I heartily hope Mr. Law will do, "and enjoy the fruits of his labour."

Mr. Law is of opinion that, to give such a return, the cacao must be farmed in a very different way from the usual plan; that the trees must not be left shaded, as now, by Bois Immortelles, sixty to eighty feet high, during their whole life. The trees, he says with reason, impoverish the soil by their roots. The shade causes excess of moisture, chills, weakens and retards the plants; encourages parasitic moss and insects; and, moreover, is least useful in the very months in which the sun is hottest, viz. February, March, and April, which are just the months in which the Bois Immortelles shed their leaves. He believes that the cacao needs no shade after the third year; and that, till then, shade would be amply given by plantains and maize set between the trees, which would, in the very first year, repay the planter some 6,500 dollars on his first outlay of some 8,000. It is not for me to give an

[1] "How to Establish and Cultivate an Estate of One Square Mile in Cacao:" a Paper read to the Scientific Association of Trinidad, 1865.

opinion upon the correctness of his estimates: but the past history of Trinidad shows so many failures of the cacao crop, that even a practically ignorant man may be excused for guessing that there is something wrong in the old Spanish system; and that with cacao, as with wheat and every other known crop, improved culture means improved produce and steadier profits.

As an advocate of "petite culture," I heartily hope that such may be the case. I have hinted in these volumes my belief that exclusive sugar cultivation, on the large scale, has been the bane of the West Indies.

I went out thither with a somewhat foregone conclusion in that direction. But it was at least founded on what I believed to be facts. And it was, certainly, verified by the fresh facts which I saw there. I returned with a belief stronger than ever, that exclusive sugar cultivation had put a premium on unskilled slave-labour, to the disadvantage of skilled white-labour; and to the disadvantage, also, of any attempt to educate and raise the Negro, whom it was not worth while to civilize, as long as he was needed merely as an instrument exerting brute strength. It seems to me, also, that to the exclusive cultivation of sugar is owing, more than to any other cause, that frightful decrease throughout th islands of the white population, of which most English people are, I believe, quite unaware. Do they know, for instance, that Barbados could in Cromwell's time send three thousand white volunteers, and St. Kitts and Nevis a thousand, to help in the gallant conquest of Jamaica? Do they know that in 1676 Barbados was reported to maintain, as against 80,000 black, 70,000 free whites; while in 1851 the island contained more than 120,000 Negros and people of colour, as against only 15,824 whites? That St. Kitts held, even as late as 1761, 7,000 whites; but in 1826—before emancipation—only 1,600? Or that little Montserrat, which held, about 1648, 1,000 white families, and had a militia of 360 effective men, held in 1787 only 1,300 whites, in 1828 only 315, and in 1851 only 150?

It will be said that this ugly decrease in the white population is owing to the unfitness of the climate. I believe it to have been produced rather by the introduction of sugar cultivation, at which the white man cannot work. These early settlers had grants of ten acres apiece; at least in Barbados. They grew not only provisions enough for themselves, but tobacco, cotton, and indigo—products now all but obliterated out of the British islands. They made cotton hammocks, and sold them abroad as well as in the island. They might, had they been wisely educated to perceive and use the natural wealth around them, have made money out of many other wild products. But the profits of sugar-growing were so enormous, in spite of their uncertainty, that, during the greater part of the eighteenth century, their little freeholds were bought up, and converted into cane-pieces by their wealthier neighbours, who could afford to buy slaves and sugar-mills. They sought their fortunes in other lands: and so was exterminated a race of yeomen, who might have been at this day a source of strength and honour, not only to the colonies, but to England herself.

It may be that the extermination was not altogether undeserved; that they were not sufficiently educated or skilful to carry out that "petite culture" which requires—as I have said already—not only intellect and practical education, but a hereditary and traditional experience, such as is possessed by the Belgians, the Piedmontese, and, above all, by the charming peasantry of Provence and Languedoc, the fathers (as far as Western Europe is concerned) of all our agriculture. It may be, too, that as the sugar cultivation increased, they were tempted more and more, in the old hard drinking days, by the special poison of the West Indies—new rum, to the destruction both of soul and body. Be that as it may, their extirpation helped to make inevitable the vicious system of large estates cultivated by slaves; a system which is judged by its own results; for it was ruinate before emancipation; and emancipation only gave the coup de grâce. The "Latifundia perdidere" the Antilles, as they did Italy of old. The vicious system brought its own Nemesis.

The ruin of the West Indies at the end of the great French war was principally owing to that exclusive cultivation of the cane, which forced the planter to depend on a single article of produce, and left him embarrassed every time prices fell suddenly, or the canes failed from drought or hurricane. We all know what would be thought of an European farmer who thus staked his capital on one venture. "He is a bad farmer," says the proverb, "who does not stand on four legs, and, if he can, on five." If his wheat fails, he has his barley—if his barley, he has his sheep—if his sheep, he has his fatting oxen. The Provençal, the model farmer, can retreat on his almonds if his mulberries fail; on his olives, if his vines fail; on his maize, if his wheat fails. The West Indian might have had—the Cuban has—his tobacco; his indigo too; his coffee, or—as in Trinidad—his cacao and his arrow-root; and half-a-dozen crops more: indeed, had his intellect—and he had intellect in plenty—been diverted from the fatal fixed idea of making money as fast as possible by sugar, he might have ere now discovered in America, or imported from the East, plants for cultivation far more valuable than that Bread-fruit tree, of which such high hopes were once entertained, as a food for the Negro. As it was, his very green crops were neglected, till, in some islands at least, he could not feed his cattle and mules with certainty; while the sugar-cane, to which everything else had been sacrificed, proved sometimes, indeed, a valuable servant: but too often a tyrannous and capricious master.

But those days are past; and better ones have dawned, with better education, and a wider knowledge of the world and of science. What West Indians have to learn—some of them have learnt it already—is that if they can compete with other countries only by improved and more scientific cultivation and manufacture, as they themselves confess, then they can carry out the new methods only by more skilful labour. They therefore require now, as they never required before, to give the labouring classes a practical education; to quicken their intellect, and to teach them habits of self-dependent and originative action, which are—as in the case of the Prussian soldier, and of the English sailor and railway servant—perfectly compatible with strict discipline. Let them take warning from the English manufacturing system, which condemns a human intellect to waste itself in perpetually heading pins, or opening and shutting trap-doors, and punishes itself by producing a class of workpeople who alternate between reckless comfort and moody discontent. Let them be sure that they will help rather than injure the labour-market of the colony, by making the labourer also a small free-holding peasant. He will learn more in his own provision ground—properly tilled—than he will in the cane-piece: and he will take to the cane-piece and use for his employer the self-helpfulness which he has learnt in the provision ground. It is so in England. Our best agricultural day-labourers are, without exception, those who cultivate some scrap of ground, or follow some petty occupation, which prevents their depending entirely on wage-labour. And so I believe it will be in the West Indies. Let the land-policy of the late Governor be followed up. Let squatting be rigidly forbidden. Let no man hold possession of land without having earned, or inherited, money enough to purchase it, as a guarantee of his ability and respectability, or—as in the case of Coolies past their indentures —as a commutation for rights which he has earned in likewise. But let the coloured man of every race be encouraged to become a landholder and a producer in his own small way. He will thus, not only by what he produces, but by what he consumes, add largely to the wealth of the colony; while his increased wants, and those of his children, till they too can purchase land, will draw him and his sons and

Guava.

daughters to the sugar-estates, as intelligent and helpful day-labourers.

So it may be: and I cannot but trust, from what I have seen of the temper of the gentlemen of Trinidad, that so it will be.

CHAPTER XVII. (AND LAST).

HOMEWARD BOUND.

AT last we were homeward bound. We had been seven weeks in the island. We had promised to be back in England, if possible, within the three months; and we had a certain pride in keeping our promise, not only for its own sake, but for the sake of the dear West Indies. We wished to show those at home how easy it was to get there; how easy to get home again. Moreover, though going to sea in the Shannon was not quite the same "as going to sea in a sieve," our stay-at-home friends were of the same mind as those of the dear little Jumblies, whom Mr. Lear has made immortal in his "New Book of Nonsense"; and we were bound to come back as soon as possible, and not "in twenty years or more," if we wished them to say:

" If we live,
We too will go to sea in a sieve,
To the Hills of the Chankly bore."

So we left. But it was sore leaving. People had been very kind; and were ready to be kinder still; while we, busy—perhaps too busy—over our Natural History collections, had seen very little of our neighbours; had been able to accept very few of the invitations which were showered on us, and which would, I doubt not, have given us opportunities for liking the islanders still more than we liked them already.

Another cause made our leaving sore to us. The hunger for travel had been aroused—above all for travel westward—and would not be satisfied. Up the Oroonoco we longed to go: but could not. To La Guayra and Caraccas we longed to go: but dared not. Thanks to Spanish Republican barbarism, the only regular communication with that once magnificent capital of Northern Venezuela was by a filthy steamer, the Regos Ferreos, which had become, from her very looks, a byword in the port. On board of her some friends of ours had lately been glad to sleep in a dog-hutch on deck, to escape the filth and vermin of the berths; and went hungry for want of decent food. Caraccas itself was going through one of its periodic revolutions—it has not got through the fever fit yet—and neither life nor property were safe.

But the longing to go westward was on us nevertheless. It seemed hard to turn back after getting so far along the great path of the human race; and one had to reason with oneself—Foolish soul, whither would you go? You cannot go westward for ever. If you go up the Oroonoco, you will long to go up the Meta. If you get to Sta. Fe de Bogota, you will not be content till you cross the Andes and see Cotopaxi and Chimborazo. When you look down on the Pacific, you will be craving to go to the Gallapagos, after Darwin; and then to the Marquesas, after Herman Melville; and then to the Fijis, after Seeman; and then to Borneo, after Brooke; and then to the Archipelago, after Wallace; and then to Hindostan, and round the world. And when you get home, the westward fever will be stronger on you than ever, and you will crave to start again. Go home at once, like a reasonable man, and do your duty, and thank God for what you have been allowed to see; and try to become of the same mind as that most brilliant of old ladies, who boasted that she had not been abroad since she saw the Apotheosis of Voltaire, before the French Revolution; and did not care to go, as long as all manner of clever people were kind enough to go instead, and write charming books about what they had seen for her.

But the westward fever was slow to cool: and with wistful eyes we watched the sun by day, and Venus and the moon by night, sink down into the gulf, to lighten lands which we should never see. A few days more, and we were steaming out to the Bocas—which we had begun to love as the gates of a new home—heaped with presents to the last minute, some of them from persons we hardly knew. Behind us Port of Spain sank into haze: before us Monos rose, tall, dark, and grim—if Monos could be grim—in moonless night. We ran on, and past the island; this time we were going, not through the Boca de Monos, but through the next, the Umbrella Bocas. It was too dark to see houses, palm-trees, aught but the ragged outline of the hills against the northern sky, and beneath, sparks of light in sheltered coves, some of which were already, to one of us, well-beloved nooks. There was the great gulf of the Boca de Monos. There was Morrison's—our good Scotch host of seven weeks since; and the glasses were turned on it, to see, if possible, through the dusk, the almond-tree and the coco-grove for the last time. Ah, well—When we next meet, what will he be, and where? And where the handsome Creole wife, and the little brown Cupid who danced all naked in the log canoe, till the white gentlemen, swimming round, upset him; and canoe, and boy, and men rolled and splashed about like a shoal of seals at play, beneath the cliff with the Seguines and Cereuses; while the ripple lapped the Moriche-nuts about the roots of the Manchineel bush, and the skippers leaped and flashed outside, like silver splinters? And here, where we steamed along, was the very spot where we had seen the shark's back-fin when we rowed back from the first Guacharo cave. And it was all over.

We are such stuff as dreams are made of. And as in a dream, or rather as part of a dream, and myself a phantom and a play-actor, I looked out over the side, and saw on the right the black walls of Monos, on the left the black walls of Huevos—a gate even grander, though not as narrow, as that of Monos; and the Umbrella Rock, capped with Matapalo and Cactus, and night-blowing Cereus, dim in the dusk. And now we were outside. The roar of the surf, the tumble of the sea, the rush of the trade-wind, told us that at once. Out in the great sea, with Grenada, and kind friends in it, ahead; not to be seen or reached till morning light. But we looked astern and not ahead. We could see into and through the gap in Huevos, through which we had tried to reach the Guacharo cave. Inside that notch in the cliffs must be the wooded bay, whence we picked up the shells among the fallen leaves and flowers. From under that dark wall beyond it the Guacharos must be just trooping out for their nightly forage, as they had trooped out since— He alone who made them knows how long. The outline of Huevos, the outline of Monos, were growing lower and greyer astern. A long, ragged haze, far loftier than that on the starboard quarter, signified the Northern Mountains; and far off on the port quarter lay a flat bank of cloud, amid which rose, or seemed to rise, the Cordillera of the Main, and the hills where jaguars lie. Canopus blazed high astern, and Fomalhaut below him to the west, as if bidding us a kind farewell. Orion and Aldebaran spangled the zenith. The young moon lay on her back in the far west, thin and pale, over Cumana and the Cordillera, with Venus, ragged and red with earth mist, just beneath. And low ahead, with the pointers horizontal, glimmered the cold pole-star, for which we were steering, out of the summer into the winter once more. We grew chill as we looked at him; and shuddered, it may be, cowered for a moment, at the thought of "Nifelheim," the home of frosts and fogs, towards which we were bound.

However, we were not yet out of the Tropics. We had still nearly a fortnight before us in which to feel sure there was a sun in heaven; a fortnight more of the "warm champagne" atmosphere which was giving fresh life and health to us both. And up the islands we went, wiser, but not sadder, than when we went down them; casting wistful eyes, though, to windward, for there away—and scarcely out of sight—lay Tobago, to which we had a most kind invitation; and gladly would we have looked at that beautiful and fertile little spot, and have pictured to ourselves Robinson Crusoe and Man Friday pacing along the coral beach in one of its little southern coves. More wistfully still did we look to windward when we thought of Barbados, and of the kind people who were ready to welcome us into that prosperous and civilized little cane-garden, which deserves—and has deserved for now two hundred years, far more than poor old Ireland—the name of "The Emerald Gem of the Western World."

But it could not be. A few hours at Grenada, and a few hours at St. Lucia, were all the stoppages possible to us. The steamer only passes once a fortnight, and it is necessary to spend that time on each island which is visited, unless the traveller commits himself—which he cannot well do if he has a lady with him—to the chances and changes of coasting schooners. More frequent and easy intercommunication is needed throughout the Antilles. The good people, whether white or coloured, need to see more of each other, and more of visitors from home. Whether a small weekly steamer between the islands would pay in money I know not. That it would pay morally and socially, I am sure. Perhaps, when the telegraph is laid down along the islands, the need of more steamers will be felt and supplied.

Very pleasant was the run up to St. Thomas's, not merely on account of the scenery, but because we had once more—contrary to our expectation—the most agreeable of captains. His French cultivation—he had been brought up in Provence—joined to brilliant natural talents, had made him as good a talker as he doubtless is a sailor; and the charm of his conversation, about all matters on earth, and some above the earth, will not be soon forgotten by those who went up with him to St. Thomas's, and left him there with regret.

We transhipped to the Neva, Captain Woolward — to whom I must tender my thanks, as I do to Captain Bax, of the Shannon, for all kinds of civility. We slept a night in the harbour, the town having just then a clean bill of health; and were very glad to find ourselves, during the next few days, none the worse for having done so. On remarking, the first evening, that I did not smell the harbour after all, I was comforted by the answer that —" When a man did, he had better go below and make his will." It is a pity that the most important harbour in the Caribbean sea should be so unhealthy. No doubt it offers advantages for traffic which can be found nowhere else: and there the steamers must continue to assemble, yellow fever or none. But why should not a hotel be built for the passengers in some healthy and airy spot outside the basin—on the south slope of Water Island, for instance, or on Buck Island—where they might land at once, and sleep in pure fresh air and sea-breeze? The establishment of such an hotel would surely, when once known, attract to the West Indies many travellers to whom St. Thomas's is now as much a name of fear as Colon or the Panama.

We left St. Thomas's by a different track from that by which we came to it. We ran northward up the magnificent landlocked channel between Tortola and Virgin Gorda, to pass to leeward of Virgin Gorda and Anegada, and so northward toward the gulf-stream.

This channel has borne the name of Drake, I presume, ever since the year 1575. For in the account of that fatal, though successful voyage, which cost the lives both of Sir John Hawkins, who died off Porto Rico, and Sir Francis Drake, who died off Porto Bello, where Hosier and the greater part of the crews of a noble British fleet perished a hundred and fifty years afterward, it is written in Hakluyt how—after running up N. and N.W. past Saba—the fleet "stood away S.W., and on the 8th of November, being a Saturday, we came to an anker some 7 or 8 leagues off among certain broken Ilands called Las Virgines, which have bene accounted dangerous: but we found there a very good rode, had it bene for a thousand sails of ships in 7 & 8 fadomes, fine sand, good ankorage, high Ilands on either side, but no fresh water that we could find: here is much fish to be taken with nets and hookes: also we stayed on shore and fowled. Here Sir John Hawkins was extreme sick" (he died within ten days), "which his sickness began upon newes of the taking of the Francis" (his sternmost vessel). "The 18th day wee weied and stood north and by east into a lesser sound, which Sir Francis in his barge discovered the night before; and ankored in 13 fadomes, having hie steepe hiles on either side, some league distant from our first riding.

"The 12 in the morning we weied and set sayle into the Sea due south through a small streit but without danger," —possibly the very gap in which the Rhone's wreck now lies—" and then stode west and by north for S. Juan de Puerto Rico."

This northerly course is, plainly, the most advantageous for a homeward-bound ship, as it strikes the gulf-stream soonest, and keeps in it longest. Conversely, the southerly route by the Azores is best for outward-bound ships; as it escapes most of the gulf-stream, and traverses the still Sargasso Sea, and even the extremity of the westward equatorial current.

Strange as these Virgin Isles had looked when seen from the south, outside, and at the distance of a few miles, they looked still more strange when we were fairly threading our way between them, sometimes not a rifle-shot from the cliffs, with the white coral banks gleaming under our keel. Had they ever carried a Tropic vegetation? Had the hills of Tortola and Virgin Gorda, in shape and size much like those which surround a sea-loch in the Western Islands, ever been furred with forests like those of Guadaloupe or St. Lucia?

The loftier were now mere mounds of almost barren earth; the lower were often, like "Fallen Jerusalem," mere long earthless moles, as of minute Cyclopean masonry. But what had destroyed their vegetation, if it ever existed? Were they not, too, the mere remnants of a submerged and destroyed land, connected now only by the coral shoals? So it seemed to us, as we ran out past the magnificent harbour at the back of Virgin Gorda, where, in the old war times, the merchantmen of all the West Indies used to collect, to be conveyed homeward by the naval squadron, and across a shallow sea white with coral beds. We passed to leeward of the island, or rather reef, of Anegada, so low that it could only be discerned, at a few miles' distance, by the breaking surf and a few bushes; and then plunged, as it were, suddenly out of shallow white water into deep azure ocean. An upheaval of only forty fathoms would, I believe, join all these islands to each other, and to the great mountain island of Porto Rico to the west. The same upheaval would connect with each other Anguilla, St. Martin, and St. Bartholomew, to the east. But Santa Cruz, though so near St. Thomas's, and the Virgin Gordas to the south, would still be parted from them by a gulf nearly 2,000 fathoms deep—a gulf which marks still, probably, the separation of two ancient continents, or at least two archipelagos.

Much light has been thrown on this curious problem

since our return, by an American naturalist, Mr. Bland, in a paper read before the American Philosophical Society, on "The Geology and Physical Geography of the West Indies, with reference to the distribution of Mollusca." It is plain that of all animals, land-shells and reptiles give the surest tokens of any former connection of islands, being neither able to swim or fly from one to another, and very unlikely to be carried by birds or currents. Judging, therefore, as he has a right to do, by the similarity of the land-shells, Mr. Bland is of opinion that Porto Rico, the Virgins, and the Anguilla group, once formed continuous dry land, connected with Cuba, the Bahamas, and Hayti; and that their shell-fauna is of a Mexican and Central American type. The shell-fauna of the islands to the south, on the contrary, from Barbuda and St. Kitts down to Trinidad, is South American: but of two types, one Venezuelan, the other Guianan. It seems, from Mr. Bland's researches, that there must have existed once not merely an extension of the North American Continent south-eastward, but that very extension of the South American Continent northward, at which I have hinted more than once in these pages. Moreover—a fact which I certainly did not expect—the western side of this supposed land, namely Trinidad, Tobago, Grenada, the Grenadines, St. Vincent, and St. Lucia, have, as far as land-shells are concerned, a Venezuelan fauna; while the eastern side of it, namely Barbados, Martinique, Dominica, Guadaloupe, Antigua, &c., have, most strangely, the fauna of Guiana.

If this be so, a glance at the map will show the vast destruction of Tropic land during almost the very latest geological epoch; and show, too, how little, in the present imperfect state of our knowledge, we ought to dare any speculations as to the absence of man, as well as of other creatures, on those great lands now destroyed. For, to supply the dry land which Mr. Bland's theory needs, we shall have to conceive a junction, reaching over at least five degrees of latitude, between the north of British Guiana and Barbados; and may freely indulge in the dream that the waters of the Oroonoco, when they ran over the lowlands of Trinidad, passed east of Tobago; then northward between Barbados and St. Lucia; then turned westward between the latter island and Martinique; and that the mighty estuary formed—for a great part at least of that line—the original barrier which kept the land-shells of Venezuela apart from those of Guiana. A "stretch of the imagination," doubtless: but no greater stretch than will be required by any explanation of the facts whatsoever.

And so, thanking Mr. Bland heartily for his valuable contribution to the infant science of Bio-Geology—I take leave, in these pages at least, of the Earthly Paradise.

Our run homeward was quite as successful as our run out. The magnificent Neva, her captain and her officers, were what these Royal Mail steamers and their crews are—without, I believe, an exception—all that we could wish. Our passengers, certainly, were neither so numerous nor so agreeable as when going out; and the most notable personage among them was a keen-eyed strong-jawed little Corsican, who had been lately hired—so ran his story—by the coloured insurgents of Hayti, to put down the President—alias (as usual in such Republics) Tyrant—Salnave.

He seemed, by his own account, to have done his work effectually. Seven thousand lives were lost in the attack on Salnave's quarters in Port au Prince. Whole families were bayonetted, to save the trouble of judging and shooting them. Women were not spared: and—if all that I have heard of Hayti be true—some of them did not deserve to be spared. The noble old French buildings of the city were ruined—the Corsican said, not by his artillery, but by Salnave's. He had slain Salnave himself; and was now going back to France, to claim his rights as a French citizen, carrying with him Salnave's sword, which was wrapped in a newspaper, save when taken out to be brandished on the main deck. One could not but be interested in the valiant adventurer. He seemed a man such as Red Republics and Revolutions breed, and need; very capable of doing rough work, and not likely to be hampered by scruples as to the manner of doing it. If he is, as I take for granted, busy in France just now, he will leave his mark behind.

The voyage, however, seemed likely to be a dull one; and to relieve the monotony, a wild-beast show was determined on, ere the weather grew too cold. So one day all the new curiosities were brought on deck at noon; and if some great zoologist had been on board, he would have found materials in our show for more than one interesting lecture. The doctor contributed an Alligator, some 2ft. 6in. long; another officer, a curiously-marked Ant-eater—of a species unknown to me. It was common, he said, in the Isthmus of Panama; and seemed the most foolish and helpless of beasts. As no ants were procurable, it was fed on raw yolk of egg, which it contrived to suck in with its long tongue—not enough, however, to keep it alive during the voyage.

The chief engineer exhibited a live "Tarantula," or bird-catching spider, who was very safely barred into its box with strips of iron, as a bite from it is rather worse than that of an English adder.

We showed a Vulturine Parrot and a Kinkajou. The Kinkajou, by the bye, got loose one night, and displayed his natural inclination, by instantly catching a rat, and dancing between decks with it in his mouth: but was so tame withal, that he let the stewardess stroke him in passing. The good lady mistook him for a cat; and when she discovered next morning that she had been handling a "loose wild beast," her horror was as great as her thankfulness for the supposed escape. In curious contrast to the natural tameness of the Kinkajou was the natural untameness of a beautiful little Night-Monkey, belonging to the Purser. Its great owl's eyes were instinct with nothing but abject terror of everybody and everything; and it was a miracle that ere the voyage was over it did not die of mere fright. How is it, en passant, that some animals are naturally fearless and tameable, others not; and that even in the same family? Among the South American monkeys the Howlers are untameable; the Sapajous less so; while the Spider Monkeys are instinctively gentle and fond of man: as may be seen in the case of the very fine Marimonda (Ateles Beelzebub) now dying, I fear, in the Zoological Gardens at Bristol.

As we got into colder latitudes, we began to lose our pets. The Ant-eater departed first: then the doctor, who kept his alligator in a tub on his cabin floor, was awoke by doleful wails, as of a babe. Being pretty sure that there was not likely to be one on board, and certainly not in his cabin, he naturally struck a light, and discovered the alligator, who had never uttered a sound before, outside his tub on the floor, bewailing bitterly his fate. Whether he "wept crocodile tears" besides the doctor could not discover; but it was at least clear, that if swans sing before they die, alligators do so likewise: for the poor thing was dead next morning.

It was time, after this, to stow the pets warm between decks, and as near the galley-fires as they could be put. For now, as we neared the "roaring forties," there fell on us a gale from the north-west, and would not cease.

The wind was, of course, right a-beam; the sea soon ran very high. The Neva, being a long screw, was lively enough, and too lively; for she soon showed a chronic inclination to roll, and that suddenly, by fits and starts. The fiddles were on the tables for nearly a week: but they did not prevent more than one of us finding his dinner suddenly in his lap instead of his stomach. However, no one was hurt, nor even frightened: save two poor ladies—not from Trinidad—who spent their doleful days and nights in screaming, telling their beads, drinking weak brandy-and-water, and informing the hunted stewardess that if they had known what horrors they were about to endure, they would have gone to Europe in—a sailing vessel. The foreigners—who are usually, I know not why, bad sailors—soon vanished to their berths: so did the ladies: even those who were not ill jammed themselves into their berths, and lay there, for fear of falls and bruises; while the Englishmen, and a coloured man or two—the coloured men usually stand the sea well—had the deck all to themselves; and slopped about, holding on, and longing for a monkey's tail; but on the whole rather liking it.

For, after all, it is a glorious pastime to find oneself in a real gale of wind, in a big ship, with not a rock to run against within a thousand miles. One seems in such danger; and one is so safe. And gradually the sense of security grows, and grows into a sense of victory, as with the boy who fears his first fence, plucks up heart for the second, is rather pleased at the third, and craves for the triumph of the fourth and of all the rest, sorry at last when the run is over. And when a man—not being sea-sick—has once discovered that the apparent heel of the ship in rolling is at least four times less than it looks, and that she will jump upright again in a quarter of a minute like a fisher's float; has learnt to get his trunk out from under his berth, and put it back again, by jamming his forehead against the berth-side and his heels against the ship's wall; has learnt—if he sleep aft—to sleep through the firing of the screw, though it does shake all the marrow in his backbone; and has, above all, made a solemn vow to shave and bathe every morning, let the ship be as lively as she will: then he will find a full gale a finer tonic, and a finer stirrer of wholesome appetite, than all the drugs of Apothecaries' Hall.

This particular gale, however, began to get a little too strong. We had a sail or two set, to steady the ship: on the second night one split with a crack like a cannon; and was tied up in an instant, cordage and strips, into inextricable knots.

The next night I was woke by a slap which shook the Neva from stem to stern, and made her stagger and writhe like a live thing struck across the loins. Then a dull rush of water which there was no mistaking. We had shipped a green sea. Well, I could not bale it out again; and there was plenty of room for it on board. So, after ascertaining that R—— was not frightened, I went back to my berth and slept again, somewhat wondering that the roll of the screw was all but silent.

Next morning we found that a sea had walked in over the bridge, breaking it, and washing off it the first officer and the look-out man—luckily they fell into a sail and not overboard; put out the galley-fires, so that we got a cold breakfast; and eased the ship; for the shock turned the indicator in the engine-room to "Ease her." The engineer, thinking that the captain had given the order, obeyed it. The captain turned out into the wet to know who had eased his ship, and then returned to bed, wisely remarking, that the ship knew her own business best; and as she had chosen to ease the engines herself, eased she should be, his orders being "not to prosecute a voyage so as to endanger the lives of the passengers or the property of the Company."

So we went on easily for sixteen hours, the wise captain judging—and his judgment proved true—that the centre of the storm was crossing our course ahead; and that if we waited, it would pass us. So, as he expected, we came after a day or two into an almost windless sea, where smooth mountainous waves, the relics of the storm, were weltering aimlessly up and down under a dark sad sky.

Soon we began to sight ship after ship, and found ourselves on the great south-western high-road of the Atlantic; and found ourselves, too, nearing Niftheim day by day. Colder and colder grew the wind, lower the sun, darker the cloud-world overhead; and we went on deck each morning, with some additional garment on, sorely against our wills. Only on the very day on which we sighted land, we had one of those treacherously beautiful days which occur, now and then, in an English February, mild, still, and shining, if not with keen joyful blaze, at least with a cheerful and tender gleam from sea and sky.

The Land's End was visible at a great distance; and as we neared the Lizard, we could see not only the lighthouses on the Cliff, and every well-known cove and rock from Mullion and Kynance round to St. Keverne, but far inland likewise. Breage Church, and the great tin-works of Wheal Vor, stood out hard against the sky. We could see up the Looe Pool to

Helston Church, and away beyond it, till we fancied that we could almost discern, across the isthmus, the sacred hill of Carnbrea.

Along the Cornish shore we ran, through a sea swarming with sails: an exciting contrast to the loneliness of the wide ocean which we had left—and so on to Plymouth Sound.

The last time I had been on that water, I was looking up in awe at Sir Edward Codrington's fleet just home from the battle of Navarino. Even then, as a mere boy, I was struck by the grand symmetry of that ample basin: the breakwater—then unfinished—lying across the centre; the heights of Bovisand and Cawsand, and those again of Mount Batten and Mount Edgecumbe, left and right; the citadel and the Hoe across the bottom of the Sound, the southern sun full on their walls, with the twin harbours and their forests of masts, winding away into dim distance on each side; and behind all and above all, the purple range of Dartmoor, with the black rain-clouds crawling along its top. And now, after nearly forty years, the place looked to me even more grand than my recollection had pictured it. The newer fortifications have added to the moral effect of the scene, without taking away from its physical beauty: and I heard without surprise —though not without pride—the foreigners express their admiration of this, their first specimen of an English Port.

We steamed away again, after landing our letters, close past the dear old Mewstone. The warrener's hut stood on it still: and I wondered whether the old he-goat, who used to terrify me as a boy, had left any long-bearded descendants. Then under the Revelstoke and Bolt Head cliffs, with just one flying glance up into the hidden nooks of delicious little Salcombe, and away south west into the night, bound for Cherbourg, and a very different scene.

We were awakened soon after midnight by the stopping of the steamer. Then a gun. After awhile another; and presently a third: but there was no reply, though our coming had been telegraphed from England; and for nearly six hours we lay in the heart of the most important French arsenal, with all our mails and passengers waiting to get ashore; and nobody deigning to notice us. True, we could do no harm there: but our delay, and other things which happened, were proofs — and I was told not uncommon ones — of that carelessness, unreadiness, and general indiscipline of French arrangements, which has helped to bring about, since then, an utter ruin.

As the day dawned through fog, we went on deck to find the ship lying inside a long breakwater bristling with cannon, which looked formidable enough: but the whole thing, I was told, was useless against modern artillery and ironclads: and there was more than one jest on board as to the possibility of running the Channel Squadron across, and smashing Cherbourg in a single night, unless the French learnt to keep a better look-out in time of war than they did in time of peace.

Just inside us lay two or three ironclads; strong and ugly: untidy, too, to a degree shocking to English eyes. All sorts of odds and ends were hanging over the side, and about the rigging; the yards were not properly squared, and so forth; till—as old sailors would say—the ships had no more decency about them than so many collier-brigs.

Beyond them were arsenals, docks, fortifications, of which of course we could not judge; and backing all, a cliff, some 200 feet high, much quarried for building-stone. An ugly place it is to look at; and, I should think, an ugly place to get into, with the wind anywhere between N.W. and N.E.; an artificial and expensive luxury, built originally as a mere menace to England, in days when France, which has had too long a moral mission to fight some one, thought of fighting us, who only wished to live in peace with our neighbours. Alas! alas! "Tu l'a voulu, George Dandin." She has fought at last: but not us.

Out of Cherbourg we steamed again, sulky enough; for the delay would cause us to get home on the Sunday evening instead of the Sunday morning; and ran northward for the Needles. With what joy we saw at last the white wall of the island glooming dim ahead. With what joy we first discerned that huge outline of a visage on Freshwater Cliff, so well known to sailors, which, as the eye catches it in one direction, is a ridiculous caricature; in another, really noble, and even beautiful. With what joy did we round the old Needles, and run past Hurst Castle; and with what shivering, too. For the wind, though dead south, came to us as a continental wind, harsh and keen from off the frozen land of France, and chilled us to the very marrow all the way up to Southampton.

But there were warm hearts and kind faces waiting us on the quay, and good news too. The gentlemen at the Customhouse courteously declined the least inspection of our luggage; and we were at once away in the train home. At first, I must confess, an English winter was a change for the worse. Fine old oaks and beeches looked to us, fresh from ceibas and balatas, like leafless brooms stuck into the ground by their handles; while the want of light was for some days painful and depressing. But we had done it;. and within the three months, as we promised. As the king in the old play says, "What has been, has been, and I've had my hour." At last we had seen it; and we could not unsee it. We could not not have been in the Tropics.

THE END.

LONDON:
R. CLAY, SONS, AND TAYLOR, PRINTERS,
BREAD STREET HILL.

Every Thursday, price 4d.; Monthly Parts, 1s. 4d. and 1s. 8d.
Subscriptions—Annual, 18s. 6d.; Half-yearly, 9s. 6d.; Quarterly, 5s.

NATURE.

A WEEKLY ILLUSTRATED JOURNAL OF SCIENCE.

Vols. I.—III., Price 10s. 6d. each.

LIST OF CONTRIBUTORS.

Abel, F.A., F.R.S., H.M. Chem. Dep., Woolwich.
Agassiz, Prof. L., Museum of Comparative Zoology, Harvard College.
Andrews, Prof. T., F.R.S., Queen's Univ., Dublin.
Bastian, Prof. H. C., F.R.S., University College.
Beale, Prof. Lionel S., F.R.S., King's College.
Berthelot, Prof., Collège de France, Paris.
Brodie, Prof. Sir C., Bart., F.R.S., Oxford.
Brown, Prof. A., Crum, Edinburgh University.
Brush, Prof. G. I., Sheffield Scientific School, Yale College.
Busk, Prof. G., F.R.S.
Clifton, Prof. R. B., Oxford.
Cooke, Prof. J. P., jun., Cambridge, U.S.A.
Dana, Prof. J. D., Newhaven, Conn., U.S.A.
Darwin, C., F.R.S.
Dumas, J. B., Sec. Imperial Acad. of Sciences, Paris.
Farrar, Rev. F. W., F.R.S., Harrow School.
Fehling, Prof. Stuttgart.
Feruet, Prof. E., Paris.
Flower, Prof. W. H., F.R.S., Royal College of Surgeons.
Foster, Prof. Michael, Royal Institution.
Foster, Prof. G. Carey, F.R.S., University College.
Frankland, Prof. E., F.R.S., Royal College of Chem.
Galloway, Prof. R., College of Science, Dublin.
Galton, Douglas, F.R.S.
Geikie, A., F.R.S., Geological Survey of Scotland.
Grant, Prof. R., F.R.S., Direc. Glasgow Observatory.
Hauer, H. Franz von, Director Geological Institute, Vienna.
Haughton, Rev. Prof. S., F.R.S.
Hirst, Prof. F.R.S., Gen. Sec. British Association.
Hooker, Dr. J. D., F.R.S., Director Royal Gardens, Kew.
Humphry, Prof., F.R.S., Cambridge.

Huxley, Prof. T. H., F.R.S., President Geological Society.
Jack, Prof., Owens College, Manchester.
Jenkin, Prof. H. C. Fleeming, F.R.S., Edinburgh University.
Jevons, Prof. W. S., Owens College, Manchester.
Johnson, Prof. S. W., Sheffield Scientific School, Yale College.
Jones, Dr. H. Bence, F.R.S., Secretary Royal Institution.
Kingsley, Rev. Canon.
Lankester, Dr. E., F.R.S.
Liveing, Prof. G. D., F.C.S., Cambridge.
Lubbock, Sir John, Bart., F.R.S.
Magnus, Prof., Berlin.
Main, P. T., Cambridge University.
Marschall, Count A. G., Vienna.
Maskelyne, N. S., British Museum.
Matthiesson, Prof. A., F.R.S., St. Bartholomew's Hospital.
Murchison, Sir Roderic I., Bart., F.R.S., President Geographical Society; Director Geological Survey.
Newton, Prof. Alfred, F.L.S., Cambridge.
Odling, Prof., F.R.S., Royal Institution.
Oliver, Prof. D., F.R.S., Royal Gardens, Kew.
Phillips, Prof. J., F.R.S., Oxford.
Quetelet, Dr. A., Secretary Royal Academy of Sciences, Brussels.
Ramsay, Prof. A. C., F.R.S., Geological Survey.
Rolleston, Prof. G., F.R.S., Oxford.
Roscoe, Prof. H. E., F.R.S., Owens College, Manchester.
Stewart, Balfour, F.R.S., Director Kew Observatory.
Sylvester, Prof. J. J., F.R.S.
Tait, Prof. P. G., Edinburgh University.
Thomson, Prof. Sir W., F.R.S.
Tyndall, Prof. J., F.R.S., Royal Institution.
Wallace, A. R., F.R.G.S.
Williamson, Prof. A., F.R.S., President Chem. Society.
Wöhler, Prof., Secretary K. Soc. der Wissenschaften, Göttingen.

MACMILLAN & CO., 16, Bedford Street, Covent Garden, LONDON, W.C.

MACMILLAN AND CO.'S PUBLICATIONS.

New Edition. 8vo., cloth, price 7s. 6d.

PROFESSOR HUXLEY'S LAY SERMONS, ADDRESSES,
AND REVIEWS. Contents :—On Improving Natural Knowledge—Emancipation, Black and White—A Liberal Education—Scientific Education—The Study of Zoology—The Physical Basis of Life—Scientific Aspects of Positivism—On a Piece of Chalk—Geological Reform—The Origin of Species, &c.

Crown 8vo., cloth limp, price 2s.

ESSAYS SELECTED FROM PROFESSOR HUXLEY'S LAY SERMONS, ADDRESSES, AND REVIEWS.

ON THE GENESIS OF SPECIES. By St. George Mivart,
F.R.S. With Numerous Illustrations. Crown 8vo., 9s.

"In no work in the English language has this great controversy been treated at once with the same broad and vigorous grasp of facts, and the same liberal and candid temper. The range and depth of Mr. Mivart's learning are as conspicuous as that unvarying courteousness of tone which we have been by no means used to meet with in most phases of the same strife."—*Saturday Review.*

TALES OF OLD JAPAN. By A. B. Mitford, Second
Secretary to the British Legation in Japan. With upwards of 30 Full-page Illustrations drawn and cut on Wood by Japanese Artists. Two Vols. crown 8vo., 21s.

"A work which adds more to our knowledge of this strange country, but so lately opened to Europeans, than a whole pile of grave blue-books or learned treatises."—*John Bull.*

THE ILIAD OF THE EAST. A Selection of Legends
drawn from Valmiki's Sanskrit Poem, "The Ramayana." By Frederika Richardson. Crown 8vo., 7s. 6d.

MACMILLAN AND CO., LONDON.

MACMILLAN AND CO.'S PUBLICATIONS.

Just ready, in Two Vols. crown 8vo. With Portraits. Price 24s.

THE LIFE OF ANTHONY ASHLEY COOPER, First Earl of SHAFTESBURY, 1621–1683. By W. D. CHRISTIE, M.A., formerly her Majesty's Minister to the Argentine Confederation and to Brazil.

This day, in Two Vols. crown 8vo., price 21s.

A MEMOIR OF CHARLES MAYNE YOUNG, TRAGEDIAN. With Extracts from his Son's Journal. By JULIAN CHARLES YOUNG, M.A., Rector of Ilmington. With Portraits and Sketches.

THE RED RIVER EXPEDITION. By CAPTAIN G. L. HUYSHE, Rifle Brigade, late on the Staff of Colonel Sir Garnet Wolseley, C.B., Commander of the Expedition. 8vo., 10s. 6d. With Maps.
[*Just ready.*

INSIDE PARIS DURING THE SIEGE: being the Diary of an Oxford Graduate. [*In the Press.*

THE WAR CORRESPONDENCE of the *DAILY NEWS*. Edited with Notes and Comments, forming a Continuous Narrative of the War between Germany and France. *Third Edition.* Two Vols., crown 8vo. With Maps. Each 7s. 6d.

THE LIFE AND WRITINGS OF ROBERT KNOX, the ANATOMIST. By his Pupil and Colleague, HENRY LONSDALE, M.D. With Portraits. Crown 8vo., 8s. 6d.

"Dr. Knox deserves to be long remembered, and the elegance and truth with which Dr. Lonsdale has written his life will materially aid in securing him this distinction."—*Pall Mall Gazette.*

MR. GLADSTONE'S JUVENTUS MUNDI. Gods and Men of the Heroic Age. With Map. *Second Edition.* Crown 8vo., 10s. 6d.

MACMILLAN AND CO., LONDON.

MACMILLAN AND CO.'S PUBLICATIONS.

HEREDITARY GENIUS: An Inquiry into its Laws and Consequences. By FRANCIS GALTON, F.R.S. 8vo., price 12s.

MR. DARWIN, in his "Descent of Man," says, "We know, through the admirable labours of Mr. Galton, that genius, which implies a wonderfully complex combination of high faculties, tends to be inherited."

COMPARATIVE LONGEVITY IN MAN AND THE LOWER ANIMALS. By E. RAY LANKESTER, B.A. Crown 8vo., price 4s. 6d.

PROFESSOR SEELEY'S LECTURES AND ESSAYS. Contents: Roman Imperialism, Three Lectures—Milton's Political Opinions—Milton's Poetry—Elementary Principles in Art—Liberal Education in Universities—English for Schools—The Church as a Teacher of Morality—The Teaching of Politics. 8vo., 10s. 6d.

THE MORNING LAND. By EDWARD DICEY. Two Vols. crown 8vo., 16s.

"The volumes are undoubtedly full of excellent reading matter. . . They are full of lifelike pictures."—*Morning Post*.

A PAINTER'S CAMP IN THE HIGHLANDS. By P. G. HAMERTON. New and Cheaper Edition. Extra fcap. 8vo., 6s.

Recently published, in crown 8vo., price 6s.

PICTURES OF COTTAGE LIFE IN THE WEST OF ENGLAND. By MARGARET E. POOLE.

"Charming stories of peasant life, written in something of George Eliot's style. . . . As literal as truth, as romantic as fiction, full of pathetic touches and strokes of genuine humour."—*Times*.

MACMILLAN AND CO., LONDON.